The greatest of Roman historians, Publius Cornelius Tacitus (*c.*56–120 CE) studied rhetoric in Rome; and his rhetorical and oratorical gifts are evident throughout his most substantial works, the incomplete but still remarkable *Annals* and *Histories*. In elegant, unsurpassed Latin prose, marked by sometimes bitter and ironic reflections on the human capacity to abuse and misuse power, Tacitus charts the violent trajectory of the Roman Empire from Augustus' death in 14 CE to the end of Domitian's rule in 96. Victoria Emma Pagán looks at Tacitus from a range of perspectives: as a literary stylist, influenced by Sallust; his notion of time; his modes of discourse; his place in historiography; and the later reception of Tacitus in the Renaissance and early modern periods. Tacitus remains of major interest to students of the Bible, as well as classicists, by virtue of his reference to 'Christus' and Nero's persecution of the Christians after the Great Fire of Rome in 64 CE. This lively survey enables its readers fully to appreciate why, in holding up a mirror to venality and greed, the work of Tacitus remains eternal.

VICTORIA EMMA PAGÁN is Professor of Classics at the University of Florida. The editor of *A Companion to Tacitus* (2012), she is in addition the author of *Conspiracy Narratives in Roman History* (2004), *Conspiracy Theory in Latin Literature* (2012) and *Rome and the Literature of Gardens* (2006).

'Victoria Pagán's lively new survey of Tacitus' works and their impact is especially interesting for her original contribution to our understanding of how twentieth- and twenty-first-century poets, painters, dramatists, composers and filmmakers have brought the historian's trenchant worldview into our own time. Recommended highly to students and general readers.'

—Ronald Mellor, Distinguished Research
Professor of Ancient History, UCLA

UNDERSTANDING CLASSICS

EDITOR: RICHARD STONEMAN (UNIVERSITY OF EXETER)

When the great Roman poets of the Augustan Age – Ovid, Virgil and Horace – composed their odes, love poetry and lyrical verse, could they have imagined that their works would one day form a cornerstone of Western civilization, or serve as the basis of study for generations of schoolchildren learning Latin? Could Aeschylus or Euripides have envisaged the remarkable popularity of contemporary stagings of their tragedies? The legacy and continuing resonance of Homer's *Iliad* and *Odyssey* – Greek poetical epics written many millennia ago – again testify to the capacity of the classics to cross the divide of thousands of years and speak powerfully and relevantly to audiences quite different from those to which they were originally addressed.

Understanding Classics is a specially commissioned series which aims to introduce the outstanding authors and thinkers of antiquity to a wide audience of appreciative modern readers, whether undergraduate students of classics, literature, philosophy and ancient history or generalists interested in the classical world. Each volume – written by leading figures internationally – will examine the historical significance of the writer or writers in question; their social, political and cultural contexts; their use of language, literature and mythology; extracts from their major works; and their reception in later European literature, art, music and culture. *Understanding Classics* will build a library of readable, authoritative introductions offering fresh and elegant surveys of the greatest literatures, philosophies and poetries of the ancient world.

UNDERSTANDING CLASSICS

TACITUS

Victoria Emma Pagán

UNDERSTANDING CLASSICS SERIES EDITOR:
RICHARD STONEMAN

Published in 2017 by
I.B.Tauris & Co. Ltd
London · New York
www.ibtauris.com

ISBN: 978 1 78076 317 0 (HB)
          978 1 78076 318 7 (PB)
eISBN: 978 1 78672 132 7
ePDF: 978 1 78673 132 6

A full CIP record for this book is available from the British Library
A full CIP record is available from the Library of Congress

Library of Congress Catalog Card Number: available

Text designed and typeset by Tetragon, London
Printed and bound in Great Britain by T.J. International, Padstow, Cornwall

MIX
Paper from
responsible sources
FSC® C013056
www.fsc.org

CONTENTS

For John, Marc, Mike, Mary and Julia

Acknowledgements

THE LENGTH OF THIS PARAGRAPH of acknowledgements is in inverse proportion to the debt I owe to the institutions and individuals who have supported my study of Tacitus ever since I first read the *Annals* with David Potter in the autumn of 1988. I would like to thank Richard Stoneman, Alex Wright and the team at I.B.Tauris for their patience, and Ellie Wolpert for her technical assistance. I am grateful for the research support provided by the University of Florida College of Liberal Arts and Sciences, Office of Research and Department of Classics. For their daily encouragement and kindness I thank my husband, son and daughter. I dedicate this book to my dear brothers and sisters. Each will know best why.

LIST OF EMPERORS

LIST OF FIGURES

ABBREVIATIONS

The works of Tacitus are abbreviated as follows:

Ag. = *Agricola*
Ann. = *Annals*
Dial. = *Dialogue on Orators*
G. = *Germania*
Hist. = *Histories*

The following abbreviations refer to works cited frequently:

Blackwell Companion: Victoria Emma Pagán (ed.), *A Companion to Tacitus* (Blackwell Companions to the Ancient World) (Oxford and Malden, MA, 2012)

Cambridge Companion: Anthony J. Woodman (ed.), *The Cambridge Companion to Tacitus* (Cambridge, 2009)

Devillers: Olivier Devillers (ed.), *Les* opera minora *et le développement de l'historiographie tacitéenne* (Bordeaux, 2014)

Heritage: Ronald Mellor (ed.), *Tacitus: The Classical Heritage* (New York and London, 1995)

Imperial Projections: Sandra R. Joshel, Margaret Malamud and Donald T. McGuire, Jr. (eds), *Imperial Projections: Ancient Rome in Modern Popular Culture* (Baltimore, MA, 2001)

Tacitus and the Tacitean Tradition: Torrey James Luce and Anthony J. Woodman (eds), *Tacitus and the Tacitean Tradition* (Princeton, NJ, 1993)

All translations are my own unless otherwise specified.

I

Prefacing a Life

IN 1728 A SCOTTISH BARRISTER named Thomas Gordon published
the first edition of his translation of the works of Tacitus, followed by a series
of his own essays. His appreciation for Tacitus is manifest:

> There is no end of specimens and examples; it is all over a wonderful
> Book, full of wisdom, full of virtue; of astonishing strokes of genius
> and superior sense. Yet he seems not to value himself upon his great
> thoughts; the finest things fall from him like common things; he says
> them naturally, and never dwells upon one, because he always has more
> to utter. When he has struck your imagination, and you want to stand
> still and ruminate, you have no time; he draws, or rather forces you
> forward, and the next thought strikes you as much; so does the third,
> and all of them; and you go on reading and wondering, yet wishing for
> leisure to ponder and recollect. But he gives you none; for from first to
> last the present reflection is always the best.[1]

Some 30 years later Reverend Thomas Hunter of Lancashire published his
Observations on Tacitus, in which he compares him with Livy and clearly
finds him wanting:

> Hence, it is, among other Causes, that you take up *Livy* with Pleasure; peruse him with Eagerness, and lay him down with Regret. *Tacitus* (after you are acquainted with his Manner and Subject) you enter upon as a Task, and consequently read him with uneasiness, throw him by with Pleasure, and resume him with Reluctancy.[2]

Eighteenth-century Britain may seem a rather oblique way of approaching Tacitus, but in this age Tacitus was called upon by the opposing parties of Whigs and Tories in heated debates over the path towards a balanced constitution.[3] Tacitus is no longer pressed into the service of modern political arguments, but the aesthetic judgements of Gordon and Hunter are still valid. Some modern readers might feel that reading Tacitus is an uneasy task gladly set aside or taken up with reluctance, so my job is to convince you to 'go on reading and wondering' and wishing for more time to ponder him.

Cornelius Tacitus (*c.*56–120 CE) is one of our richest sources for the history of the early Roman Empire. His magisterial style is peerless, his narratives are intricate and his speeches are a tour de force of rhetoric and metahistory. Therefore, his history is inextricably bound with his philosophy of human nature, and his prose is haunted by an eerily familiar sense of survivor's guilt. He is keen to portray the struggle between individual and society, perhaps most memorably characterized by the ever-troubled relationships between emperor and senators, general and soldiers, governor and provincials, and the family dramas between uncle and nephew, mother and son, husband and wife. Though his expressions are terse, his implications ring clear, and his indictment of those who fall short of his exacting moral standards still seethes with the anger he so frankly rejected.

Tacitus left five extant works. The *Life of Julius Agricola* is a biography of his father-in-law, who was governor of Britannia under the reign of Domitian. The *Germania* is a brief treatise on the customs and peoples of Germania. The *Dialogue on Orators* is a discussion among friends about the importance and decline of public speaking. Of the *Histories*, only the first five books survive. They recount the Long Year 69, when four emperors ruled Rome: Galba, Otho, Vitellius and Vespasian, founder of the Flavian dynasty. Finally, the *Annals* chronicle the Julio-Claudian emperors. The reign of Tiberius is covered in Books 1–4 and the fragments of Books 5 and 6. The books from the end of 6 to the beginning of 11 are missing: hence the entire reign of Caligula is lost. Books 11–12 cover the end of the reign of Claudius, Books 13–16 the reign of Nero. The manuscript of the *Annals* breaks off in the middle of Book 16.

In classical antiquity there are only scattered references to these works, due in part to the accidents of transmission. Tacitus appears to have been neglected in late antiquity and the Middle Ages (650–850 CE). By 1362, the Florentine scholar and poet Giovanni Boccaccio was reading *Annals* Books 11–16 and *Histories* Books 1–5; by 1473, a first edition of the *Germania* and *Dialogue on Orators* appeared in Venice. With the publication of *Annals* Books 1–6 and the *Agricola* in 1515 (in the Renaissance age of Niccolò Machiavelli), Tacitus experienced a revival of epic proportions. In the sixteenth century 45 editions of his work appeared, including the monumental edition by the Flemish philologist Justus Lipsius in 1574, and 103 more in the seventeenth. Between 1580 and 1700, 100 commentaries on the works of Tacitus were published.[4] The eighteenth century was the age of Tacitism in Britain, the nineteenth in Germany. The political thought of Tacitus cut a broad swathe across European intellectual history – and beyond. The recent scholarship of Christopher Krebs on the influence of the *Germania* in early to mid-twentieth-century Germany demonstrates the devastating grip that Tacitus held over the imagination of the emergent German nation.[5] Yet in Tacitus, postwar German artist Anselm Kiefer and American poet Frank Bidart find inspiration for works of art that confront, and perhaps even seek to heal, the traumas of World War II. In 1983, American historian Stanley Karnow opened his *Vietnam: A History* with perhaps the most famous (certainly among the most quoted) words of Tacitus: 'They make a wasteland and call it peace.'[6] The imprint of Tacitus on Western thought is indelible.

Because his language is notoriously difficult but his history indispensable, this volume aims to enhance appreciation and to provide an overview of Tacitean scholarship. Beyond these nominal objectives, however, it is my hope to introduce the reader to the fascinating world of Roman politics, history and private life that Tacitus recreated in his writing. For example, Tacitus puts before the mind's eye the Capitol consumed by flames, and although the fire was accidental, readers still feel the hollow senselessness of civil war in the pits of their stomachs. One of my students was once so moved by the opening paragraphs of the *Agricola* that he looked up from the book and declared to his classmates, 'This is not going to end well.' A preface that can evince such an emotional response from the average university student is a good place to begin.

The first sentence of the *Agricola* prefigures a major theme that recurs in all of Tacitus' works – the disconnect between honourable men and the dishonourable times in which they live:

> To hand down to posterity the deeds and characters of famous men is an ancient practice neglected not even in our times (although our age is careless of its own men) whenever some great and noteworthy virtue prevailed and rose above the vice common to states great and small, namely ignorance of and hostility towards righteousness.[7]

From the outset, history is commemorative, and Tacitus announces his intention to take part in this tradition, in spite of stumbling blocks. In assuming a lack of interest, ignorance and even hostility towards goodness, Tacitus challenges his reader to be open-minded. Anyone who continues reading the biography has been duly warned that the subject matter ahead will be provocative. Even so, his readership does not measure up to the standards of the past.

The first sentence of the *Germania* declares the subject matter immediately:

> All Germania is separated from Gaul, Rheatia and Pannonia by the Rhine and Danube Rivers, from Sarmatia and Dacia by mutual fear or by mountains; surrounding the rest is Ocean, embracing broad bays and great expanses of islands, where certain peoples and regions which war revealed have become known to us.[8]

The sentence has a Caesarean ring to it, recalling *The Gallic Wars* and Julius Caesar's famous beginning, 'All Gaul is divided into three parts.' Therefore the *Germania* summons comparison between the successes of the past and failures of the present to expand the empire, for unlike Caesar's Gaul, Germania was never fully brought under Roman rule. Comparison of past and present occupies Tacitus in the *Dialogue*, and while the treatise resists singular interpretation it lays bare the debates about the value of oratory in Roman society:

> Often you ask me, Justus Fabius, why, when earlier ages abounded with the talents and glory of so many outstanding orators, our age is particularly empty and bereft of the praise of eloquence, such that scarcely even the very name orator remains.[9]

Once again the past is invoked as a standard against which to measure the present. The first sentence of the *Histories* is the shortest of all, but this kind of compression is a hallmark of Tacitean style: 'My work commences when Servius Galba (second time) and Titus Vinius are about to be consuls.'[10] In just ten Latin words Tacitus can announce not just his method, to proceed year by year, but also his subject matter: the year 69, which saw the rise and fall of three emperors and the establishment of the Flavian dynasty – those under whom Tacitus' own career would advance. Finally, the subject of the *Annals* is the city of Rome, and again the first sentence carries an implicit comparison between past and present: 'The city of Rome from the beginning was ruled by kings; liberty and consulship were instituted by Lucius Brutus.'[11] Without any indication yet about the temporal scope of the work, the theme of liberation from tyranny will colour all that follows.

Tacitus' works and themes are our best and practically only sources of information about his life. To begin with the biography of the author implies that his life and career have a significant influence on his work and that his work cannot be understood without recourse to his life story. On the one hand, knowledge of the details of his birth, education, career and retirement could circumscribe interpretation, so that comprehension of his works would fit neatly into the established facts of his life. For instance, the couplet 'There is no frigate like a book / To take us lands away' is a more powerful metaphor when we know that the poet Emily Dickinson seldom left her own home, let alone travelled the seas. On the other hand, we need not know the details of her life in Amherst, Massachusetts to appreciate the belief in the value of education for all ('This Traverse may the poorest take / Without oppress of Toll –') and the image of a book as capable of conveying the essence of one's humanity ('How frugal is the Chariot / That bears a Human soul').[12] So why begin with the life of our author, Cornelius Tacitus? Because when we read his books we learn slightly less than we would like about Roman history and a great deal more than we might expect about his attitudes, perspectives and philosophy. The opening sentences divulge his concerns about morality, the expansion of empire, the comparison of past and present, and the conflict of tyranny and liberty. In the words of the French Renaissance philosopher Michel de Montaigne, 'If his writings tell us anything about his qualities, Tacitus was a great man, upright and courageous, not of a superstitious but of a philosophical and high-minded virtue.'[13] And yet a contemporary Jesuit treatise arrives at a radically different conclusion: 'It is enough to say that Cornelius Tacitus was a pagan, idolator [sic] and enemy of Christ our Redeemer and of the Christians.'[14] Patent ideological bias notwithstanding, the lack of evidence about the life of Tacitus minimizes the risk that a biographical approach would shackle interpretation of his works.

Because Tacitus is a historian engaged in narrating the past, he speaks of himself rarely. Since Romans held political office in such a regular sequence (called the *cursus honorum*, or course of public office), knowledge of one or two dates for an office can generate a predictable timeline for the rest of the career. Most of what we know of his life is derived from his own writing; five passages indicate exact years. Two dates are supplied from two letters of his contemporary Pliny the Younger. These literary sources provide the facts necessary to supplement a fragmentary funerary inscription.

First, the year of Tacitus' birth is inferred from the dramatic date of the *Dialogue on Orators*. The discussion is said to take place during the sixth year of Vespasian's rule, that is, the year 75 CE, and Tacitus refers to himself as a young man ('I once heard as a young man...').[15] If we roughly estimate Tacitus to have been 20 years old at the time, then he would have been born in 55 at the earliest. Thus he would have been a teenager in the year 69, when the Roman world was ravaged by civil war. Second, according to the *Agricola* Tacitus was married in the year after his father-in-law was consul, that is, in 77: 'When he was consul he promised me his daughter, a woman of great hope, and after his consulship he saw to our marriage.'[16] Third, Tacitus is not unaware that his own career advanced at a time when it was difficult for others: 'I cannot deny that I originally owed my position to Vespasian, or that I was advanced by Titus and still further promoted by Domitian.'[17] The fourth and perhaps most valuable fixed date is given in the *Annals*, where Tacitus speaks of his official duties as praetor in the year 88: 'For he [Domitian] also put on secular games, in which I was involved with considerable responsibility, since I was a member of the priesthood of the Fifteen and was at the time praetor.'[18] From this fixed office of praetorship we can estimate that Tacitus must have performed military service as a tribune before being elected quaestor in 81 or 82. Following the *cursus honorum* he would next have been elected aedile two or three years later. After the praetorship in 88, he would have held a three-year command of a legion and an appointment as a proconsul of one of the minor provinces. Finally, when he states that his father-in-law died 'four years earlier, during a long absence,'[19] we may assume that Tacitus was filling these duties abroad. The year was 93. The date of Tacitus' consulship is provided by Pliny the Younger, who records that as consul Tacitus delivered the funeral oration for Verginius Rufus, who died in 97.[20] In the year 100 Tacitus and Pliny were appointed by the Senate to a special commission in the case of Marius Priscus, and they spoke on behalf of the prosecution.[21]

A fragment of an elaborate funerary monument found on the Via Nomentana in Rome preserves the middle section of three lines of text. Most of the restoration of the inscription is based on the information from Tacitus and Pliny. It is customary to list the public offices held by the deceased; the size and alignment of extant letters allows us to infer seven public offices, not listed in chronological order: consul (in 97, as we know from Pliny, *Ep.* 2.1), member of the priesthood of the Fifteen (in 88, *Ann.* 11.11.1), member of the board of ten for adjudicating disputes (Pliny, *Ep.* 2.11), tribune of a military legion (inferred), quaestor of Augustus (in 81 or 82, inferred), tribune of the plebs (inferred) and praetor (in 88, *Ann.*

11.11.1). The most tantalizing bit of information provided by the inscription regards Tacitus' name.

The inscription preserves the letters CITO. Very few Latin names end in -*citus*, and scholars agree this must be the end of the name *Tacito* in the dative case: 'to Tacitus'. Furthermore, the name is not common. It is likely that his father's ancestors were non-Romans who received citizenship in the Republican period under the patronage of a man named Cornelius. The next fully preserved letter after a space is C followed by the bottom of what scholars take to be the letter A. From this it has been suggested that in addition to 'Tacitus' there were two more *cognomina* (Roman family names), perhaps indicating his mother's family. The fully restored dedication is conjectured thus: 'To Publius Cornelius (son of Publius) Tacitus Caecina Paetus.' The family name Caecina Paetus was common enough in the Julio-Claudian and Vespasianic periods, but relationships among them are unclear. If indeed Tacitus was related to the Caecinae Paeti, then several passages in the *Annals* and *Histories* that treat members of the family acquire added significance, for Tacitus would have been writing about his mother's relatives.[22]

Although dates for the composition of his five works can also be derived from internal references, our understanding of the cultural contexts in which Tacitus wrote his five surviving works nevertheless hinges on a chronology that is not always as accurate as we would like. In the *Agricola* references to Nerva as still alive and then Trajan as *princeps* suggest the work was begun in 97 CE and completed in 98.[23] A reference to the second consulship of Trajan in 98 is the only evidence for the date of the *Germania*.[24] The *Dialogue on Orators* was written sometime between 96 and 109, an 'uncomfortably wide'[25] margin of more than a decade that cannot be secured by internal reference; nonetheless, consensus dates it before the two major historical works. Thanks to two letters of Pliny the Younger on the eruption of Vesuvius, we know that Tacitus was working on the *Histories* in 106, and it is assumed that he finished this work before embarking on his last masterpiece, the *Annals*, the date of which hinges on an internal reference to the 'Red Sea'.[26] If this refers to the modern Red Sea, then a date after 106 is given; if the Persian Gulf is meant, then the date may be pushed as far forward as 117. Trajan was the first emperor to expand significantly beyond the limits of empire reached by Augustus. He annexed Dacia, Arabia, Armenia, Mesopotamia and Assyria, thus extending the Roman Empire to its furthest limits. Preferring consolidation over expansion, Hadrian immediately abandoned all except Dacia. So it is generally accepted that the *Annals* were begun under Trajan but not completed until after the accession of Hadrian in 117.[27] There is no evidence available on Tacitus' death.

In some ways this life is not very remarkable. Cornelius Tacitus was born during the reign of Nero and was a teenager during the civil wars of 69. He was married in the year 76 or 77 to the daughter of Julius Agricola, a man whom he admired greatly. He began his career in public service with the quaestorship in 81, after which he probably served as tribune of the plebs. Before or after that office he may have served abroad in the army. He was elected to the office of praetor, then consul, and he was so well respected that he was selected to serve on a special commission in the year 100. We then assume that he was governor of a province. Tacitus would have been just about 65 years old when Hadrian became emperor in 117, and given the length and scope of the *Annals*, we must assume that Tacitus began this monumental work under Trajan and continued it into the reign of Hadrian; how far into this reign we cannot say.

Tacitus enjoyed this comfortable and somewhat ordinary career during one of the more challenging periods of Roman history marred by varying degrees of violence and political upheaval. The death of the colourful and controversial emperor Nero brought about the end of the Julio-Claudian dynasty. Three generals tried and failed to rule Rome before the Flavian dynasty was established. Vespasian ruled well enough, but the short reign of his son Titus was followed by the despotic tyranny of Domitian. The era of the five good emperors (Nerva, Trajan, Hadrian, Antoninus Pius and Marcus Aurelius) has been called 'the period in the history of the world, during which the condition of the human race was most happy and prosperous', in the words of the eighteenth-century scholar Edward Gibbon,[28] and yet the transfer of power by adoption was no more transparent than the cognatic succession by which the Julio-Claudians stumbled along. Furthermore, while engaged in his public career, Tacitus was writing history. As Dylan Sailor neatly summarizes, 'It is exactly in this respect that Tacitus' historiographical career is remarkable: it continued apace with his political career.'[29] This is in part why Tacitus' writings are so intriguing, for he gives us history not merely as a consumer of the past but as one actively engaged in producing the history of his own times. What were those times like?

'Although interpreters of texts run the risk of ridicule when they tie a text too closely to the author's life,' warns Christopher Krebs, 'there can be no question that [Tacitus'] existence under Domitian shaped him as a writer.'[30] Domitian, last of the Flavian emperors, is traditionally remembered as a bloodthirsty tyrant, thanks to the hostile tradition as exemplified by the biographer Suetonius, who speaks of 'savage cruelty not just excessive but cunning and unexpected'.[31] The adjective 'despotic' easily attaches to a man who held continuous consulships and was censor from 84 to 96; that is, until his death. In this capacity he regulated membership of the Senate; to his credit, he made a point of admitting men from the provinces, so that the Senate began to represent the empire and not just the city of Rome. Still, he rarely summoned the Senate for any real business. According to Pliny the Younger, Domitian convened the senators for either recreation or crime.[32] As for foreign affairs, Domitian reorganized the German frontier, creating the two provinces of Upper and Lower Germany that streamlined administration and left the Romans unchallenged on the west bank of the Rhine; however, during his reign the Dacians posed a serious threat on the Danube. Domitian was able to establish peace, and he fortified the Danube against further attacks. Less sympathetic interpretations credit Domitian with seizing these opportunities for military glory that would place him on an equal footing with his father and brother, whose merits had been proven by actual military challenges. Yet Domitian's real problem, according to Suetonius, was his overly suspicious, indeed paranoid nature that drove him to execute anyone he suspected. In the end, this paranoia was the cause of his death; Domitian was assassinated in a palace conspiracy.[33] The ease with which Nerva succeeded him suggests careful planning. The sources prohibit an unbiased assessment for us as they did for Tacitus, whose consistently negative opinions of Domitian cast a strong shadow over all of his works.[34]

Domitian was succeeded by Nerva, a senior senator with a successful career in law under Nero. Since he was advanced in age and had no military experience, he adopted Trajan as co-regent, who was at the time commander of Upper Germany.[35] Upon the death of Nerva in 98, Trajan commenced his reign without event. He followed precedent and adopted Hadrian; however, because Trajan waited until he was on his deathbed to do this, the transition aroused suspicion that the adoption had been machinated by Trajan's wife without his consent. The beginning of Hadrian's reign in 117 was further marred by political difficulty. He did not reach Rome until July 118, and in the intervening months the Senate executed four former consuls on the charge of conspiracy. Palma and Celsus had supposedly plotted to kill Hadrian while hunting, Nigrinus and Lusius while sacrificing. Coincidentally, all four had served under Trajan. So Hadrian's first priority was to acquit himself of involvement in the Senate's rash actions.[36] In spite of this rough start, however, the relationship between the Senate and the *princeps* continued along the productive path led by Nerva and Trajan – in sharp contrast to the practice of Domitian.

There are valid reasons for regarding the reigns of Trajan and Hadrian as a superlatively prosperous period in Roman history, certainly when compared to the dark days of Domitian. Under Trajan and Hadrian, freedmen were no longer appointed to posts in public administration; the bureaucracy that developed was staffed by men of equestrian rank who were able to pursue meaningful careers in civil service. Imperial legislation turned to helping weaker members of the community: the lots of children, slaves and women improved. Trajan established loans to municipalities where their moderate interest paid for the children of needy families. Although it was usual and even expected of emperors to distribute large sums of cash, wine and oil to the urban populace, Trajan also provided for the distribution of grain for poor children. Public works were generously supported as well: he completed the last of the great aqueducts to the city. In addition, he built a forum complete with markets and a basilica with libraries. The complex was crowned by a column commemorating his triumph in Dacia.[37] Hadrian built a Temple of Venus and Rome, replaced Agrippa's Pantheon and constructed his mausoleum, still one of Rome's grandest landmarks on the bank of the Tiber. A new highway was constructed across the Apennine Mountains and the port at Ostia was reinforced and upgraded. Hadrian continued Vespasian's policy of state-sponsored education that supported schools and libraries. The result was an established book trade and a Greek renaissance known as the Second Sophistic, the literary movement that produced Plutarch (45–120 CE), the Greek writer best known for his *Parallel Lives*, a series of biographies of famous Greek and Roman generals and statesmen paired on the basis of similar character traits and behaviours.[38] This was Tacitus' world.

A rich source of information about Tacitus' life is found in the prefaces to his works. Prefaces are a regular feature of ancient historiography. The traditional themes include a praise of history, the reasons for the choice of subject, and the historian's attitude to his work. In the preface, the reader learns why the author wrote history, how he regarded it and what aims he intended to achieve. But these passages should be approached with some caution; the opening paragraphs are carefully contrived to predispose the reader towards the work.[39] Tacitus' introductions are highly controlled expositions of subject matter, yet they convey so much more. In what follows, we will examine the five prefaces closely. In addition to some facts that help us piece together Tacitus' biography, the prefaces also help us understand some of his motivations and concerns.

The Prefaces

We can dispense rather quickly with the *Germania*, which has no preface, and the *Dialogue on Orators*, which adheres closely to generic convention. The *Germania* divides immediately into two parts, the first describing the peoples in general, the second the individual tribes, and both exhibit the recognizable characteristics of ancient ethnography. Tacitus gives no guidance as to the purpose or intent of the work, nor does he situate it within his research agenda.[40] What may we infer from this silence? Perhaps the conventions of the genre precluded prefatory statements. Perhaps the *Germania* was not intended to stand alone but rather to serve as primary source material for other historians. Perhaps Tacitus had no personal stake in the subject matter and so felt no reason to explain himself. Writing about emperors demanded responsibilities; writing about barbarians simply did not. In the *Agricola*, *Histories* and *Annals*, Tacitus had an obligation towards the eyewitnesses or their descendants; the subject matter of the *Germania* placed no such demands on the author. And yet Domitian and Trajan campaigned against the peoples of Germania. The Flavian poet Statius wrote an epic poem about Domitian's military exploits entitled, 'On the German War', now lost to us.[41] The poem may not have been completed, perhaps because as earnest as the poet may have wished to be, the topic foundered. According to Tacitus, 'Domitian was conscious that his recent, fake triumph over Germania was a laughing stock.'[42] By not prefacing the *Germania*, Tacitus does not stake a claim in the political implications of writing about a topic that struck so close to Domitian, although for Rhiannon Ash, such pointed silence partakes in the 'anti-Domitianic stance of Tacitus' other works'.[43] We shall return to this question in Chapter IV.

After the *Germania*, Tacitus wrote the *Dialogue on Orators*, and its preface follows Ciceronian models closely in its establishment of the setting. The work is dedicated to Justus Fabius, consul in 102. He asks Tacitus why there are no talented orators in their day, and rather than venture an answer, Tacitus reports a discussion he once heard, which enables him to rely on memory and avoid the need for eloquence: 'Thus I'll not need talent but merely memory and the art of recollection.'[44] In Chapter V we shall explore the dynamics of the setting in more detail.

The prefaces of the *Agricola* and the *Histories*, by contrast, reveal a great deal of information about Tacitus. Judging from the opening paragraphs of these two works, Tacitus was acutely aware that he was living an ordinary life during extraordinary times. On this point he is noticeably self-conscious, beginning with the *Agricola*. Following on from the disconnect between past and present discussed earlier in this Preface, Tacitus laments that the reign of Domitian was a time that was hostile towards virtue of any sort. He gives two examples of upstanding statesmen and their biographers who were persecuted for praising their virtue:

> We read, when Arulenus Rusticus wrote his laudatory biography of
> Thrasea Paetus and Herennius Senecio of Helvidius Priscus, that it was

a capital crime, and not only were the authors subject to savage punishment, but also their books; a board of three men was chosen to burn the literary tributes of these famous men in the public assembly and in the forum. Doubtless they thought in that fire the voice of the Roman people, the freedom of the Senate and the conscience of humankind were being abolished. At the same time professors of philosophy were banished and all morality was driven into exile so that nothing at all honourable would present itself.[45]

This is a grim picture indeed of political persecution spanning nearly three decades. Publius Clodius Thrasea Paetus (and here we might recall the conjectured cognomen Paetus and hence a special interest on the part of Tacitus) was a senior statesman who openly opposed Nero on several occasions. His political enemies trumped up charges and he was offered his choice of death in the year 66. Before the abrupt break in the manuscript, the last paragraphs of the *Annals* relate the trial and death of Thrasea Paetus, and so from our perspective, from *Agricola* to *Annals*, this disturbing case circumscribes Tacitus' literary career. Yet even after Nero the persecutions continued, since Helvidius Priscus, praetor in 70, was executed in 74 during the reign of Vespasian for his opposition to the emperor. Arulenus Rusticus and Herennius Senecio, the biographers of these martyrs, were executed in 93, when (as we learn at the end of the *Agricola*) Tacitus was abroad. Perhaps this is why Tacitus introduces the paragraph with the Latin word *legimus*, 'we read'. By chance, in both Latin and English the tense is distinguished by pronunciation only, so that from print alone and without any telltale adverb we cannot know whether Tacitus meant 'we read in the past' or 'we read now'. Either way, the emphatic position of this verb underscores that Tacitus was not personally present as witness but had to ascertain knowledge of the executions and book burnings from written sources – which is also odd: why not consult eyewitnesses, who were surely still alive when Tacitus was composing the biography?[46]

We are given the impression that Tacitus is putting some distance between himself and these events, until the next sentence: 'Truly we have given great testimony to patience; and as the previous generation witnessed the ultimate in freedom, so we the ultimate in slavery, when informants stripped away the free exchange of speaking and listening.'[47] Tacitus thus implicates himself in the period after such persecution, and his next sentence is one of his most artful and memorable: 'We should have lost memory itself with voice, if it had been in our power to forget as it was in our power to keep silent.'[48] When freedom of speaking was so restricted, Tacitus and those of his generation kept silent rather than speak out. So perhaps Tacitus wishes to forget not only the reign of terror but the passive response to it, yet cannot forget either; it is easy to keep silent but impossible to forget. Amnesia was not an option for individuals, and unlike the Athenians who purposely decreed amnesty, a public forgetting of the traumas of civil war, the Romans never passed such legislation that required all parties to forget past wrongs.[49] The closest they came was the so-called *damnatio memoriae*, a modern term that describes the destruction of the memory of a person after his death – quite the opposite, in fact, of an amnesty meant to heal a community.[50] Therefore the Senate decree passed in 96 that the memory of Domitian be obliterated could never be a sufficient remedy. We are only two paragraphs into Tacitus' literary career, and already we are deeply immersed in the complexities of his thought.

In the third and final paragraph of the preface, Tacitus contrasts those dark days with present circumstances:

> Now at last our spirit is returning, and although at the outset of a most blessed age Nerva Caesar has combined things once incompatible – namely principate and liberty – and Nerva Trajan daily increases the happiness of the times, and although public security has not only our hope and prayer but also the trust and strength of that prayer, still the nature of human weakness is such that remedies act slower than the diseases.[51]

Tacitus credits Nerva and Trajan for the restoration of public intellectual life, and yet he concedes that there are still obstacles to honest writing. The medical metaphor makes vivid the harm done to the state by Domitian's tyranny; surely we know that it can take years to recover from an accident that occurs in just a few seconds ('Thus you can oppress genius and intellect more easily than you can restore it'[52]). Therefore, in spite of Nerva's and Trajan's best efforts, human nature is such that recovery will be slow. The second obstacle to literary revival, however, is more pointed:[53]

> What if during those 15 years (a long period of mortal life) many died by fortuitous chance and the most able by the savagery of the emperor, but a few of us were survivors, so to speak, not merely of others but even of ourselves, since we were robbed of the best years of our lives in which the young men among us arrive at old age and the old men arrive practically at their graves in utter silence?[54]

Those 15 years were 81–96, the reign of Domitian, and they cut a hole in the lives of the young and old alike. But what exactly is Tacitus asking in this question? Grammatically it begins with the interrogative 'What if', so that editors close the punctuation with a question mark. This rhetorical question does not seek so much as provide an answer: some were in fact able to survive the difficult conditions. But how? Tacitus does not say, although the implication is clear: they survived by forswearing their integrity. Under any other circumstances such behaviour would be reprehensible. Under Domitian, it was necessary.[55]

The preface of the *Agricola* leaves us with the impression that Tacitus bears a sense of guilt for having kept his head down and survived while others were felled by savage tyranny, and this impression is confirmed at the end of the work. Agricola died in 93, but Domitian still had three more years to wreak havoc: 'Agricola did not see the Senate house under siege and surrounded by arms, the slaughter of so many consular men in one massacre, the exiles and flights of so many of the most noble women.'[56] Tacitus names three prosecutors who after the death of Agricola would ruin the lives of decent Romans with their sycophantic accusations, then names four victims, and in a surprising change of grammatical subject takes responsibility for their persecutions: 'Soon *our* hands dragged Helvidius to prison; *we* were afflicted by the sight of Mauricus and Rusticus, Senecio splattered *us* with his innocent blood' (my emphasis).[57]

Tacitus vividly implicates himself and his fellow senators in the trials of these men who preferred outspoken opposition to Domitian. This Helvidius is the son of the Helvidius mentioned in the preface. Domitian had him executed, alleging that in a play he wrote about the mythological characters of Paris and Oenone he was criticizing the emperor's recent divorce.[58] Mauricus and Rusticus were brothers; by Domitian the former was banished, the latter executed, as we learnt in the Preface. In writing a laudatory biography, Tacitus aligns himself with the biographers Arulenus Rusticus and Herennius Senecio, but he does not suffer their fate. Tacitus will not confirm rumours that Agricola was poisoned, but he does note that Domitian sent far too many freedmen, physicians and messengers to gather intelligence about Agricola's dying moments.[59] We are left with the impression that Agricola was persecuted too, like Thrasea and the elder Helvidius.[60] Without going so far as to speculate about Agricola's ability or inability to survive the tyranny of Domitian, we can at least glean from the preface and the epilogue some of Tacitus' preoccupations.

These surface again in the preface of the *Histories*. Unlike the *Agricola*, which survives in its entirety, the *Histories* breaks off in Book 5, so that we cannot know how it would have ended or whether, as in the *Agricola*, Tacitus would have referred to the preface in the epilogue. The scope of the *Histories* is generally agreed to cover the years 69–96 in probably 12 books, from the revolt against Galba to the assassination of Domitian.[61] Tacitus thus lived through the period; he was a contemporary of the events he narrates. As it is, the five extant books cover the tumultuous civil wars and establishment of the Flavian dynasty; we can only imagine how he would have treated the assassination of Domitian. The preface of the *Histories* is noticeably short. As we have seen, the first sentence announces the starting point. The second sentence defends the choice: Republican history has already been treated sufficiently, while the Augustan era permanently changed the enterprise of writing history. People came to prefer flattery and criticism to truth, and so Tacitus must explain himself:

> Galba, Otho, Vitellius were known to me neither for help nor for harm.
> I shall not deny that my career was begun under Vespasian, advanced

by Titus and extended quite far under Domitian: but those professing truth inviolate must speak without partiality and without hatred.[62]

The three unsuccessful usurpers are easily dismissed; their successes and failures were too short-lived to matter. However, the Flavians need more explanation, and Tacitus makes masterful use of the Latin language here. He begins with litotes, a rhetorical figure that allows him to understate his case by negating the contrary: 'I shall not deny', meaning 'I affirm'. Second, note that the verbs are passive (retained in the English), suggesting receipt rather than pursuit of favour. Third, he implies that he is among 'those professing truth', but nothing in the Latin (or in the English) explicitly states a commitment on his part.[63] However, he does commit to writing another history:

> But if my life should last long enough, I have set aside for my old age
> the principate of Divine Nerva and the imperial command of Trajan,
> material richer and safer, in the rare happiness of the times when one
> is allowed to think what you wish and say what you think.[64]

The promise of a history of Nerva and Trajan was first made in the preface to the *Agricola*: 'I shall not regret, even if in language unskilled and plain, recounting the history of our earlier servitude and the testimony of our present happiness.'[65] The reign of Domitian (the 'history of our earlier servitude') was delivered in the lost portion of the *Histories*, as Tacitus himself states in the *Annals*: 'in the books I composed on the history of the emperor Domitian'.[66] Twice, then, Tacitus contemplates writing a history of Nerva and Trajan, but as far as we know he never fulfilled the promise. Instead, he elected to retreat to the reign of Tiberius with his *Annals*, and there he makes one final promise to write about the age of Augustus: 'As for the deaths of the others, I will relate the rest of their age, if, after finishing what I have begun, I should prolong my life to yet more work.'[67] Instead of moving forward to the history of his own times, Tacitus retreats further into the past.

The preface of the *Histories* concludes with a stylistic flourish. Under Nerva and Trajan a historian can enjoy the ideal – and uncommon – circumstances, 'the rare happiness' for writing history. Nerva and Trajan also provide material that is 'richer and safer'. The comparative adjectives suggest that the subject of the *Histories* was less rich and less safe. Perhaps the civil wars that occupy Books 1–5 were unsatisfying and the events of the Flavian dynasty that would have occupied Books 6–12 were increasingly unsafe to write about. The stability of the reigns of Nerva and Trajan prove that the damages wrought by civil war and the tyranny of Domitian were temporary.[68] However, the rhetorically balanced aphorism draws so much attention to itself as to invite speculation. Outspokenness (the ability to 'say what you think') is a central concept of free speech, to be prized and protected. Its absence and presence can be measured; thus, freedom of speech was denied by Domitian, who did not tolerate criticism, and returned by Nerva and Trajan, who presumably did – although we are led to believe that they did not need to tolerate criticism because they did nothing to invite it. Far less tangible (or audible, to be more precise) is freedom of thought, the ability to 'think what you wish'. To judge whether thoughts were critical of one regime or supportive of another implies that thoughts were (and continued to be) monitored. Twice Tacitus pledged to write about Nerva and Trajan, but never delivered on his promise, as far as we know. Furthermore, as Brian Jones points out, a man named Calpurnius Piso was favoured by Domitian, exiled by Nerva and Trajan and killed by Hadrian, while Avidius Nigrinus, hostile towards Domitian, was also executed by Hadrian.[69] These deaths may be dismissed as incidental, but they do attest to an uneven treatment of senators after Domitian. Had the times really improved?[70]

While the *Agricola* and the *Histories* begin with apologies for a career advanced under tyranny, the *Annals* opens confidently:

> The city of Rome from the beginning was ruled by kings; liberty and consulship were instituted by Lucius Brutus. Dictatorships were assumed temporarily; the power of the boards of ten men did not extend beyond two years, nor did the consular right of military tribunes last for long. The dictatorships of Cinna and Sulla were not prolonged, and the power of Pompey and Crassus yielded quickly to Julius Caesar, the arms of Lepidus and Antony to Augustus, who under the name of *princeps* took command of a world worn out by civil war.[71]

In just two Latin sentences, Tacitus has covered a period of 800 years of history and condensed the entirety of Livy's monumental opus, which began with the foundation of the city of Rome and ended with the death of Cicero in 43 BCE, and which was followed by 22 more books on contemporary events of the Augustan age. Tacitus creates a palpable tension between the very long period of time under consideration and the very short intervals of time during which any one person held political office. Furthermore, Tacitus lays the foundation for a work about the Julio-Claudian dynasty by naming Julius Caesar and his heir Augustus. The stage is set for Tiberius.

This sweeping political history is followed immediately by a brief literary history:

> The successes and failures of the ancient Roman people have been memorialized by famous writers; the age of Augustus was not lacking talented intellect, until historians were deterred by glowing flattery. The histories of Tiberius, Gaius, Claudius and Nero were falsified by contemporary historians because of fear. After the emperors died, recent hatred dictated their histories.[72]

We can assume that Livy would have fallen into the first category of 'famous writers', for elsewhere Tacitus refers to him as 'pre-eminently famous for eloquence and honesty'.[73] The contemporary historical sources for the age of Augustus, the historians who lived during his reign and who recorded events first-hand, are lost to us. Asinius Pollio's history would have covered the years 60–42 BCE, from the first triumvirate to the battle of Philippi, the very period of time that Tacitus specified in his previous sentence. Aufidius Bassus and Servilius Nonianus wrote histories of the Tiberian principate, but Tacitus does not refer to them by name and they do not survive for us. The surviving portions of the work of Velleius Paterculus (also not mentioned by Tacitus) are characterized by the flattery that Tacitus abjures. Pliny the Elder and Cluvius Rufus wrote histories of the later Julio-Claudian period, but these do not survive either. We are quite hampered in our ability to assess Tacitus' statements.

Tacitus was not the only one to recognize the problems of bias in historical writing. Pliny the Younger preserves a snippet of a conversation between
the Flavian historian Cluvius Rufus and Verginius Rufus (whose funeral
oration Tacitus delivered in 97): 'You know, Verginius, that history must
be faithful to fact; so if you read anything in my histories which is other
than you wish, I beg you ignore it.' Verginius replied to this, 'Do you forget,
Cluvius, that I did what I did so that you could be free to write what you
please?'[74] Verginius refused the acclamation of his soldiers, but once Nero
was dead he accepted Galba as emperor;[75] yet apparently this agile naviga-
tion of treacherous political waters still did not protect the writing of history. Cluvius' work terminated either at the end of 68 or with the death of
Nero, and he did not write about the civil war, in which he was a partisan
of Galba, Otho and Vitellius in turn.[76] Tacitus, on the contrary, did write
about the age in which he lived and served office, so in the next sentence
he sets himself apart from the rest:

> From this point forward, it is my plan to hand down a few things about
> the last days of Augustus, followed by the principate of Tiberius and the
> rest, without anger and eagerness, whose causes I keep at arm's length.[77]

In the prefaces of the *Agricola* and *Histories*, Tacitus was keen to acknowledge
the favour received under the Flavians and to prove that it would not affect
his ability to write honestly. In the preface of the *Annals*, on the other hand,
he explains the causes of bias so that he can reject them soundly. Yet if the
contemporary historians of the Julio-Claudians were unable to escape bias,
then what are we to make of Tacitus' own earlier works about the Flavians?

The Plan

In part this book will attempt to answer this question by exploring the
intricate relationship between who Tacitus was and what he wrote. His
authorial voice emerges throughout his texts, not just in the prefaces. His
choices of subject matter, distribution of topics, character development

and chronological placement are, I believe, closely related to his attitudes and outlook. Along the way we will learn about the reigns of Tiberius, Claudius and Nero, and about the disastrous civil wars of 69. But more abiding are the lessons about human nature, and especially about how people cope with absolute power: how they wield and react to the authority placed in their hands and over their heads. To what extent is power secured at the centre, and to what extent is it threatened by forces on the periphery? Just how much influence could a person have on the outcome of events?

Each chapter shall keep closely to Tacitus' texts to examine the content of his works and his method of writing history. Because it is difficult to follow the complicated narratives of the *Histories* and *Annals* unless one is familiar with the major players, the next chapter, 'Nobles and Nobodies', will introduce some of the members of the Julio-Claudian and Flavian families and their supporters and detractors. Other characters are stereotypes that Tacitus carefully develops: the fawning senator, the obstreperous barbarian, the vicious informant. Elite figures dominate the pages of Roman history, yet Tacitus includes the names and deeds of non-elites in narratives that are freighted with moral lessons.

Chapter III, 'Words and Deeds', then examines how Tacitus constructs his narratives by revealing events in one of two ways: speeches in which characters speak for themselves, or summary descriptions delivered in the third person. In selecting the mode of presentation, Tacitus can exercise control over the story. He can signal his sources or include corroborating details so that the veracity of the story is taken out of his hands. He can also convey information by suggestion, innuendo, insinuation or implication. Either characters speak for themselves, or their words are reported. In such indirect discourse, quotation marks are suppressed and the conjunction 'that' is usually inserted before the reported speech, which is in a dependent clause. Tacitus' use of indirect discourse is so significant that in her recent translation of the *Annals*, Cynthia Damon has attempted to capture its artistry, opting to print reported speech and thought in italics for 'the immediacy they give to the words and thoughts of Tacitus' memorable characters'. Translation of the Latin subject in the accusative case and the verb in the infinitive form is too easily naturalized in English; italics make the difference visible. According to Damon, 'Indirect quotations strike the eye in Tacitus' Latin and because he uses them so often and to such good effect they should do so in English as well.'[78] In addition to these traditional forms of direct speech (*oratio recta*) and indirect speech (*oratio obliqua*), free indirect discourse is a form of reporting a character's speech or thought that delays or even suppresses the reporting verb of saying or thinking, and these different modes allow for information to be processed in different ways. Speech that is highlighted by direct discourse or decentralized in free indirect discourse can, for example, emphasize certain themes or characterizations, lend a degree of suspense, contribute to the overall sense of aesthetic pleasure and appeal to the reader's emotions more or less directly. In part the difficulties in reading Tacitus stem from his seamless transitions from one mode to the next, which complicate the reader's ability to discern easily who is speaking or whose ideas are being represented. Furthermore, Tacitus moves back and forth between omniscience and the limited point of view of one character. In part, then, Tacitus is inscrutable because of such shifts to this so-called internal focalization; and in these shifts, again Tacitus is able to insert his own opinions. The result is a sort of echo chamber: one can never be quite sure whether the opinions expressed are those of the times narrated or those of Tacitus' own day.

Chapter IV, 'Romans and Others', argues that the *Germania*, far from being an anomalous work, is critical for understanding Tacitus. The *Germania* contains themes and concerns that are central to Tacitus' way of thinking. For example, the perpetual confrontation between freedom and slavery and the theme of tyrannical dissimulation evident in the *Histories* and *Annals* already begin to surface in the *Germania*. Rome is of course at the forefront of the treatise, but hybridity blurs the distinction between the centre of the empire and the provinces on the periphery. Tacitus resists a one-to-one correspondence between the near and the far, the morally good and the morally reprehensible. Instead of neat maps that indicate precisely where morality resides, intricate patterns convey implicit value judgements about the limits of empire, whether fixed by Augustus or extended by Trajan; hence the monograph is constructed along an axis of praise and criticism for Romans and Germani alike.

Chapter V, 'Then and Now', traces critical correspondences between the *Dialogue on Orators* and the *Annals*, to demonstrate how Tacitus revisits themes such as the decline of oratory as seen in the comparison of past to present, the periodization of a genre according to political regime and the influence of politics on the art of persuasion. To achieve this, Tacitus takes a fair number of chronological liberties. For example, the *Annals* begin with the accession of Tiberius; however, the digression on the origin of law allows Tacitus to comment on a number of events that predate the reign of Tiberius, while the digression on luxury leads him beyond the reign of Nero to speak of Vespasian as chiefly responsible for frugal behaviour.[79] Of course, ancient historians had long since used digressions for chronological in- and extrusions; likewise, temporal displacement is the historian's prerogative. Tacitus is therefore not the only historian to bend time to his purpose, but his extant writings treat time in such a way as to generate a unique matrix that affords us glimpses of moments in the history of imperial Rome like no other. Moreover, in Tacitus' treatment of time, especially in the pervasive comparisons of (degenerate) present to (honourable) past, his moralizing tone rings clear.

This brings us to the core problem when reading Tacitus: how to separate the opinions inserted by the historian at the time of writing from genuine opinions held by the subjects of his writing. To what extent did current affairs of the period obtrude upon the events he is writing about? Among its many purposes and achievements, Sir Ronald Syme's monumental *Tacitus* in two volumes is a thoroughgoing demonstration of the influence of contemporary events in Tacitus' own lifetime upon his writing. While the argument is orchestrated across hundreds of pages, it crystallizes here:

> The early chapters of Book I [of the *Annals*] depict political behaviour, pitilessly – the fraudulent protestations of loyal subjects, discreetly modulated between mourning and rejoicing, and the eager rush to voluntary enslavement. State ceremonial, public professions, and secret conflicts – the whole thing may seem to hint and foreshadow the accession of Hadrian.[80]

Syme announces unequivocally the narrative principles governing the structure of Tacitus' *Annals*. We have come to call this kind of historical explanation 'metahistory', and if we are suspicious of the motives behind Tacitus' narratives of the Julio-Claudians, then we can be doubly suspicious of the motives behind Syme's two-volume *Tacitus*, written during the Cold War.

With this in mind, the sixth and final chapter, 'Yesterday and Today', will explore the influence of Tacitus across the ages, and again the *Germania* will prove central, for the work earned Tacitus the title of 'father of ancient Germanic studies'.[81] The rapidly growing field of classical reception studies aims to explore the transmission, interpretation, rewriting and rethinking of ancient Greek and Roman material as it is reworked in the contexts of other cultures. After a necessarily brief survey of the reception of Tacitus from late antiquity to the Middle Ages, Renaissance, early modern period and the nineteenth century, we will turn to three different twentieth-century iterations of the story of Germanicus in the *Annals*, which has proven irresistible. The saga of Germanicus' death is the subject of *Germanicus*, a play published by South African writer Nicolaas Petrus van Wyk Louw in 1956. The return to the Teutoburg Forest, as told in the first book of the *Annals*, is reimagined in Anselm Kiefer's painting *Varus* (1976) and in the poem 'The Return', by Frank Bidart (1997). Through their interpretations of Tacitus on stage, on canvas and in verse, these artists and writers harness the power of Tacitus' dark imagery to convey the fallibility and finitude of the human condition.

II

Nobles and Nobodies

AMONG HIS MANY COMPLAINTS about Tacitus, Reverend Thomas Hunter grumbled, 'Tacitus has too many Actors and Figures in his Piece which breed Confusion.'[1] Indeed, the cast of characters in the works of Tacitus is daunting: approximately 1,000 individuals are named (only 70 of which are women), and about 300 of these are known only from Tacitus. Of course, he was writing history, and so the pages should be filled with the lives and deeds of the principal actors and those with whom they lived and interacted ('So many names and agents, such is the nature of senatorial annals,' says Ronald Syme).[2] The cast is further complicated by the Roman system of nomenclature, which Tacitus manipulates for effect; then, behind these characters, are the ancestors of those on the page, whose deeds and exploits performed a decade, a generation or even a century earlier influenced the state of affairs under discussion but are not fully explained because they fall outside the temporal scope of the narrative. Readers of Tacitus are therefore expected to come to the text with quite a bit of prior knowledge, and it is the aim of this chapter to explore Tacitus' treatment of the Julio-Claudians who inhabit the *Annals* and then the emperors and their factions in the

Histories, remembering, of course, that the *Histories* were written before the *Annals* (Tacitus was always on the retreat, selecting topics ever further in the past). To complement the prosopography of mainly elite persons, the second part of the chapter attempts to resurrect and analyse Tacitus' portrayals of non-elites. For now, we will set aside the *Dialogue on Orators*, *Agricola* and *Germania*, since the dramatis personae of these works are manageable given their contexts.

Nobles

Tacitus begins the *Annals* with the death of Augustus, who suffered the worst fate to befall any potentate: he had no sons. As Tacitus says, 'As sturdy as the fortune of Augustus was in matters of state, so unfavourable was it within his own home.'[3] With only a daughter (whom he banished for adultery) and a string of untimely funerals for his grandsons, Augustus was obliged to adopt Tiberius, thereby merging the Julian with the Claudian clan. The result is a complicated nexus of family relationships that tends to fatigue modern readers before they turn the first page; yet readers who despair amidst the tangled branches of the Julio-Claudian family tree should remember that no one would have liked to give us a simpler line of accession more than Augustus himself.

Augustus had one daughter, Julia, by his second wife Scribonia, whom he divorced. Julia married Augustus' close friend and general, Marcus Agrippa. They had three sons and two daughters. Gaius and Lucius died as children, and the third son, Agrippa Postumus, was killed upon the ascension of Tiberius in the year 14. Julia the Younger was sent into exile as punishment for adultery; no offspring survived. Thus Agrippina the Elder was the only child of Julia and Marcus Agrippa to have children, the only blood heirs of Augustus.

After divorcing Scribonia, Augustus married Livia, who had two sons by her first husband Tiberius Claudius Nero: Tiberius (emperor) and Nero Claudius Drusus, or Drusus, as he was known. As sons of Tiberius 'Claudius' Nero, these two sons of Livia introduce the 'Claudian' element into the dynasty. Drusus was married to Antonia the Younger, daughter of Augustus' only sister Octavia. They had three children: Livilla, Claudius (emperor) and Germanicus. After Marcus Agrippa died, Tiberius was forced to marry Julia, in an attempt to strengthen the family bond so that Livia's son was married to Augustus' daughter, but the marriage was a fruitless disaster.

The marriage of Agrippina the Elder and Germanicus united the granddaughter of Augustus with the grandson of Livia. Of their six children, Gaius 'Caligula' became emperor, and Agrippina the Younger was the mother of Nero. She was also married for a time to her uncle, the emperor Claudius, who had two children by his third wife, Valeria Messalina: Britannicus and Octavia. These were murdered by Nero, whose only daughter Claudia Augusta died in infancy. When Nero took his own life in 68, the dynasty came to an end (see Figure 2.1).

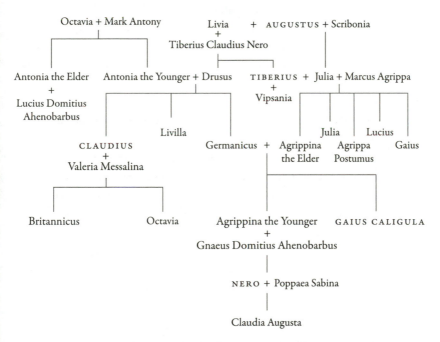

2.1 The family of Augustus, selected.
Emperors are indicated by capital letters.

A key figure in the family lineage is Augustus' sister Octavia, betrothed to the triumvir Mark Antony in an attempt to strengthen political bonds. Eventually Mark Antony became Augustus' rival and committed suicide with Queen Cleopatra, but his daughter Antonia the Younger married Drusus, son of Livia, and their son Claudius became emperor. Yet Peter Wiseman reminds us that 'Claudius was not a Caesar either by blood or by adoption'; indeed, Claudius was the grandson of Mark Antony, Augustus' one-time enemy! Caligula was Augustus' great-grandson, Nero his great-great-grandson. Therefore, Claudius' reign was 'a usurpation, an anomalous interruption in the dynastic succession of Augustus' family'.[4]

While the Julio-Claudian family tree may provide vertical structure to the hexads of the *Annals*, for Tacitus the significance of the dynasty lies in the peripheral relationships. He is interested in the members of court who did not come to power but whose marriages and alliances influenced the balance of power. So let us expand upon Figure 2.1.

Augustus' sister Octavia had two daughters. Antonia the Younger, whom we mentioned above, was mother of Claudius and Germanicus. Antonia the Elder married Lucius Domitius Ahenobarbus. His obituary includes information about his father and grandfather:

> His father, powerful at sea during the civil war, brought credit until he joined partisans of Antony and later Julius Caesar. His grandfather had fallen at the Battle of Pharsalus fighting for the cause of the optimates. He himself was chosen to marry Antonia the Elder, daughter of Octavia, then crossed the Elbe River with an army that penetrated deeper into Germania than any before, and for these exploits he obtained the triumphal insignia.[5]

These facts about the ancestors of Lucius Domitius Ahenobarbus corroborate a passing statement that Tacitus makes later on, when his son, Gnaeus Domitius Ahenobarbus, marries Agrippina the Younger:

> Then Tiberius ordered the marriage to be celebrated in Rome, when he handed his granddaughter Agrippina the Younger born of Germanicus to Gn. Domitius Ahenobarbus in the presence of witnesses. Besides the

antiquity of his family line, in Domitius Tiberius had selected blood
ties to the Caesars, for Domitius could call Octavia his grandmother
and through her Augustus his great-uncle.[6]

The marriage was intended to strengthen political alliances. Given that their
son Nero became emperor, the strategy appears to have worked.

Of course, not all marriages produced such lasting results. Tiberius'
first wife Vipsania is a fascinating character in her own right. She was the
only daughter of Marcus Agrippa by his first wife, Caecilia Metella (before
he married Julia). Vipsania was betrothed to Tiberius in her infancy and
they had one son, Drusus the Younger. After Tiberius was forced to divorce
Vipsania so that he could marry Julia, Vipsania married Asinius Gallus –
who could therefore never be on friendly terms with Tiberius. Their five
sons (see Figure 2.2) did not fare well: Gaius Asinius Pollio was exiled and
executed in 45; Marcus Asinius Agrippa died in 26; Asinius Saloninus died
in 22; under the emperor Claudius, Servius Asinius Celer was killed and the
youngest son Asinius Gallus exiled. Thus Tacitus says of her death:

> A few days later Drusus the Younger's mother Vipsania died, the only
> one of all of the children of Agrippa whose death was not violent, for
> the rest were either openly cut down by the sword or believed to have
> been poisoned or starved.[7]

Tacitus is referring to Agrippa's five children by Julia. Lucius died of natural
causes, Gaius of a wound; poison was suspected in both cases.[8] Agrippa
Postumus was murdered, 'the first crime' of Tiberius' principate, according
to Tacitus.[9] Julia the Younger died in exile. Vipsania's peaceful end contrasts
sharply with the terrible death of Agrippina the Elder:

> News was heard of Agrippina the Elder, who I reckon had lived on,
> sustained by hope, after the death of Sejanus, and after no effort was
> spared on savagery she took her own life, unless of course such an end
> is merely pretence when food is withheld, so as to seem undertaken of
> one's own accord.[10]

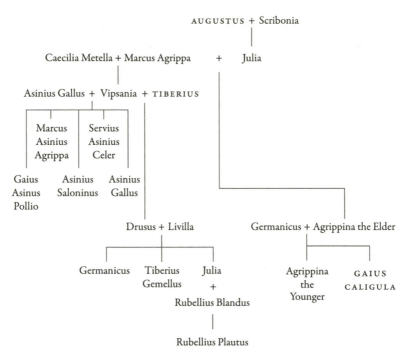

2.2 The family of Vipsania, selected.
Emperors are indicated by capital letters.

Of the sons of Vipsania, then, Drusus the Younger had the most successful career both in military command and in political office. From the outset, his father Tiberius put him in charge of quelling the mutiny of the legions in the military zone of Germania upon his accession in 14. The following year father and son were consuls. After the death of Germanicus, Tiberius asked the Senate to bestow tribunician power on his son, following the example of Augustus who had similarly designated his heir.

Drusus the Younger was qualified: he had eight years of military experience, a triumph and two consulships.[11] He was married to Livilla, sister of Claudius and Germanicus; they had twin boys and a girl. Because he was clearly in line to succeed Tiberius, he was a major obstacle to Sejanus, the sinister praetorian prefect who sought power for himself, and the rivalry was bitter: Sejanus seduced Livilla and imposed himself upon Tiberius to such an extent that Drusus the Younger complained publicly of his pre-sumptuousness. Sejanus acted quickly: Drusus the Younger was poisoned. Livilla was now widowed, and Sejanus sought her hand in marriage, but Tiberius soundly rejected him – not least because of his inferior birth and status. Eventually Livilla committed suicide after the fall of Sejanus. As for the children, one twin died at the age of four; the other, Tiberius Gemellus, was murdered by Caligula. Daughter Julia was married to Rubellius Blandus, and their son was executed by Nero. This was effectively the end of Tiberius' line (see Figure 2.2).

Vertical relationships lend continuity from the first to the third hexad; for example, the marriage at the end of *Annals* Book 3 produced the emperor who occupies *Annals* Books 13–16. Horizontal relationships among siblings and their spouses enrich the narrative of the *Annals*, with further possibilities to demonstrate tyranny as well as nobility.

There are also characters whose families and fates extend from the *Annals* into the *Histories*. Ellen O'Gorman has demonstrated that the Pisones, whose overarching presence unites Tacitus' historical works, constituted what she calls a 'virtual' dynasty.[12] In fact, 27 different Calpurnii Pisones are attested from the imperial period.[13] Furthermore, in 1884 nine funerary altars that belonged to the Licinian family were discovered in Rome, pro-viding physical evidence of the nexus of relationships that Tacitus exploits in his narrative.[14]

O'Gorman identifies five Pisones whose stories span Tacitus' historical writings. The first is Gnaeus Calpurnius Piso, appointed by Tiberius as governor of Syria in the year 17:

> Tiberius appointed Gnaeus Piso, a man of violent temper and unac-customed to deference, whose fierceness was inherited from his father Piso, who during the civil war helped the insurgent partisans in Africa against Julius Caesar, but then soon followed Brutus and Cassius and upon his return refrained from seeking office until at last he was named by Augustus to accept the consulship. In addition to his father's spirit the noble rank and wealth of his wife Plancina also advanced his cause.[15]

Tacitus suggests that Gnaeus Piso was deployed specifically to hinder Germanicus, whose popularity, experience and descent made him a rival to Tiberius' son Drusus the Younger. According to Tacitus, Piso 'hardly doubted that he was appointed to Syria for the purpose of checking Germanicus' hopes. Some believe he was given secret orders by Tiberius.'[16] In Syria, Piso bribed the soldiers, replaced strict commanders with lax, and generally demoralized the legions in Germanicus' absence. When Germanicus returned from a visit to Egypt (a breach of protocol, since senators were prohibited from entering this particular imperial province) and discovered his orders reversed, they quarrelled openly. Germanicus contracted an illness, and Piso left for Seleucia. Germanicus died, and Piso was charged with murder by poison. Before the trial was finished, Piso took his own life. The inscription of the *senatus consultum de Gn. Pisone patre* describes Piso's rivalry with Germanicus, his insubordination and his punishments, as well as the investigation of his death and the thanksgiving decreed because the death of Germanicus had been avenged.[17]

Second is Gaius Calpurnius Piso, the nominal head of a conspiracy to assassinate Nero. In 65 CE, soldiers, senators and equestrians banded together out of hatred for Nero and agreed to assassinate him and give their support to Gaius Piso, whom Tacitus describes as follows:

> He was born of the Calpurnian line and on his father's noble side was connected to many notable families. He had a good reputation among the commoners for his virtue, or at least an appearance of virtue. For he used his eloquence in defence of fellow citizens, his generosity towards friends, and towards strangers he exercised gentle speech and conduct. In addition, he was tall and handsome, but not very serious in his ways or reserved in his spending. He indulged in laziness, magnificence and occasionally luxury. This met the approval of the common folk who, when the attraction of vice is so much the stronger, are not looking for some higher authority that is restrictive or extremely severe.[18]

Germanicus' enemy Gnaeus Piso had a violent and arrogant temperament. He pursued ambition through his military career and social advancement through his marriage to Plancina. The Neronian conspirator Gaius Piso, on the other hand, although similarly noted for his noble lineage, was merely easy-going and good-looking, with no military or political experience to speak of. His indulgent lifestyle would ensure that those who were comfortable under Nero would remain so. Thus in their choice of Piso the conspirators do not seem to seek real regime change. The freedman of one of the conspirators informed Nero, and the plot was leaked. In their panic, conspirators betrayed one another, and Gaius Piso committed suicide.[19]

Third is Lucius Calpurnius Piso Frugi Licinianus, adopted by Galba on 10 January 69. Galba's adoption of Piso occupies *Histories* 1.12–20, paragraphs 'fuller, more accurate, and more richly elaborated than those in the parallel sources',[20] perhaps because the scene is meant to evoke Nerva's more recent adoption of Trajan. Once again, Tacitus takes the time to remark about the high standing of the Pisones as well as questionable character traits, which he implies are inherited:

> [Calpurnius] Piso was the son of Marcus Crassus and Scribonia, noble therefore on both sides, and possessed of the ancient ways in appearance and demeanour; by righteous judgement he was considered severe and he was less well disposed towards those who regarded him as anything less. This part of his character was as pleasing to his adoptive father as it was suspected by those whom it worried.[21]

As Gnaeus Piso sought to usurp Germanicus and Gaius Piso was proposed as an alternative to Nero, so Calpurnius Piso is intended to be Galba's successor and therefore replacement. Gaius and Calpurnius appear to be chosen because they can approximate Nero and Galba with minimal risk of imposing any real change. Once Galba was assassinated, it was as if the adoption meant nothing. Piso merely bought himself some time by hiding in the Temple of Vesta before he was dragged out and slaughtered on the steps by the henchmen of Otho. His funeral rites were performed by his brother Scribonianus and his wife Verania, who ransomed the severed head from the greedy assassins who had saved it for sale.[22] Piso's collected remains were then deposited in the Licinian tomb together with those of his brother and father, and as Patrick Kragelund notes, even the inscription avoids any mention that Piso was ever Caesar:[23] 'To the shades of Lucius Calpurnius Piso Frugi Licinianus, member of the priesthood of the Fifteen, and to the shades of Verania Gemina, daughter of the consul and augur Quintus Veranius, wife of Piso Frugi.'

The fall of Vitellius in 69 meant the end of the civil war and the establishment of the Flavian dynasty, but it did not bring immediate peace. In the aftermath, as Rome awaited the arrival of Vespasian, partisans sought vengeance and the Senate quarrelled bitterly. In this atmosphere of unrest, Mucianus put to death Calpurnius Galerianus:

> He was the son of Gaius Piso [the Neronian conspirator]. Although he had done nothing, nevertheless his well-known name and youthful attractiveness were the talk of the common crowd in a city still in turmoil and happy with new gossip; there were those who spread idle rumour of his seeking the principate. By the order of Mucianus he was put under military arrest. In case his death within the city might be more conspicuous, at the fourth stone from the city on the Appian Way he had him killed by draining the blood from his veins.[24]

With each successive Piso, the story shortens. Gnaeus was appointed governor of Syria in 17 and died two years later. Gaius headed the Pisonian conspiracy in 65 and died within the year. Calpurnius was the adoptive heir of Galba for only four days. Galerianus is introduced and dispatched in the space of one paragraph. Yet even this Piso, like the others, is 'an aspiring emperor'.[25]

The very last Piso in Tacitus is Lucius Piso, the proconsul of Africa and the cousin and father-in-law of Galerianus. Africa contained pockets of anti-Flavian support that encouraged Lucius Piso to assume command of Vitellianist supporters, on the grounds that Gaul was wavering and the legions in Germania were ready to revolt. News reached Lucius Piso that his death had been ordered, and yet he did not take up arms, even though the people of Carthage rushed into the marketplace and demanded that Lucius Piso appear in public. Instead, when the messenger from Vespasian's general Mucianus arrived, Lucius Piso had him killed on the spot, and upbraided the citizens of Carthage. Quitting his duties, he did not venture out in public. The popular uproar, the execution of the messenger and general rumour worried Valerius Festus, commander of the legions in Africa, who ordered the cavalry to put Lucius Piso to death. Tacitus describes the scene:

> They set out immediately just before dawn and burst into the house of the proconsul with swords drawn. Most of them did not know Piso, because Festus had chosen Phoenician and Moorish auxiliary troops for the assassination. Not far from the bedroom they happened to meet a slave, and when they asked him who and where Piso was, the slave replied with an obvious lie that he was Piso, and they killed him on the spot. Not much later Piso was killed, for there was present one who knew him: Baebius Massa, one of the procurators of Africa, a man even then hateful to anyone good and soon to be a recurrent cause of the evils which we would soon bear.[26]

Festus followed the murder with arrests, punishments and rewards so that the affair would have all the trappings of a legitimate revolt, which he could then claim to have suppressed. So for the fifth and final time, then, Tacitus tells the story of a Piso who would have been emperor, leading O'Gorman to ask, 'What if?' What if Piso had unseated Germanicus? Or Gaius Piso had replaced Nero? Or Piso Licinianus had succeeded Galba? Or the son of Gaius really had sought the principate? Or Lucius Piso had revolted in Africa against Vespasian? The repeated attempts suggest a weakness in a system that would let these men come as close as they did to ruling the empire, but Tacitus is also interested in the resilience of the principate. It should have been easy to assassinate the last Piso in his own home, yet the centurions misfired and had to rely on an informant whose description slips almost imperceptibly into the first person: Tacitus knew this man.

Baebius Massa was an equestrian procurator of Africa in 70 and was promoted to the Senate by Vespasian as a reward for his part in the suppression of this so-called revolt. His approval by the Flavian regime continued until the time of Domitian, whose favour he enjoyed and to whom he served as an informant so notoriously that Juvenal lambasts him in his first satire, wondering openly who could contain himself at the approach of 'the man who informed on his powerful friend, the man who will soon grab any scraps left from the carcass of the nobility, the man feared even by Massa?'[27] In 91 Baebius Massa was governor of Baetica (western Spain), his last recorded post. Two years later he was accused of plundering the province. Pliny the Younger and Herennius Senecio (who was from Baetica) were chosen to prosecute, and Tacitus mentions the trial briefly at the end of the *Agricola* in such a way as to imply that Baebius Massa was still an active threat even after this case.[28] Pliny seems rather proud to have been chosen by the Senate, for he describes in a letter to Tacitus his involvement in the case, in the hopes that Tacitus will include it in the relevant part of his *Histories*.[29] We cannot know whether or to what extent the trial of Baebius Massa would have been included in the *Histories* after Book 5, but his passing mention in the *Agricola* followed by this detailed account of his part in the African revolt and the hint of future trouble suggests that Pliny was right to be hopeful.

Our survey of characters has thus progressed from the Julio-Claudians, who died long before Tacitus began writing the *Annals*, to a newly risen senator whom Tacitus knew. Another useful way to keep track of the hundreds of people mentioned by Tacitus is to recognize common features that establish categories of stock characters. In 1952, Elisabeth Walker Henry first published a study of the *Annals* in which she identified the tyrant and his entourage of the opportunist, the informer, the victim and the collaborator. The tyrants Tiberius and Nero could not have maintained their power without some assistance from collaborators, notably the praetorian prefects. Yet in spite of their loyalty to their *principes*, Sejanus and Burrus were replaced by Macro and Tigellinus. Collaborators were no safer than victims. As collaborators and victims are in a sense codependent, so too Walker posits that the Noble Savage and the Intransigent are likewise complementary. The former criticizes the Roman Empire from his or her position as non-Roman (for example, Arminius, chief of the Cherusci; Caratacus, chief of the Catuvellauni; and Boudicca, queen of the Iceni), while the latter also refuses to comply but from within Roman society (for example, the senators Cremutius Cordus and Thrasea Paetus).[30]

Equipped with these categories, the reader can anticipate attitudes, behaviours and outcomes based on the actions of similar types. So the tyrant is driven by a lust for power that, once gained, then causes resentment in his subjects; his excessive power makes him an object of suspicion. At the same time, however, the tyrant is suspicious of those around him. He is afraid of rebellions, conspiracies, plots and assassination. When these fears exceed reason, the tyrant becomes paranoid. Excessive power also leads to excessive behaviour, and the tyrant is thus traditionally depicted as immoral and debauched. Finally, Walker notes, the tyrant's overall effect on society is disastrous.[31] Tacitus' tyrants are Tiberius, Nero and Domitian.

Attached to the tyrant are the opportunist and informer, distinguished by their social class. Both are egotistical, arrogant and lack self-respect; however, the former is usually a freedman, while the latter is usually of higher rank, even a senator. These men do whatever it takes to advance themselves at the expense of others. They do not adhere to traditional Roman values of honesty, faith or trust. Preying on the tyrant's suspicious nature, they accuse or denounce anyone if they think it will increase their standing, yet as Steven Rutledge has shown, informants were not guaranteed political or social advancement; if anything, they stood to lose ground within a conservative society that valued traditional means of competition and advancement.[32] Thus Baebius Massa is all the more reprehensible a character for profiting by his betrayal of Lucius Piso – and whoever else Tacitus is alluding to in *Histories* 4.50.

For example, Fulcinius Trio, a senator under Tiberius, was an informer who appears to adhere to the character type. According to Rutledge, Fulcinius was from a family that could trace ancestors all the way back to the Republic, but none appear to have held the consulship.[33] In the year 16, Tiberius was friends with a man named Libo Drusus, whose friend Firmius Catus convinced him to dabble in astrology and magic. Tiberius ignored the rumours of this questionable behaviour, until a certain Junius (otherwise unknown) was asked to perform necromancy. Junius alerted Fulcinius Trio, whose 'talent among informers and greed for evil notoriety [was] well known.'[34] Fulcinius thus initiated the proceedings against Libo Drusus, who committed suicide before the verdict was rendered. Tiberius swore that the hasty suicide prevented his intervention on the defendant's behalf, even though he was guilty.[35] So from this episode, we learn that Fulcinius, who already had a reputation, was an effective prosecutor. Four years later, Fulcinius Trio is involved in an even higher-profile case that likewise resulted in the suicide of the defendant. He was part of the team that prosecuted Piso for the murder of Germanicus. When the trial was over, Tiberius rewarded the prosecutors Vitellius (uncle of the future emperor), Veranius and Servaeus with priesthoods, while 'to Fulcinius he promised recommendation to office, but warned him not to ruin his eloquence with violence.'[36] The promise seems to have been kept, for Fulcinius was suffect consul in 31, the year that Tiberius' praetorian prefect Sejanus fell from power:

> At the end of the year a long-growing enmity between the consuls [Fulcinius Trio and Memmius Regulus] came to a head. For Trio, ready to take up hostilities and practised in the forum, struck at Regulus indirectly for being slow to indict the henchmen of Sejanus. Regulus, on the other hand, who retained self-control unless attacked, not only blunted his colleague's attack but was ready to drag him into court accused of conspiracy. Although many senators asked them to set aside their hatred that was bound to end in disaster, they remained hostile and threatening until they left office.[37]

At work here is what Joseph Roisman calls the rhetoric of conspiracy, whereby the allegation of conspiracy is 'more easily made than refuted'.[38] The consuls hurl the accusations at one another without need for rigorous proof. Indeed, their name-calling backfired, because the next year Haterius Agrippa accused them both of conspiracy since neither of them had pursued their earlier accusations.[39] At that time, the senators did not take action, but four years later, Tiberius continued to punish doubtful or forgotten offences. Under this cloud, Fulcinius Trio committed suicide rather than await prosecution; yet even from beyond the grave he continued his vociferous denunciations, for in his will he inserted accusations against Macro (Sejanus' successor), Tiberius' freedmen and Tiberius himself. Whether guilty or innocent of conspiracy, Fulcinius Trio was true to his character type to the end. He was an informant who attacked social superiors and who eventually paid the price for his talent.

So how are we to judge Fulcinius Trio? He was part of the team that prosecuted Libo Drusus, whom Tiberius actually trusted, and who was perhaps entrapped by Firmius Catus to engage in activities that he would not have otherwise. Yet, if Libo Drusus' actions were not so innocent, then perhaps he could have been perceived by Fulcinius Trio as seeking advice about the possibilities of overthrowing Tiberius. Fulcinius Trio could then have been seen as acting to preserve the life of the *princeps* and to safeguard the regime. Likewise in the case against Piso: Fulcinius Trio was part of the team that prosecuted the murderer of Germanicus. When it came to the treasonous Sejanus, he felt that his colleague Regulus had not been vigorous enough in prosecuting the supporters. So while Tacitus implies that Fulcinius was overly eager to ruin lives, it is also possible that he had good intentions. In his suicide, he finally became the victim, for like Libo Drusus, we can never know whether he was guilty or whether he was innocent but unwilling to suffer an unjust trial. Whether by choice or by necessity, informants dwell in a morally ambiguous state.[40]

Victims are another of Walker's stock characters. They elicit our pity and die dramatically before our eyes. Consider Britannicus, the son of Claudius, who should have come to power upon his father's death but was sidelined by the machinations of Claudius' wife Agrippina the Younger, who saw to it that her son Nero was hailed emperor instead. Tacitus paints a vivid picture. At a festival a few days before Britannicus' fourteenth birthday, Nero ordered his stepbrother to sing for the party guests. Unlike Hamlet, who exposed his uncle's nefarious plot by staging the allegorical 'Murder of Gonzago', Britannicus sang loud and clear about his being cast out of his father's home and robbed of his patrimony: 'Whence arose a pity all the more manifest because night and recklessness had stripped away any pretence,' Tacitus says.[41] Nero became furious and ordered poison to be prepared. Again Britannicus' youth and helplessness are underscored by the fact that the poison administered by his tutors passed through his bowels without consequence, either because it was simply ineffective or because it was diluted. So a second, successful attempt was made on the boy's life.

Tacitus describes in detail the children's table at the family dinner and the trick by which the poison was added to the drink after it had been sampled by the slave. Death was immediate. Nero remained composed, but his mother's shocked response suggested that she was not privy to the plot. In the same moment that Britannicus thus falls victim to Nero's tyranny, Tacitus hints that Agrippina the Younger will herself become a victim of Nero: 'She realized that her last source of aid had been stripped from her and was now a precedent for murder.' The scene ends with the pitiable response of Octavia, Britannicus' sister, soon to be Nero's victim: 'Octavia too, though still quite young, had learned to hide grief, charity, all emotion. Thus after a brief silence the happiness of the dinner resumed.'[42]

Walker herself realized the limitations of such a generalizing approach (which is also limited to the *Annals* and therefore only partial in its analysis). Artificial distinctions rapidly break down and inconsistencies surface. Assumptions swallow the details. Differences are elided. Stereotypes reinscribe rather than expose prejudices. To counteract the forces of generalization, prosopography minds the particular, with close attention to the names themselves.[43] Adjectives derived from the *nomen* indicate adoption; for example, the complete name of Scipio the Younger was Publius Cornelius Scipio Africanus Aemilianus: Africanus denoted his exploits in Africa, Aemilianus his adoption from the Aemilian *gens*. In understanding the complex relationships of characters in Tacitus, it is important to pay attention to the *gens*. For example, there are 23 different Cornelii mentioned by Tacitus (himself a Cornelius), not including those from whom the name Cornelius was omitted. The families of Aemilius, Antonius, Calpurnius, Cassius, Claudius, Domitius, Julius, Junius, Pompeius, Sulpicius, Valerius and eventually Vitellius contribute grandfathers, fathers and sons to history, so that what emerges is a picture of elite social and political circles, tightly drawn and fiercely guarded. So for example while it is helpful to think of Rubellius Plautus as a victim executed by the tyrant Nero, his plight takes on added significance when we reconnect him to his father, the Rubellius Blandus whose marriage to Julia, granddaughter of Tiberius, is embedded in Tacitus' account of the massacre of the detainees associated with the conspiracy of Sejanus.[44] Yet prosopography has its shortcomings too, for it only enables the reconstruction of elite society, which was designated by *gens*. We learn a great deal about the powerful families of Rome, and next to nothing about ordinary men and women. So we will close this chapter with an examination of those people mentioned in Tacitus by one name only, whose names appear only once, or whose part in the narrative is minimal.

Nobodies

History belongs to the nobility, at least until revolt or conspiracy threatens stability. Only then does Tacitus provide the names of individuals who would otherwise remain invisible. When Tiberius became *princeps*, the legions in Pannonia revolted, for no other reason (according to Tacitus) than that the change in regime abolished discipline and promised hope of booty from civil war (*Histories* Book 1 is rife with such motives). It was summer, and the commander Junius Blaesus authorized furlough. Idleness led to disaffection, which one legionnaire used to his advantage: 'In camp there was a certain Percennius, once a leader of a theatrical troupe but lately a common soldier, a smooth talker who knew from his acting experience how to stir up a crowd.'[45] He succeeded in agitating the other soldiers, who agreed to make their demands to Tiberius via envoys. While they waited, the mutiny rekindled, and amidst the outbreak another common soldier (Tacitus uses the same Latin phrase, *gregarius miles*) took centre stage: 'and a certain Vibulenus, a common soldier, was lifted before the platform of Blaesus on the shoulders of the bystanders among the throng and addressed an audience intent on what he prepared to say.'[46]

Vibulenus proceeded to fabricate a story about his brother, who he claimed had been murdered by the general's henchmen and denied burial. His performance was effective at arousing the indignation of the soldiers, but the truth got out quickly that he had no brother. The soldiers plundered the camp and killed a centurion named Lucilius, whom they had nicknamed 'Bring Another', because he would whip the soldiers so vigorously that when the rod broke he would call for another.[47] Tiberius sent his son Drusus, who quelled the mutiny and ordered the deaths of Percennius and Vibulenus.

At the same time and for the same reasons, a revolt also broke out in the region of Germania, and here again Tacitus embellishes the narrative with a high level of detail. Germanicus is sent to settle the troops, and upon his arrival they swarm him. Some grasp his hand as if to kiss it, but instead thrust it in their mouths so that he feels their toothless gums, proof of their old age and right to retirement. He addresses the troops, who complain of low pay, hazardous duty and unfair service. They go so far as to offer him their allegiance and even threaten him when he tries to leave, but he protests that he would rather die than usurp Tiberius. He draws his sword as if to plunge it into his own breast, when a certain soldier named Calusidius offers his, saying 'Take mine – it's sharper.'[48]

Percennius, Vibulenus, Lucilius and Calusidius lend the narrative at least a high degree of verisimilitude, if not veracity. In his commentary, F. R. D. Goodyear remarks of the episode that 'artistic convenience may have got the better of historical truth'.[49] Yet the names of low-born individuals drive home the powerful ideological message that only a few men are capable of ruling the empire. Tiberius' rule was not seriously threatened by these revolts.

Nor was Nero unseated by the Pisonian conspiracy, although the threat was within his midst and not on the frontiers. Nowhere else does Tacitus load his narrative with the names of so many individuals as in his account of the Pisonian conspiracy. After introducing Gaius Piso Tacitus lists the ringleaders, notable men whose incentives varied. Plautius Lateranus was the nephew of Aulus Plautius, who under Claudius, Tacitus tells us in the *Agricola*, was the first governor of Britannia of consular rank.[50] This distinguished military service induced Claudius to spare the nephew Plautius Lateranus from the death penalty when he was found guilty of adultery with Messalina. Nero reinstated Plautius Lateranus to the Senate and designated him consul for the year 65. Therefore he joined the conspiracy, says Tacitus, 'not because of any insult but out of love of the Republic' (*amor rei publicae*).[51] Of course this noble motive is undercut by Lateranus' immoral behaviour; still, if men indebted to Nero were willing to conspire, then surely men with personal motives joined without hesitation. Together with Plautius Lateranus, Tacitus mentions the poet Lucan, nephew of Seneca the Younger, whose distinguished position in Nero's court should likewise have protected him. However, after Nero heard the first three books of Lucan's epic poem, *The Civil War*, their relationship cooled. When Lucan went so far as to write a poem, 'On the Burning of the City', blaming Nero for the Great Fire of Rome that had occurred the year before, Nero banned his poetry.[52] Two more senators enlisted in the conspiracy, with rather similar motives, for Flavius Scaevinus was self-indulgent and lazy and Afranius Quintianus wanted to avenge a personal insult.[53] Then Tacitus lists conspirators of equestrian rank Vulcatius Araricus, Julius Augurinus, Munatius Gratus and Marcus Festus, and centurions Maximus Scaurus and Venetus Paulus. Clearly Tacitus consulted his sources or interviewed his elders; however, besides confirming his research method, the inclusion of names which only appear once reinforces the exceptionality of the conspiracy.

Unique names also give the conspiracy an extraordinary level of detail. The plot was beginning to unravel under rumours that after the assassination of Nero the centurions intended to kill Piso and install Seneca. Nor could the centurions bear the arrogance of the prefect Faenius Rufus, whose implication in the conspiracy was manifest, and so 'he was seized and bound by a soldier named Cassius who because of his distinctive physical strength was standing nearby.'[54] More detail is lavished on the single appearance of a tribune named Veianius Niger, who botched the execution of the conspirator Subrius Flavus:

> He ordered a pit to be dug in the nearby field, which Flavus criticized as too shallow and narrow, saying to the soldiers who surrounded him, 'Not even this according to regulation.' Boldly he offered his neck on command, saying, 'Would that you strike as boldly!' Trembling noticeably, Veianius Niger scarcely decapitated him with two blows, but boasted his savagery to Nero, saying he killed him with one and a half.[55]

For the once-named Veianius Niger Tacitus constructs the noun *sesquiplaga*, 'a stroke and a half', a word which appears nowhere else in extant Latin literature. The anecdote allows Tacitus to cast positive light on the

Pisonian conspirators and demonstrate the utter depravity of Nero and his henchmen. The similarly once-named Gerellanus never even carried out his orders, because the consul Vestinus simply committed suicide.[56] Perhaps these displays of incompetence are meant to bring some comic relief to the tragedy of the Pisonian conspiracy;[57] they certainly underscore its unique status as a historical event.

We have seen how an intricate web of relationships among the nobility binds the *Histories* and *Annals* in a seamless narrative: the simple mention of one senator's name can evoke a nexus of intrigue; a family member's good deed decades ago can save a life; marriage alliances can afford protection; adoption can consolidate power. Thus pathos is heightened when Tacitus lists by name the victims of the Pisonian conspiracy, men and women with no connections and therefore no safeguards, 'the rank and file',[58] as he calls them. Cluvidienus Quietus, Julius Agrippa, Blitius Catulinus, Petronius Priscus, Iulius Altinus, Caedicia, Caesennius Maximus, Novius Priscus, Artoria Flaccilla, Egnatia Maximilla: named only upon banishment, exiles never to be heard from again.

If non-elites could find a rare opportunity to make history in a mutiny or a conspiracy, then in the ensuing civil wars of 69 they were instrumental. Galba attempted to stabilize his rule by adopting Piso, but all the while Otho was scheming against him. Otho enlisted the help of his freedman Onomastus, who secured the help of two soldiers, a junior officer named Veturius and Barbius Proculus, whose task it was to circulate the daily watchword. 'Thus, two common soldiers undertook to transfer command of the Roman Empire – and actually transferred it,'[59] since, unlike the botched Pisonian conspiracy, this plot was carefully guarded: 'only a few were privy to knowledge of the crime.'[60]

Otho continued to rely upon the soldiers. In an attempt to secure the mountain passes into Gaul, Otho moved north against Gallia Narbonensis with the help of three generals. Suedius Clemens appears only here in Tacitus, and it is unlikely that he would have surfaced in the *Histories* after the accession of Vespasian. Antonius Novellus' career is otherwise unknown. Aemilius Pacensis appears elsewhere in the *Histories*, but his *cognomen* is unusual.[61] These three nonentities are completely ineffectual, according to Tacitus: Suedius Clemens commanded only for popularity; Antonius Novellus possessed no authority; and Aemilius Pacensis was thrown into chains by his insubordinate troops.[62]

They sailed northward along the coast of Italy as though it were a foreign country. Their plundering was all the more frightful because nobody resisted. A hastily gathered band of mountaineers was quickly routed in a skirmish that only goaded the Othonians' bloodlust; therefore they sacked the coastal Ligurian town of Albintimilium (also known as Intimilium) because battle had yielded no booty and the country folk who owned nothing valuable were impossible to capture because they were fast and knew the terrain. Tacitus illustrates the ignominy of the Othonians with an anecdote:

> A Ligurian woman added to the horror with her noble example (*prae-claro exemplo*). She had hidden her son, and when the soldiers believed that she was also hiding money and therefore tortured her to find out where he was hidden, pointing to her belly she replied that he was hidden there. Thereafter no threats or even fear of death caused her to waver in the consistency of her brave words.[63]

The power of this brief story lies in the stark juxtaposition of specificity and generalization. The maritime expedition began from Ostia in early March of 69, and Albintimilium appears in the extant *Histories* only here.[64] The gesture, words and response of the woman are transmitted intact (the Latin infinitive, *latere*, preserves in indirect discourse the substance of her direct response, 'he is hidden here'). These details of time, space and speech allow the reader to recreate the scene in the mind's eye. Such vividness increases the emotional response, yet the particulars of the passage are offset by the generalities. The woman, her son and her tormenters are not named, and the use of torture is routine and not unexpected.[65] Her gesture is symbolic and not unprecedented in Latin literature; for example, Nero's own mother pointed to her womb and declared 'Strike here' when her assassins came for her.[66] Most stark is the juxtaposition of the strength of an unnamed and unarmed woman that renders the brutality of a band of bloodthirsty soldiers impotent.[67]

In the *Annals,* Tacitus revisits the paradigm of a woman's constancy in the face of violent injustice. Although tortured for information against the Pisonian conspirators, the freedwoman Epicharis remained silent, in contrast to the cowardly senator Scaevinus and equestrian Natalis, who immediately denounced the conspiracy. Tacitus compares Epicharis' willingness to die to the indifference of the conspirators towards their own cause – with a familiar prepositional phrase:

> With a more noble example (*clariore exemplo*), a woman – a freedwoman at that – died by defending others and those practically unknown to her under such terrible compulsion, when free men and noble men, Roman senators and equestrians, untouched by torture each betrayed the dearest of his relatives.[68]

As the example of the Ligurian woman shows how depraved the soldiers of Otho were, so the example of Epicharis damns the Pisonian conspirators. When citizens turn on fellow citizens, whether in civil war or conspiracy, humble women are more reliable than men of any rank. The Ligurian woman is thus a type of character Walker might have included in her catalogue. She might also have included under such a rubric Agricola's mother:

> His mother was Julia Procilla, a woman of singular virtue. Reared in her care and kindness he spent his childhood and adolescence pursuing the cultivation of every respectable skill. She protected him from the enticements of troublemakers. [...] I recall his telling that he had latched on to the study of philosophy more fiercely than was becoming of a Roman and a senator, and would have continued his study if his mother's prudence had not checked his excited and ardent spirit.[69]

Recent commentators have noted that this section on Agricola's mother is 'very much longer than that on his father'.[70] Tacitus relates her tragic death:

> The following year Agricola's soul and home were struck by a terrible loss. For the fleet of Otho while wandering idly plundered as if a foreign

territory Intimilii, part of Liguria, killed Agricola's mother on her own property, and seized the very property and the better part of her inheritance, which was the cause of her murder.[71]

Scholars have recognized behind the Ligurian woman the fate of Agricola's mother, but they are divided on Tacitus' motives. Rhiannon Ash credits Tacitus with self-control that 'enhances his credibility as a historian by not narrating the murder of Julia Procilla, Agricola's mother (*Agr.* 7.1), killed in this very attack'.[72] Gwyn Morgan, on the other hand, is more suspicious: 'It might in any case have been difficult for Tacitus to report the expedition's activities objectively, since the mother of Agricola, his own father-in-law, was one of the victims.'[73] In the tale of the nameless Ligurian woman, Tacitus found a way to remember the mother of his beloved father-in-law.

A century before Reverend Hunter, the French Jesuit René Rapin (1621–87) was also put off by the vast number of characters in Tacitus' histories, whom he found indistinguishable: 'In a word, all his Characters are alike.'[74] Yet as I hope to have shown, at work in all of the characters Tacitus writes about is a process of elaboration that restores to the imagination who they were. Such a dynamic process mediates the characters of the past and the audience of the present. So the question 'Who are Tacitus' main characters?' is not as important as how he recreated and evaluated them. What unites the characters in Tacitus, regardless of status or gender, are his clear moral judgements on their motives and actions. Some, like Vipsania, he finds blameless; others, like Tiberius, irredeemable. Some, like Germanicus, enjoy as much approval as they provoke disapproval, but Tacitus' opinion and its reasons are never unclear. The most straightforward approach is to trace family lineage by naming ancestors. At times politically motivated, marriages then add a horizontal aspect to the vertical ancestry. These methods result in character types that help simplify the complexities of Roman society across diverse episodes that span generations, yet Tacitus can also be precise and include the exact names of characters who are otherwise vanished from history. In the next chapter, we shall explore how Tacitus manipulates narrative processes that restore to the imagination a vision of history that likewise conveys his pervasive moral concerns.

III

WORDS AND DEEDS

THE WRITINGS OF TACITUS differ from modern expectations of history; as a result, Tacitus has been routinely condemned for his historical inaccuracy. Since the nineteenth century, empirical history has dominated, and modern historians strive for objective truth about the past based on data. Not so in antiquity: classical historiography is a genre in which historians narrated past events so as to persuade their readers of the importance of their ancestors and their contributions to the *res publica* ('public affairs', the distinctly Roman conception of governance and civic duty). A less generous assessment would accuse ancient historians of deliberate mendacity; however, the rules of the game were different, and judgement by modern standards is not fair. While it is possible to glean historical facts from ancient historiography, the precise reconstruction of political, social or economic developments was not the primary aim. Instead, the ancient historians set out to provide examples of virtue, honour and excellence to emulate or examples of vice, shame and wickedness to avoid. Accordingly, ancient historiography is markedly moral in its tone.

Traditionally, Quintus Fabius Pictor is credited as the first historian of Rome; he wrote in the second half of the third century BCE. He is followed by Lucius Cincius Alimentus, Aulus Postumius Albinus and Gaius Acilius.

Although their writings survive only in mere scraps and fragments, it is worth recognizing these founders of the Roman historiographical tradition for one remarkable reason: they wrote in the Greek language.[1] Presumably by writing Roman history in Greek, these historians promoted Roman culture and values to an increasingly Greek audience, as Roman conquest slowly progressed eastward across the Mediterranean.

Marcus Porcius Cato (Cato the Censor, 234–149 BCE) pioneered the art of Latin prose- and history-writing in the Latin language. The shift in language, from Greek to Latin, is accompanied by a shift in form as well, from annals to monograph. According to Cicero,

> history was nothing but a compilation of annals [...] the *pontifex maximus* [chief priest] used to commit to writing all the events of the year, record them on a white tablet and post it up at his house so that the people could become acquainted with it, and still today these records are called the *annales maximi*.[2]

Over time, historians fleshed out these annalistic lists with episodes of cultural history, folk tales and *aetia*, or explanations for the origins of customs and institutions. The writing of history was also a way for a historian to recount and praise the achievements of his ancestors.

Tacitus rarely uses superlatives, so when he calls Sallust 'the most brilliant author of Roman history', his praise must be deliberate.[3] During the triumvirate of Octavian, Antony and Lepidus (44–35 BCE), Sallust wrote the *War Against Catiline* and the *War Against Jugurtha*; he died before completing *The Histories*. With his characteristic *breuitas* (brevity) and *inconcinnitas* (unconnectedness), Sallust is a natural model for Tacitus. *Breuitas* aids memory (shorter things are easier to remember), and so ancient authors used it to make their material more accessible to readers. The first rule of *breuitas* is to achieve only enough: brevity is satisfying. Second, *breuitas* demands that the beginning of the work not indulge in background information but commence at a suitable stage of the event. Repetition is avoided, and the work must end when further narrative would no longer be relevant. Nevertheless, *breuitas* admits digressions, which must themselves observe the cardinal principles of brevity – provided they are justified by the context. Digressions contain material that is integral not only to the narrative but also to the philosophical conception of history. According to the favourable Thomas Gordon, Tacitus 'is remarkable for a surprising brevity: But let his words be ever so few, his thought and matter are always abundant.'[4] As for the unconnectedness and avoidance of balanced structure, grammatical parallelism is replaced by variation calculated for purpose and effect. Variation keeps the reader alert. In tones that are slightly off-key, so to speak, one can hear disdain for the conventional. If Tacitus seems to speak from the moral high ground, it is in part because he holds common parlance at arm's length.

The Augustan historian Livy also warrants the superlative 'most eloquent', and is 'famous above all for his eloquence and reliability'.[5] In spite of the tremendous scope of Livy's monumental undertaking (the history of Rome from its beginnings to the death of Cicero), his purpose is unified: to expose the infinite variety of human behaviour so the reader can discover examples of goodness to imitate and warnings of evil to avoid. And as Judith Ginsburg has demonstrated, Livy's annual narrative was a model of traditional practice that Tacitus shaped to his own purposes. Thus in content and in form, Livy is a source of inspiration for Tacitus.[6]

In gathering information and composing his history, Tacitus' method consists of autopsy, interview and documentary evidence. He consults previous scholarship for both facts and style. Above all, Tacitus, like all ancient historians, engages in imaginative reconstruction or *inuentio*. Rhetorical amplification was an acceptable way for ancient historians to develop the facts; the actual was further supported by the probable. 'The invention of circumstantial detail,' says Peter Wiseman, 'was a way to reach the truth.'[7] In part this chapter will attempt to identify the implications of *inuentio* for understanding Tacitus.

One could argue that history does not occur until pen hits paper. Events take place, but until they are recorded in written form, they cannot be accessed by others as history. This is troublesome, since a pen is held by a person who may have an agenda beyond the recording of facts or events. History is personal, to the extent that it is told by a person with a method and a goal. Tacitus' veracity is not at stake: no matter what his ideological propensity, no matter how sensational the story, at the core he is account-able to the men who lived through the events of the *Agricola*, the *Histories* and even the later books of the *Annals*. Nor was Tacitus in the business of writing what might have happened (as much as his works may encourage speculation); rather, he operated under the Aristotelian law of probability and necessity in relating particular (and not universal) events.[8] Our aim in this chapter is to explore Tacitus' methods of storytelling, especially in the *Agricola*, *Histories* and *Annals*. Broadly speaking, his stories unfold in one of two ways: either in the words characters speak for themselves or in the third-person descriptions of their deeds. In the end, how Tacitus writes history leads inevitably to why he writes history.

Words

Let us begin with words. In Tacitus' works speeches are set apart from the rest of the narrative by introductory phrases, sentences, even paragraphs that explain the context and setting. The speaker proceeds in the first person and addresses an internal audience in the second person. In Latin, such directly quoted speeches are referred to as *oratio recta*, and English translations use quotation marks. Of course, writers may also use indirect discourse, *oratio obliqua*, in which the contents of the speech are reported in dependent clauses introduced by a verb of speaking. Even in English, indirect discourse is easy to spot: 'He said that the British are coming.' Yet indirect discourse is flexible. Sometimes the speaker is not identified by name, but is one voice representing a group; sometimes the reporting verb of saying is delayed or suppressed altogether and must therefore be supplied by the reader; some-times Tacitus uses *oratio obliqua* to report not what a character says but what he thinks. Nominative singular participles ('believing', 'reckoning', 'judging', 'contemplating', etc.) are particularly effective ways of shifting the point of view to the internal motivations of the character.

One paragraph from the *Histories* demonstrates the varieties of indirect discourse at Tacitus' disposal. In January 69, Galba needed to secure his position, which was undermined in Rome and in the provinces:

A few days after the first of January letters were brought from Pompeius
Propinquus, procurator of Belgica: the legions of Upper Germania,
having broken the obligation of their oath, were demanding another
emperor, but conceded to the Senate and the Roman people the decision
of the choice in order that their revolt might be more leniently received.
This event brought to fruition the plans of Galba, already for some
time contemplating adoption in his own mind and with close friends.
In fact, there was throughout the entire city during those months no
more frequent topic of conversation, at first simply due to the liberty
and inclination for gossip, then because of Galba's feeble old age. Few
had any judgement or love of the Republic; many with foolish hope,
depending on whether he was anyone's friend or dependent, were
nominating this man or that with ambitious rumours.[9]

In the first sentence, the letters of Pompeius Propinquus are clearly identified as the source of the indirect discourse that informs Galba of the revolt,
the demand, the concession and its reason. Although the verb of saying is
suppressed, the pragmatics are clearly indicated; it is as if we are watching
Galba read the letters. In the second sentence, Galba is clearly identified
as the subject and so the source of the reported information; however, the
participle 'contemplating' and the prepositional phrase 'in his own mind'
shift the point of view from the external, physical letters, to the internal,
abstract thoughts of the emperor. Galba also discussed adoption with 'close
friends', but they are not named. From these close friends, the discussion
radiates outward to the general populace. Although no longer technically
in *oratio obliqua*, still the substance of the popular conversations is related:
Galba's feeble old age and potential nominees for adoption. The paragraph
thus ranges from the formal indirect discourse of Pompeius Propinquus'
letters, to a shift to the internal point of view of Galba, and finally to the
rumours of the people.

Such a range of indirect modes has the effect of distancing the audience
from the speaker. The content is embedded within a letter, within Galba's
thoughts and within the rumours that circulated in the city. Direct discourse
should, therefore, restore the speaker to the audience and elevate the content

of the speech; however, even direct speeches in ancient historiography bear the imprint of the author.

In his history of the Peloponnesian War, Thucydides records some of the most memorable speeches of Greek literature: Pericles' funeral oration in praise of Athens; the Melian dialogue that dramatizes arguments against joining the Athenian league; the Mytilenian debate over punishment for revolt. At the outset of his history, Thucydides anticipates potential objections to his version of what was spoken:

> With reference to the speeches in this history, some were delivered before the war began, others while it was going on; some I heard myself, others I got from various quarters; it was in all cases difficult to carry them word for word in one's memory, so my habit has been to make the speakers say what was in my opinion demanded of them by the various occasions, of course adhering as closely as possible to the general sense of what they really said.[10]

Thucydides puts into practice the ancient rhetorical notion of *inuentio*, which according to Cicero is 'the devising of matter true or lifelike which will make a case appear convincing'.[11] An ancient historian's narrative technique, his skill and ability in constructing a historical narrative, is in large part the exercise of invention, the creation of complete narratives out of slender and selected remnants of evidence from the past.

Although Tacitus is nowhere as explicit as Thucydides, he was forced to respond to even more pressing constraints than forgetfulness or lack of witnesses; before a historian can even begin to write history, he must have some access to the primary sources. When Thucydides could not remember a speech, he could interview an audience member, since the speeches he reports were given in public assemblies. At the beginning of the *Histories*, Tacitus defines the difficulties that beset historians writing after Actium, that is, after the establishment of the principate:

> After the battle of Actium, and peace depended on the conferral of all power on one man, great intellects faded. At the same time truth

was refracted in many ways, first by an unawareness of the Republic as if it were a foreign state, soon by a desire to flatter or again by a hatred towards overlords. Thus between the hostile and the subservient no one cared about posterity.[12]

Tacitus does not need to mention by name the great Republican historians who had at their disposal the raw material for their histories. But when all power devolved to one person, information was less public because events took place in closed chambers or between individuals rather than in an open forum. Furthermore, this concentration of power caused a general ignorance about politics, until citizens were so uninformed as to become foreigners in their own state. Their history was no longer their own; rather, it was the exclusive purview of the *princeps*. This explains in part why Tacitus frequently shifts the point of view to the internal thoughts of a character. When important decisions were being made by one person, deliberations no longer took place in the open; Tacitus had no choice but to record the thoughts of his characters.[13] Olivier Devillers summarizes the effect of this alienation:

> The concentration of power, presented as a major historical fact throughout the book, is also a determining factor in the writing of history. Since it obstructs access to information, it leads Tacitus to adopt a subjective method of reconstructing the past.[14]

In composing his speeches, Tacitus laboured under the conventional constraints identified by Thucydides and compounded by the trouble caused by the principate.

Two speeches from the *Agricola* (one spoken by rebel Britons, the other by their chieftain, Calgacus) and one from the *Annals* (by Claudius) demonstrate Tacitus' range of form and content. Tacitus does not record forensic speeches given by litigants, although he does report on criminal trials throughout the *Annals*.[15] Instead, like Thucydides, he reproduces deliberative and epideictic speeches. The *Agricola* contains an example of each: the deliberative speech of the rebels in indirect discourse and the epideictic speech of Calgacus quoted directly.

Before describing Agricola's governorship of Britannia, Tacitus provides background information on the island, its inhabitants and the Roman occupation before Agricola's arrival. In the year 58, during the reign of Nero, Suetonius Paulinus was appointed governor. He thought it was necessary to subdue the island of Mona (modern Anglesey), yet his departure left Britannia open to attack: 'When fear was alleviated by his absence, the Britons discussed among themselves the evils of slavery, compared insults and exaggerated by putting their own spin on things.'[16] Grammatically, Tacitus shifts from the finite, indicative verbs of the preceding sentence to three historical infinitives, 'discussed [...] compared [...] exaggerated', that convey a livelier sense of narration. The historical infinitives then set up the speech in indirect discourse, in which we learn the Britons' chief complaints against the Romans.

No one speaker is specified; rather, Tacitus presents a composite sense of dissatisfaction. He reports using dependent clauses in which personal and possessive pronouns are shifted from the first to the third person. Translators must therefore make a choice: either to retain the third-person pronouns which in English make no distinction between 'they' who are speaking (Latin *se*) and 'they' who are spoken of (Latin *eos*), or to revert the pronouns to the first person, which obfuscates the dependent clauses of indirect discourse in Latin but nonetheless clarifies the subjects and objects. I have opted for the latter:

> Nothing is gained by patience but that heavier burdens are exacted as if from men who tolerate them easily. Once individual kings ruled us; now two are imposed: a legate savage towards our lives, a procurator towards our possessions. Their quarrels are as injurious to their subjects as their agreements. Centurions combine the violence and insult of the one, slaves of the other. Nothing is exempt from their greed, nothing from their lust. In battle the stronger strips the enemy; in our case, however, cowards and weaklings rob our homes, abduct our children and force us to enlist, as if we do not know how to die for the sake of our country. Indeed, how few Romans have crossed the channel, if we Britons should count our own numbers? Germania shook off the yoke

and it was defended by a river, not an ocean. We fight for fatherland, wives, parents, they for greed and luxury. They will retreat, just like Divine Julius, once we imitate the virtue of our ancestors. Don't be afraid because of the outcome of one or two battles. The fortunate may have greater drive, but greater resolution is in the hands of the miserable. Even the gods pity Britannia now, since they detain the Roman chief and his army on another island. We are deliberating: that's the hardest part, for in situations such as this it is more dangerous to be caught than to dare.[17]

This nameless Briton makes suspiciously masterful use of rhetorical figures such as anaphora, antithesis and asyndeton, as well as the history of the Roman attempts at occupation of Germania, and the result is an artfully balanced speech that achieves its persuasive goal, for the Britons revolt under the leadership of Queen Boudicca. He is even so clever as to refer to his speech as deliberative (the Latin verb is *deliberare*), in which speakers persuade an assembly of the best policy or action to take. Although the use of the interrogative ('How few Romans have crossed the channel?') and imperative ('Don't be afraid') lend the speech a sense of dramatic dialogue between the speaker and his attentive audience, nevertheless the entire speech is, grammatically speaking, the historian's report.

The revolt of Boudicca is told in greater detail in the *Annals*, in which the scope of the work permitted fuller treatment than in the slender biography. For the revolt Tacitus probably had at his disposal the memoirs of Suetonius Paulinus, which would have provided details about the disposition of Roman troops and the course of the battle in which he was eventually victorious. Particular facts, such as the construction of flat-bottomed vessels for infantry and the fording or swimming of the cavalry, would have originated from such memoirs. In the *Annals*, Tacitus specifies why Suetonius invaded the island of Mona: its population was gaining strength and it had become a refuge for fugitives. Furthermore, Suetonius could not brook a rival. He sought by the subjugation of Britannia to upstage the exploits of Domitius Corbulo in Armenia.[18] From the *Annals* we learn that Boudicca belonged to the tribe of the Iceni who initiated the revolt;

they suborned the Trinobantes and others who had their reasons for joining. In the *Annals*, as in the *Agricola*, the Britons seem to discuss among themselves the evils of slavery, compare insults and exaggerate by putting their own spin on things:

> Because of insults and fear of worse, although they had been reduced to the status of province, they seized arms, with the Trinobantes incited to rebellion and others who had not yet been broken by slavery who promised in secret conspiracies to regain their liberty. Their most bitter hatred was reserved for the veterans recently settled in the colony of Camulodunum, where they were driving them out of their homes, ejecting them from their farms and calling them captives and slaves. The soldiers egged on the impertinence of the veterans, who enjoyed a similar lifestyle and hoped for similar lawlessness. Furthermore, a temple to the Divine Claudius built as if an altar to eternal domination was on permanent view before them, and priests chosen on the pretence of religious ceremony were squandering entire fortunes.[19]

The comparative expression 'fear of worse', the superlative 'most bitter hatred', the name-calling, the comparison of the temple to an altar of eternal domination, the assertion of pretence and the hyperbolic adjective 'entire' all serve to exaggerate and exacerbate the causes of the rebels, framed in terms of slavery and freedom. In the *Agricola*, the speech of the Britons (albeit in indirect discourse) is referred to as deliberative and therefore presumably spoken in a public setting, perhaps before a tribal council. In the *Annals*, however, the rebels conspire in secret. Differences in treatment can be attributed not only to generic convention but also to character development. In the *Agricola*, Suetonius is a minor figure, just one of the many governors of Britannia who got it wrong before Agricola came along. In the *Annals*, however, Tacitus carefully colours our initial opinion of Suetonius. A leading man of consular rank who attained great distinction for his campaigns in Britannia,[20] Suetonius would go on to be victorious at Cremona, only to be captured by Vitellius, who pardoned him on the grounds that he must have deliberately undermined Otho's cause (even though the circumstances of the treachery were completely accidental).[21]

Let us turn to our second example from the *Agricola*. Agricola's greatest accomplishment as governor of Britannia was his victory against the tribes of Caledonia (the Highlands of Scotland) in the seventh and last year of his command. Agricola had harassed the coastal tribes as far as Mons Graupius. There, Tacitus tells us, 30,000 armed men joined against the Romans under the leadership of Calgacus, who 'before the host gathered around, clamouring for battle, is said to have spoken in this way'.[22] Thus, unlike the indirect discourse of a nameless speaker that is signalled semantically (with the verbs 'discussed [...] compared [...] exaggerated') and syntactically (with subordinate clauses in the third person), the speech is attributed directly to Calgacus, the subject of the participle *locutus* ('to have spoken'). Verbs and pronouns are in the first person. Thus, a voice other than Tacitus' appears to take over the narrative and confront the reader directly.

Since the tribes are already gathered against the Romans, there is nothing to deliberate. Calgacus' speech does not persuade the tribes to resist so much as it praises their valour and criticizes the Romans in the manner of epideictic oratory. He begins by appealing to their distant location that has kept them beyond the reach of the Romans: 'To this day our very remoteness has protected us at land's end on the edge of freedom.'[23] There is nothing beyond them but waves and rocks and Romans, whose oppression is inescapable. Calgacus then pronounces one of the most withering condemnations of Roman imperialism in Latin literature:

> Robbers of the world, after there is nothing left on land to steal, they scour the sea; if the enemy is rich, they are greedy; if poor, they are ambitious. These are men whom neither East nor West has satisfied. They alone of all desire wealth and poverty with equal zeal. What they call 'empire' is by any other name plunder, slaughter and rape. And where they make a wasteland, they call it peace.[24]

This speech, with its finely crafted parallelism, antithesis and candour, holds a mirror to Roman identity, a topic we will address in the next chapter. From criticism of the Romans, Calgacus then embarks on praise of the Caledonian spirit and reflects on their strengths and the opportunities that lean in their favour. The Roman forts are unprotected, their leaders are aged, the occupied towns disaffected and disloyal. The speech closes with the rebels hemmed in on all sides by the spectre of slavery: 'Whether you bear it for eternity or avenge it once and for all will be decided on this field. Therefore as you are about to go forth into battle, think of your ancestors and your posterity.'[25] In this speech, Tacitus continues to hone the theme of past and present, then and now. Like the indirect speech of the deliberating Britons, the epideictic speech of Calgacus also enumerates anti-Roman sentiments in a profusion of rhetorical and stylistic ornament that could only originate from a learned author like Tacitus. The reader is left with the impression that in spite of the formality of direct discourse that purports to convey the speaker's words directly, the speech of Calgacus is a meditation by Tacitus on themes of freedom, slavery and Roman identity cast in terms that would resonate with his senatorial audience.

Our third example is from the *Annals*. A fortuitous archaeological discovery affords us a rare opportunity to compare the speech of Claudius with primary evidence. In 1528 a bronze tablet was unearthed in Lyons; on it is inscribed a speech of the emperor Claudius that was displayed in Lugdunum (modern Lyons and capital of the Roman province of Gallia Lugdunensis). Of course, the inscription may not record Claudius' every word precisely and may have been altered to fit the medium – or at least epigraphical convention. In fact, the text of the inscription is incomplete. The top of the tablet is missing, so that the beginning of the speech is lost. And since the speech was inscribed in two columns, there is also a lacuna in the middle section, between the bottom of the first column and the top of the second. Still, enough survives for general comparison.[26]

In the year 48, the Senate debated whether it should extend the right to hold public office at Rome to nobility from Gallia Comata, the rural province north of Gallia Narbonensis. Tacitus begins his account of the debate with the objections of some senators given in indirect discourse, introduced as 'lots of various rumours', and presented in a privy council meeting *apud principem*, 'before the emperor'.[27] No individual senator is credited with the objections; rather, they are condensed and combined: 'And with various opposition it was argued before the emperor, some asserting that Italy was not so weak as to be unable to supply the Senate for its own city.'[28]

In Latin, the participle *adseuerantium*, 'some asserting', introduces the subordinate clause 'that…'. The rest of the paragraph is thus rendered in indirect discourse. Two more objections were raised: firstly, the Gauls had a long history of violence towards Rome; and secondly, their admission to the ranks of public office would cheapen the honour. The overall effect of this extended indirect discourse, introduced by a plural participle whose antecedent is indefinite, is that the entire Senate appears to oppose the measure against Claudius. Tacitus presents Claudius' reply in the strongest of terms: 'The emperor, hardly troubled by these sorts of arguments, immediately rebutted and with the Senate convened thus began.'[29]

Unlike the council meeting which took place in the emperor's private chambers, this speech was given before a fully convened Senate and therefore was preserved in the *acta senatus*, the proceedings of the Senate. Thus in this debate we see Tacitus manage the historian's abiding problem of access to information.[30] If Tacitus did not have recourse to the substance of the arguments presented in chambers, then perhaps he reconstructed them based on the published speech of Claudius to the Senate.[31]

Tacitus' Claudius does not respond to the three objections directly; rather, his robust arguments for admission of the Gauls simultaneously discredit the senators' protests. First, he acknowledges that the Italian peninsula has for generations provided Rome with nobility, yet so has Spain and Gallia Narbonensis. He then harkens back to the failed policies of the Athenians and Spartans and compares the strategy of the legendary Romulus:

> What else contributed to the fall of Athens and Sparta, although they were military superpowers, but that they sequestered the conquered because they were foreign born? Our founder Romulus, on the other hand, was so wise that on the same day he considered several peoples his enemy, he considered them fellow citizens.[32]

Claudius admits the aggression of the Gauls towards Rome, but he also reminds the senators of the humiliation that Rome suffered at the hands of Italian tribes. Yes, it took Julius Caesar ten years to subjugate Gaul, but subsequently they have offered no resistance.[33] The speech closes with a rhetorical flourish:

> Senators, everything now credited with the greatest antiquity was once new: plebeians became magistrates after patricians, Latins after plebeians, the nations of Italy after the Latins. One day this too will grow old, and what we defend today with precedents will one day rank among precedents.[34]

The power of this passage derives partly from the skilful combination of brachylogy (the omission of the verb altogether; in my translation I supplied the factitive verb 'became') and polyptoton (the repetition of the nouns 'plebeians', 'Latins' and in the final sentence, 'precedent', in different cases). In the same stroke, omission compresses the language of the sentence while repetition expands it.

How then does Tacitus' speech compare with the version preserved in the inscription? Obviously he did not consult this exact physical copy of the speech. It is more likely that he consulted the *acta senatus*, the records of the Senate. Norma Miller identified seven similarities in argument between the inscription and Tacitus' rendition: (1) the sentiment that everything was once new; (2) non-Roman kings once ruled Rome; (3) plebeians were once restricted from holding office; (4) Romans increased empire through warfare; (5) citizenship was gradually extended; (6) provincial senators had already been admitted; and (7) although the Gauls were once aggressive, peace had prevailed for a hundred years at that point in time.[35] Yet the treatment of these seven arguments differs markedly. Tacitus reworked the primary source material to fit the form and style of his *Annals*. Furthermore, the speech in the *Annals* contains three pieces that are absent from the extant inscription. According to Miller, the inscription makes no mention of the narrow citizenship policies of Athens and Sparta. In the *Annals*, Claudius begins the speech with reference to his ancestors and the origin of the *gens*

Claudia.[36] One could argue that these two insertions were not necessarily Tacitean invention; rather, they may have been included in the original but lost in the lacunae at the beginning and in the middle of the inscription. However, the third item identified by Miller is most likely a Tacitean insertion. In the *Annals*, Claudius argues: 'That elected offices were entrusted to the sons of freedmen is nothing hitherto unknown, as most are mistaken in thinking, but it was repeatedly practised in the Republic.'[37]

Even without confirmation from the inscription (assuming such a bit was not lost), this sentence is inconsistent with a debate about not the social status but the ethnic origin of potential senators. The request for the privilege of holding office was made by the *primores* from Gallia Comata; the Latin word denotes the chief or leading men of high rank or position. They are not seeking the right for their freedmen but for themselves. Later in *Annals* Book 11, Tacitus will portray Claudius as dependent upon his freedmen, who are able to manipulate and control him; such a characterization partakes of the hostile attitude towards Claudius that dominates the historical tradition.[38] Therefore the addition of a sentence about freedmen, while irrelevant to the present argument, contributes to this portrait and keeps a negative impression of imperial freedmen in the forefront of the reader's mind.

The Lyons Tablet can only take us so far. In general, we learn that: Tacitus had primary source material; he consulted it; he revised it to fit the work at hand; and he revised it in ways that would not have raised serious objections in his readership. He probably used it not only as a general template for Claudius' speech but also to infer the substance of the senators' objections that had been voiced behind closed doors; thus, Tacitus is seen negotiating a deficit in source material.

The speeches in Tacitus reveal the way people deal with power, whether in their hands or over their heads. The tribes in Britannia only come forward with complaints when the immediate threat of Suetonius Paulinus' presence is removed. Nor do they feel safe in voicing criticism individually, yet their common animosity towards the Romans unites them as no other force had yet. The mere act of speaking ('We are deliberating') gives them the confidence to oppose the Roman forces. The speech of Calgacus is longer, more pointed and more crafted, as if to turn the art of persuasion, as practised by the Romans, against the Romans themselves. Yet the speeches of the rebels and of Calgacus do not advance the outcome for the Britons; the Romans were victorious against Boudicca and at the battle of Mons Graupius. Rather, the force of these speeches lies in their depictions of Roman cultural identity, which we will explore in more detail in the next chapter. For now, it is important to examine how claims of freedom and denials of slavery, which resound in spirited speeches of resistance to Roman rule, collapse under pressure. Claudius' speech to the Senate likewise enacts a struggle for power between Senate and *princeps*; objections to the admission of the *primores Galliae* were apparently strong enough to warrant formal response, and after Claudius' speech, the Senate issued an official decree granting the Aedui the right to become senators at Rome.[39] Silent throughout the debate are the *primores Galliae* themselves; their advantages to the Roman Senate can only be inferred from the disadvantages, namely that they are too wealthy and they have proven capable of successful resistance. Ultimately, the speeches in Tacitus, whether in *oratio obliqua* or *oratio recta*, are more than displays of the art of persuasion or plot development. They are the battlegrounds of ideologies.

Even the shortest of speeches can carry high stakes. At least a dozen times in the *Annals* Tacitus insists upon the authentic status of the words he reports and claims to record the direct quotation verbatim. Seven of these are clearly delineated by the postpositive Latin verb *inquit*, 'he or she said', and the rest are explicitly marked as direct quotations. The first example occurs at the very outset of Tiberius' reign, when it was unclear how the duties of state should be apportioned. Tiberius said he was unequal to the task and would assume only that part of the state which was entrusted to him, to which Asinius Gallus (the senator who married Tiberius' beloved Vipsania) said: 'May I ask, Caesar, which part of the state do you wish to be entrusted to you?'[40] Later, when Tiberius said he would cast a vote in a trial, Gnaeus Piso (enemy of Germanicus) said, 'In what order will you vote, Caesar? If first, I will have a vote to follow. If last, I fear I will dissent out of ignorance.'[41] These questions challenge Tiberius' authority and substantiate the otherwise unexpressed concerns of a silent Senate that is normally left guessing the wishes of the *princeps*. Asinius Gallus was one of Tiberius' most ardent enemies, Gnaeus Piso a most loyal friend.[42] Whether petulant or innocent, the questions expose Tiberius' inconsistency and pretence. Tiberius' charade is exposed again when the slave Clemens is arrested for instigating civil unrest by impersonating Agrippa Postumus. When Tiberius asks how he came to assume his identity, Clemens sneers, 'The same way you became Caesar,'[43] insinuating that he has assumed a position to which he, like Tiberius, has no legal claim. Even as he is dying, Tiberius puts up a show of strength, although he is surprisingly candid about his lack of a successor. Embracing one grandson, Tiberius Gemellus (see Figure 2.2), he predicts the future to his other (adopted) grandson, Caligula: 'You will kill him, and someone else will kill you.'[44] To the end Tiberius remains master of dissimulation, concealing his own death while exposing Caligula's crime.

The Neronian books of the *Annals* contain the greatest number of direct quotations. Agrippina the Younger is quoted twice. When astrologers predict that her son will one day rule and kill his mother, she says, 'Let him kill, so long as he rules.'[45] With these words Agrippina parodies the often cited quotation (it is found in Cicero, Seneca and Suetonius) from the Republican playwright Accius in his tragedy about the tyrant Atreus: 'Let them hate, so long as they fear.'[46] Upon her death she instructs the centurions, 'Strike my womb,'[47] with the gesture made by the nameless Ligurian woman of *Histories* Book 3. The death of Seneca is narrated at length; since he died so slowly he had several opportunities to address his friends and loved ones. First, in indirect discourse he reprimands his friends for their unmanly displays of emotion.[48] Then when his wife Paulina resolves to commit suicide with him, he says:

> I would have shown you the consolation of life, but you prefer the honour of death, and I will not begrudge you an example. In an end so brave as this may self-possession be equally within the power of us both, although in your death there is more distinction.[49]

In fact Nero forbade her death and ordered her arms to be bound to stop the bleeding; she lived a few years longer, pale and weakened by the ordeal.[50]

As he was dying, Seneca dictated to his secretaries, but these words Tacitus overtly refuses to include: 'I decline to paraphrase for the general public what has been published in his own words.'[51] Curiously, Tacitus uses the verb *inuertere*, 'to paraphrase', which suggests a degree of inversion from the original. We might well wonder how faithful Tacitus' reproductions are.[52]

Twice Tacitus specifies quotations as *ipsa uerba*, the very words spoken. When Nero is brought the head of Rubellius Plautus (discussed in Chapter II), Tacitus promises a direct quote: 'I will report the very words of the emperor.' Unfortunately the manuscript fails, leaving only the beginning of a question that perhaps Nero asked himself: 'Why [...] Nero...'[53] Nero's remark must have circulated widely, since a version of it is recorded by the later historian Dio Cassius, in which Nero said, 'I did not know he had such a big nose!'[54]

In the last chapter we saw how the Pisonian conspirator Subrius Flavus scoffed at his executioners for digging his grave too shallow and too narrow, and Tacitus quotes him: 'Not even this according to regulation.'[55] When Nero asked Subrius Flavus why he joined the Pisonian conspiracy, he said these very words, *ipsa uerba*: 'I hated you, and no soldier was more faithful to you while you deserved it. I began to hate you after you killed your mother and your wife and you became a charioteer, an actor and an arsonist.'[56]

Like the impostor Clemens, in the face of death Subrius Flavus has nothing to lose by speaking the truth to the emperor's face. Tacitus explains that he has included this particular quotation 'because, unlike the words of Seneca which were published, the sentiments of a soldier, forcible though plain, ought no less to be known.'[57] While such a statement of method does not clarify Tacitus' source for the quotations, it does indicate an awareness that such direct quotations convey powerful emotions and moral implications.

The final instance of a direct quotation in the *Annals* is the dying words of yet another of Nero's victims, the Stoic philosopher and senatorial dissident, Thrasea Paetus:

> We are pouring a libation to Jupiter the Liberator. Look here, young man,
> and may the gods ward off the omen. But you have been born in times
> when it is better to strengthen the spirit with examples of constancy.[58]

Seneca also poured a libation to Jupiter the Liberator, and the suicides of both philosophers are framed as re-enactments of the death of Socrates, whose last words were so carefully preserved (or represented) by Plato.[59] Tacitus' account of Thrasea's last words is thus endorsed by literary tradition.

Each of the speakers of these direct quotes in the *Annals* suffered a violent end. Tiberius' enemy Asinius Gallus starved in prison; Germanicus' enemy Gnaeus Piso committed suicide under highly suspicious circumstances; the impostor Clemens was put to death; Tiberius was smothered; Agrippina the Younger was stabbed; Subrius Flavus was executed; Seneca and Thrasea were forced to commit suicide. Their status as dying persons with very little left to lose valorizes the substance of the quotations, which no doubt circulated in sources available to Tacitus.[60] In form, however, we may detect a degree of literary stylization; for example, Agrippina the Younger riffs on a familiar line from tragedy, Thrasea echoes Seneca, and both recall Plato's accounts of the death of Socrates. Furthermore, the outspokenness exhibited by these individuals contributes to the tyrannical character portrayals of Tiberius and Nero. At the very least, the verb 'paraphrase' should alert us to the artistry inherent in the transmission of *ipsa uerba*.

The numerous instances of *ipsa uerba* could imply that direct quotations are somehow more reliable than indirect quotations. When a historian is able to quote directly, he somehow brings us closer to the historical events that speak for themselves. However, when reading Tacitus it is important to resist this temptation; we should not assume that direct discourse carries more validity than indirect discourse.[61] Although the speech of Claudius is presented in direct discourse in the *Annals* such that a reader may assume it reproduces what Claudius said, it contains not a single verbatim quote from the Lyons Tablet. In this case, Tacitus did not lack sufficient evidence for what he might have quoted; rather, he shaped the evidence in such a way as to maintain a degree of verisimilitude. In the end, the difference between direct and indirect discourse – even *ipsa uerba* – is less significant than the content, which delivers not just the substance of the characters' words but also the reminder of Tacitus as ever-present narrator and ultimate speaker. In spite of his wholly unfavourable opinion of Tacitus, Reverend Hunter is correct:

''tis generally *Tacitus* that makes the Speech, conducts the Action, and forms the Thought.'[62]

Deeds

As for deeds, Tacitus' subject matter is far-ranging. He deals with events as distant as Britannia and Syria, as near as the forum and the Palatine, as recent as his own childhood and as bygone as three generations past; therefore, structure is critical to comprehension and cohesion. In general, Tacitus organizes his material chronologically. The *Agricola* treats each of the governors of Britannia in turn, and then narrates in order the seven years of Agricola's governorship. From what remains of the *Annals* we can infer three neat hexads: Books 1–6 treat Tiberius, 7–12 Caligula and Claudius, 13–18 Nero. Tacitus marks the transition from one year to the next with the regular formula, 'in the consulship of', followed by the names of the two consuls for the year. Furthermore, for each year Tacitus usually records a combination of domestic and foreign affairs. The same consular formula is deployed from the outset of the *Histories*: 'My work commences when Servius Galba (second time) and Titus Vinius are about to be consuls.' Yet Tacitus is not constrained by these formulaic prescriptions; as Judith Ginsburg has demonstrated, he is 'perfectly capable of manipulating the conventions of annalistic history to his own advantage.'[63] Tacitus uses two principal devices to shape his narrative: description and comment.[64]

Tacitus rarely describes objects, and unlike the biographer Suetonius, he does not regularly describe physical features or physiognomy. Instead he tends to linger on places of devastation, for example the Teutoburg Forest littered with the bones of Varius' legions or the Capitol burnt to the ground.[65] Tacitus can appeal to the senses in order to engage readers so fully that they become eyewitnesses themselves. Such vividness, or *enargeia*, as it was called in Greek, puts the event before the reader's eye; the Latin *euidentia* retains the etymological root from the verb *uidere*, to see. Yet vivid descriptions must also answer to physical reality; hence sizes, dimensions and distances must appear to be accurate or at least feasible. *Enargeia* and panoramic scenes tend to heighten emotional affect, yet Tacitus uses them sparingly.[66] Instead he colours episodes with small details that should perhaps otherwise go unmentioned, for several of his details push the limits of generic decorum.

Of course ancient historians rely on anecdotes, self-contained stories that deliver a single detached incident for its value as inherently interesting or striking – or even shocking. So Tacitus records that Nero probably engaged in incest with his mother Agrippina the Younger and that while in Alexandria Vespasian cured the blind and healed the lame.[67] Compared to other writers of the day, however, Tacitus incorporates anecdotes less frequently. When the year 57 offers little to narrate, Tacitus refuses to indulge in insignificant pulp:

> When Nero was consul for the second time with Lucius Piso, few things happened worthy of mention, unless one takes pleasure in filling scrolls with praise of foundations and structures for the huge amphitheatre built on the Campus Martius, whereas it has been an established usage, suitable to the dignity of the Roman people, to reserve distinguished deeds for the annals of history and such stories as these for the daily journals.[68]

Commentators have conjectured that Pliny the Elder was the target of this barbed criticism because his *Natural History* is packed with details, including notice of a very large beam of wood brought to Rome for this very amphitheatre.[69] Regardless of the intended recipient, Tacitus' point is that without proper material historians cannot do their job – although apparently it is better to fill the void with sarcasm than with trivia. Furthermore, it cannot be the case that nothing happened in the year 57 or that records of the events were unattainable; rather, the deliberate exclusion of historical events makes Nero's tedious reign seem interminable.[70]

Earlier in the *Annals*, Tacitus lists those things that qualify as worthy of history:

> I am not unaware that several of the items which I have related and which I shall relate seem perhaps paltry and trifling to recall, but no one

> should compare our annals with the writings of those who composed the antiquities of the Roman people. They used to recount huge wars, sacks of cities, kings routed and captured, or whenever they turned to domestic affairs, they used to recount the strife of consuls against tribunes, agrarian and grain laws, contests between commoners and nobility, all with free scope. Our work is confined and undistinguished, peace unbroken (ha!) or modestly troubled, the sad affairs of Rome and a *princeps* uninterested in extending empire. Still it will not be without use to examine those events that seem minor at first glance but from which often arise the great movements of history.[71]

Here then are the standards of generic decorum which Tacitus refuses to exceed, at least for the year 57. As Martin and Woodman observe, most ancient historians claim superiority over their predecessors, but Tacitus overtly proclaims his work to be inferior.[72] His problem is not a lack of talent; rather, he is at a loss for good old-fashioned *res gestae*, grand events fit for the annals of history, and access to that information is limited.

When Tacitus does narrate the history available to him, he sometimes includes material that, while it may not be wholly objectionable, is certainly unexpected. He embellishes his accounts with details given in a single sentence, sometimes even a mere phrase. For example, a band of ruthless informants needed more evidence to convict their hapless victim. It was too risky to hide behind doors where they would be easily discovered, so 'three of these senators hid themselves in the space between the roof and the ceiling [...] and pressed their ears to the cracks and crevices.'[73] It is bad enough that distinguished gentlemen should stoop to spying, but to abandon personal dignity by crawling into a cramped, stuffy space and cupping a hand to the ear compounds the sense of disgust.

As praetorian prefect, Sejanus worked his way up to becoming Tiberius' trusted advisor; he was ambitious and continually plotted ways to increase his political influence. Unfortunately, the relevant section of nearly three years of the *Annals* is missing, in which Tacitus might have explained why exactly Sejanus fell from power; nevertheless, when the narrative resumes, Sejanus is dead and the Senate has decided that his children should be killed. When the executioner drags them to prison, the son surmises the danger. As for the daughter, 'she was so unaware that she repeatedly asked what she had done wrong and where she was being taken and repeatedly said that she would not do so any more and that she could be chastised with a spanking.'[74]

Surely this qualifies as *enargeia*, for the sight of the innocent girl is enhanced by the sort of pleas that parents regularly hear. Tacitus successfully arouses pity, but he does not stop there. The executioner baulks because there is no precedent for the capital punishment of a virgin. So he rapes her first, 'while the rope was yet on her neck'. Although Tacitus is not responsible for this lurid detail, which was handed down by 'historians of the time',[75] nevertheless, by choosing to include it, he quickly turns pity into disgust.

Tacitus records the deaths by starvation of Asinius Gallus, the outspoken enemy of Tiberius, and Drusus, the second son of Germanicus. However, we also learn that Drusus in his distress was reduced to 'chewing the stuffing of his mattress'.[76] This unseemly detail bothered the nineteenth-century Swiss scholar Johann Caspar von Orelli so much that he excised it on the grounds that Tacitus would not have used such an undignified expression.[77] Although Orelli is the only editor to go to such lengths to defend decorum as to violate the text, his sensibility is indicative of what is expected of history. Yet Tacitus thwarts expectations.

The outrages of the reign of Nero provided plenty of colourful material for Tacitus, and the later books of the *Annals* contain more anecdotes than any other portion of Tacitus' works, as for example when Nero dressed as a slave and wandered the streets of Rome in search of a good brawl,[78] or when he dressed as a bride and married a freedman named Pythagoras.[79] Yet Tacitus also includes details that embellish narratives of more straightforward historical events: two examples suffice. First of all, when the general Domitius Corbulo was on campaign in Armenia, winter hindered his operations. Tents were difficult to pitch in the frozen ground, frostbite was common, and some died of exposure. Again, the picture is complete, but Tacitus appends a final detail, probably gleaned from Corbulo's memoirs: 'The hands of a soldier carrying a bundle of wood were so frozen that they fell off while clinging to the load, his arms reduced to stumps.'[80] This image is presented just four paragraphs after Tacitus decried the paucity of historical material and the silliness of reporting on building construction; however, when good material is at hand, he obviously enhances it to arouse emotions such as pity and fear.

Tacitus also builds suspense in his narrative of the failed Pisonian conspiracy. The courtesan Epicharis divulges the conspiracy to Proculus, captain of the fleet, but withholds names; as a result, Proculus can give Nero only her name. The rest of the conspirators are protected for the moment. Although tortured for information, Epicharis remains silent. Rather than prolong her torment, she kills herself – by fashioning a noose 'from the band she took from her breast' (English translation demands the periphrasis; in Latin, one word suffices: *fascia*).[81] In relating such visceral details Tacitus heightens the emotional effects of the episodes; such physicality humanizes *res gestae*, the noble exploits worthy of literary composition.

Historians are not supposed to talk about senators' ears pressed against cracks in the ceiling, ropes tied around virgins' necks, mattress stuffing, arms reduced to stumps, and brassieres. When he wants, Tacitus can be prim. By avoiding the word 'shovels' (Latin *palae*) and referring instead to 'those things by means of which earth is dug or turf cut',[82] Tacitus became the man who refused to call a spade a spade.[83] More often, however, he provides details from everyday life which would be much more at home in Roman verse satire, a genre that delivers hard-hitting invective, bombast and anger to pass judgement on Roman society and especially morality. For Ronald Syme, 'Tacitus and Juvenal could be regarded as parallel and coeval phenomena. Style, tone, and sentiments are comparable.'[84] Indeed, as satire pointedly criticizes human nature, so Tacitus can be snide: for example, when the army cursed the horrors of civil war but continued to strip the bodies of their kinsmen, Tacitus observes, 'They speak of crime committed, yet they do it themselves.'[85]

This witticism brings us to the second principal device by which Tacitus shapes his narrative: comment. Tacitus regularly appends *sententiae*, aphorisms or maxims that deliver a general moral principle applicable beyond their specific situations. *Sententiae* demonstrate the difference between the normative and the exceptional by stating a commonly held social ethos ('they speak of crime committed') against which a behaviour is measured ('yet do it themselves'). The result is a communal moral obligation so obvious as to gain universal acceptance.[86] With his *sententiae*, Tacitus thus illustrates the disintegration of communal moral obligations. Cynthia Damon catalogues more than 50 *sententiae* and epigrams from the first book of the *Histories* alone.[87] Tacitus' *sententiae* deliver grim, undeniable truths. For example, when Domitian insults Agricola, Tacitus remarks: 'It is human nature to hate the person whom you have harmed.'[88] The obituary of Galba concludes, 'By common consent he was capable to rule – if only he hadn't.'[89] The death of Nero conveyed one very important lesson, as relevant in the year 69 as in Tacitus' own day, for both Trajan and Hadrian were proclaimed abroad: 'The secret of empire is that emperors can be made elsewhere than Rome.'[90]

Such epigrams strengthen the moral fibre of the text, but we should also be alert to their corrosive properties. Tacitus' *sententiae* are embedded in their own historically specific contexts, yet because they are concise and succinct they can be easily excerpted (as they have been here) and thrust into changing contexts that erode the original sense. Divorced from their immediate circumstances to fulfil different needs, *sententiae* have the potential to bury under self-evident and unquestionable truths any contest over the questionable distribution of power and unjust social practices that guaranteed inequality. So although Tacitus is in the business of historical specificity, he uses *sententiae* to achieve moral generalities, at the expense of inconvenient realities. In doing so, he is no different from the Roman writers of his day, who, if they stopped to think about the morality of oppression at all, did not do so for long.

Since epigrams and *sententiae* are repositories for community values, they are especially useful for providing moral guidance to the reader. For Tacitus, this is one of the purposes of history:

> I do not intend to pursue individual proceedings, unless noteworthy for their integrity or conspicuous for their disgrace, because I take this to be the particular function of history, that virtues not be silenced and that fear for one's reputation in the future attend those crooked words and deeds.[91]

Although Tacitus cannot always satisfy the prerequisites of old-fashioned Republican history, whether because access to information was limited or because people stopped engaging in noble exploits altogether, he can succeed in providing some degree of moral instruction, even if by negative example. Yet deterrence is only effective if readers fear that their names too may one day appear in the annals of history, that they too may one day be the target of invective.[92] Whether in his speeches or in his descriptive passages, in his words or deeds, Tacitus surmounts the difficulties of writing history after Actium, such that his works are not nearly as narrowly circumscribed and boring as he would have us believe.

IV

ROMANS AND OTHERS

ETHNOGRAPHIES IN LATIN LITERATURE give us a glimpse of Roman ethnocentricity, since the authors assume that Rome was the cultural and political centre of the known world. The custom of describing far-off places dates back to the sixth century BCE and the Ionian historians, and in the fifth century Herodotus wrote at length about Egypt in *Histories* Book 2. The extensive campaigns of Alexander the Great then opened up new lands and peoples to the Greeks for Hellenistic historians to write about. Ethnographic digressions were expected to include information about location, physical geography, climate, crops and natural and mineral resources, as well as social and political institutions, religious customs and military organization.

Such digressions are not unusual in Latin literature. Julius Caesar wrote about the customs of the Gauls and the Germanic people in his commentary on the Gallic war. Sallust included an excursus on the geography and people of North Africa in the *War Against Jugurtha*. From the fragments of his *Histories*, we can piece together descriptions of Sarmatia, Corsica, Taurus, Crete and Pontus. Tacitus himself inserted a digression on the geography and people of the island of Britannia in the *Agricola*.[1] However, the *Germania* is unique as the only extant work in Latin literature devoted exclusively to a group of people.[2] Furthermore, as the shortest of all of Tacitus' works the *Germania* alone is devoid of speeches direct or indirect; as a result, it is his most transparent work, since he need not invent or pretend to record the words of others. Tacitus as narrator is the only person who speaks in the *Germania*; there are no main characters whose words or deeds command centre stage. Additionally, the treatise does not adhere to an annalistic chronology (James Rives calls it 'largely ahistorical'[3]), and as we already saw in Chapter I, it lacks a preface. In a word, the *Germania* is an anomaly. For this reason, it is arguably the most important work for understanding Tacitus.

Following the convention adopted by Rives, in this book the Latin noun 'Germani' is used of the people, Germania the place, and the English adjective Germanic when necessary. The modern adjective and nouns German, Germans and Germany are purposely avoided, since Tacitus describes ancient tribes and parts of northern Europe that encompassed more than modern Germany.[4] The title of the monograph as transmitted in the manuscripts is 'On the origin and geographical situation of the Germani'. Tacitus clearly designed the monograph in two halves; the first follows in the tradition of ancient ethnographies with information about the social, political, economic and cultural institutions of the Germani in general and as a whole, and the second half adheres more closely to the Hellenistic tradition of the guided tour, or 'periegesis', since Tacitus 'leads us around' the lands and provides specific details about individual tribes.[5]

In the first sentence, Tacitus draws the physical boundaries of Germania: east of the Rhine, north of the Danube and south of the North and Baltic Seas. This area encompasses the modern countries of (from west to east) Belgium, the Netherlands, Germany, Denmark, Poland, the Czech Republic, Austria, Slovakia and Hungary. The Germani are descended from the god Tuisto by his son Mannus, whose sons bestowed names on the three major divisions of peoples, the Ingaevones, Hermiones and Istaevones (*G.* 2.2). Hercules is said to have lived among them, and according to legend Odysseus visited and founded the town of Asciburgium (modern Moers-Asberg; *G.* 3.2), although the attribution is likely false, since archaeological evidence reveals that the town was probably founded as a military camp under Drusus.[6] Next Tacitus describes the soil and its capabilities before going into detail about military equipment and organization (*G.* 5–8). He then turns to the religion of the Germani; this section is surprisingly brief. Tacitus uses the Roman names for deities whose Germanic names are known (for example, Mercury instead of Woden; *G.* 9.1). A paragraph comparing and contrasting the Roman and Germanic practices of taking auspices and augury leads to a discussion of public deliberation and assemblies (*G.* 10–11), and just two paragraphs describe the attitude of the Germani towards war and peace (*G.* 14–15). We learn next about daily life and customs: urban planning and architecture, clothing, marriage, child-rearing, hospitality, entertainment and slaves (*G.* 16–25). After a brief paragraph on the economy (loans, land distribution and cultivation; *G.* 26), the first half closes with a description of funerary practices (*G.* 27.1).

Such a strong closural device thus naturalizes the exotic customs of the Germani by framing them within the familiar rhythms of life and death. It also necessitates an equally strong justification for further progress on a subject that has reached such a natural conclusion as death. Therefore, Tacitus proclaims his intention for the second half of the monograph:

> These are the things we have learned in general about the origin and customs of all the peoples of Germania. Now I shall set forth the institutions and rituals of each tribe individually, to what extent they differ and which tribes have crossed over from Germania into Gaul.[7]

Epic and didactic poetry offer similar examples of proems in the middle, especially when the poet is about to embark on a lengthy catalogue, as Tacitus is about to do.[8] Starting in the west, Tacitus begins with tribes that do not observe the clear-cut distinction between Gaul and Germania as set forth in the first chapter. For example, the Vangiones, Triboci and Nemetes were Germanic tribes who lived in the Romanized province of Gallia Belgica (*G.* 28). Then there are those tribes east of the Rhine that were under Roman hegemony, for example the Batavi, Chatti and Mattiaci (*G.* 29–31). Beyond were the Usipi, Tencteri, Bructeri, Chamavi and Angrivarii (*G.* 32–4); to the north the Chauci, Cherusci, Cimbri, Semnones and Langobardi (*G.* 35–7); to the east the many tribes that are generally classed as Suebi, including Hermunduri, Marcomani, Quadi and Gotones (*G.* 38–44). Tacitus interrupts his tour through Germania with a digression on the 200-year history of Roman interaction with the tribes under discussion (*G.* 37.2). So while normally ethnography is a digression from history, in the *Germania* history is a digression from ethnography.[9]

The penultimate paragraph of the monograph is a digression on amber, collected on the shores of the Baltic Sea by the Aestii, who did not know its use or value until they traded it with the Romans for handsome prices. With a second-person verb, Tacitus invites the reader to behold a specimen in the making: 'Still you would gather that it is the sap of trees, because there often shines through it certain creatures that creep or even fly which trapped in the liquid are enclosed in the soon hardening material.'[10] This is useful information about Roman trade with northern Germanic tribes; it is also a metaphor for the delicate process of imperialism. As the insects are lured and captured by the resin, so the tribes of Germani are lured by the price and eventually trapped into supplying a commodity for the Roman luxury market.

The Peucini, Veneti and Fenni are so far east on the border of Suebia that they might qualify as being Sarmatian (i.e. Scythian) rather than Germanic in origin (*G.* 46). Although similar to the Germani in speech and settlement patterns, they are filthy, lazy and clearly the product of inter-tribal marriage. The Fenni are poor; they have no weapons, horses or homes, and rely on herbs for food and hides for clothing. At this outermost limit, Tacitus prudently ends the monograph: 'The rest is the stuff of fable, for example, Hellusii and Oxiones with the faces and countenances of men but the bodies and limbs of wild beasts. I shall quit here on the grounds that such information is undiscoverable.'[11]

Ancient ethnographers were comfortable reporting such marvellous and fantastic wonders; for example, Ctesias of Cnidus records unicorns, mantichoras, griffins and tribes with no heads but eyes and a mouth on the chest.[12] But Tacitus rejects the generic convention. As is the case with most ancient ethnographers, it is highly unlikely that he visited any of the places he talks about in the *Germania*. Instead, he relies on earlier written information. Tacitus had recourse to at least two sources which are no longer extant. The first was by Aufidius Bassus, Roman historian of the Julio-Claudian era, who wrote the *Bellum Germanicum*, a history of the Germanic war which covered the campaigns of Tiberius, perhaps from 4 CE when he resumed command of Germany, to 16, when the recovery of the standards of Quinctilius Varus was commemorated with a triumphal arch.[13] The second was by Pliny the Elder, who wrote 20 books on the German wars, according to his nephew Pliny the Younger.[14]

In the Augustan age, the historian Livy would have included wars with the Germani in the lost portion of his monumental history, and the geographer Strabo included information not found elsewhere.[15] The Tiberian historian Velleius Paterculus covered the period of Germanic and Roman interaction from Caesar to the reign of Tiberius, albeit in cursory form. In the middle of the *Germania*, Tacitus calls Julius Caesar the *summus auctorum*, the highest authority.[16] In spite of the many sources available to him, Tacitus nonetheless draws the *Germania* to a close because he has reached the limits of discovery.

The closing statement of the *Germania* also reveals that of the many cultural differences between the Germani and the Romans and the enduring political conflicts between them, hybridity elicits the most anxiety. From the outset we learn that the Germani were autochthonous and untainted by intermarriage.[17] Families were kept pure and simple, since men were content to take only one wife, women received only one husband and their children were never handed over to wet nurses but fed by their own mothers.[18] Such purity becomes a defining feature of the Germani; once they intermarry with the neighbouring tribes of Suebia, they begin to lose their claim to Germanic identity.[19] This sort of rhetoric fuelled the nineteenth-century German nationalism that twisted Tacitus' language of purity into proto-Nazi racial paradigms.[20] When Tacitus reaches the ultimate hybrid of half-man half-beast, the entire enterprise comes to a halt. Tacitus' overt judgements about hybridity (including his ultimate silence) help us understand the more latent concerns about the erosion of Roman identity that suffuse all of his works.

The identity of the Other, in our case the Germani, is developed through a carefully crafted series of antitheses with the Romans. Roman cultural identity thus becomes the standard against which the Other is measured, or more often the standard by which the Other is negated entirely. The barbarian way of life matters only to the extent that it confirms the Roman way of life. Hybridity therefore poses a special concern, since it threatens to erode the distinctions between two cultures. The abstract beast-men at the end of the *Germania* can be easily dismissed, but the concrete results of social, economic and cultural exchange are a pervasive threat to Roman identity. In the *Annals*, for example, we read of Arminius, the Cheruscan freedom fighter who was rightfully regarded as one of Rome's deadliest enemies. Yet he was a citizen with equestrian status; his son Thumelicus was raised in Ravenna, and his nephew Italicus installed by the emperor Claudius as king of the tribe. The boundaries between Roman and Other were distressingly permeable.

Scholarly discussions of the *Germania* and of the broader genre of ancient ethnography routinely address the way such texts deploy colonial discourse in the interest of building and maintaining imperial ideologies and hierarchies.[21] Normally such analyses seek the various mechanisms for asserting the necessity of imperialist oppression. Common to all such texts is the dichotomy between 'us' and 'them', and as we shall see, the *Germania* is no exception. Yet the relationship between colonizer and colonized is mutually beneficial in spite of the inherent inequality that defines the terms: the colonizer advances economically and politically; the colonized makes use of new technologies. Locked in their mutual dependence, they can neither trust nor afford to distrust each other. This mutual dependence helps explain in part the sustained theme of liberty and its proper limits in the *Germania*, since both parties are in a sense enslaved to the other. As Rives observes, the Romans place a high premium on personal liberty so long as obedience and discipline are observed, while the Germani undervalue obedience and discipline and overvalue freedom.[22] The love of liberty is a defining characteristic of the Germani in the heartland; however, the more distant tribes in the east obey kings. The Sitones are technically still Germanic, but they differ in one important respect: 'A woman rules. So far do they fall not just below liberty but even below slavery.'[23] A spectrum of responses to authority thus emerges, and in this sense the *Germania* speaks to some of the same themes as the *Annals*, since the relationship between the senatorial class and the *princeps* is likewise one of mutual dependence, and political equilibrium depends upon a balance between liberty and obedience that both parties must observe in order to prosper. The balance was not always easy to strike, as Tacitus records in the *Annals*:

> It is handed down to memory that whenever Tiberius left the Senate house, he would always exclaim in Greek, 'What men, so ready to be enslaved!' Clearly even he, who did not appreciate public displays of freedom, was disgusted by such protracted exhibitions of slavery.[24]

Like the Romans and the Germani, Tiberius and the Senate needed each other as much as they resented each other.

This brings us to the dirty little secret of the *Germania*: in a work where only four individual Germani but 17 Romans are mentioned by name,[25] we are bound to learn far more about the Romans and about Tacitus' philosophy of writing history than we will ever learn about the Germani, whose written records are problematic and whose archaeological remains are uneven in quality and frequency. In what follows, the reliability and credibility of the *Germania* are not at issue; rather, attention to Tacitus' rhetoric can help highlight some important ideologies that may even illuminate our understanding of his other works. In keeping with the design of the *Germania*, this chapter falls into two parts; the first examines literary allusions, first-person statements and comparisons between the Germani and the Romans as seen in paragraphs 1–27. The second half of the *Germania* proves as allusive as the first, as Tacitus reconstructs the history of the interaction between the Germani and the Romans, but only to a certain point. Domitian campaigned against the Chatti in 83, and after he was assassinated in 96, Trajan was active enough on the Rhine to have warranted at least a passing mention; however, on these events Tacitus is silent. In the conclusion, we shall explore the implications of these omissions as part of the larger complex of criticism and praise that underpins Tacitus' representations of Romans and Others.

Literary Qualities

Tacitus' opening sentence invites comparison with Julius Caesar's *Gallic Wars*. Both use the adjective *omnis*: 'All Germania'; 'All Gaul'. Thus both claim to be comprehensive. Next they set their subject matter apart from other lands and peoples: 'All Germania is separated from Gaul and Rhaetia by the Rhine, from Pannonia by the Danube'; 'All Gaul is divided into three parts.' Caesar then names the Aquitani, Galli and Belgae, who are noteworthy for their bravery derived in part by their contact with the Germani, 'who live across the Rhine and with whom they wage war continuously'.[26] Helvetians, too, Caesar tells us, surpass the Gauls in courage, 'because they contend with the Germani on practically a daily basis, either by keeping them within their territory or by waging war against them in their own territories'.[27] Caesar's Germani are a source of constant warfare to the Gauls; for Tacitus, the Germani will be a source of constant warfare for the Romans. Later in the *Germania*, Tacitus will reckon that the conquest of Germania has been going on for 210 years, from news of the Cimbrian migration in 113 BCE to the reign of Trajan in 98 CE.[28] Tacitus thus outstrips his model, for his monograph covers far more history in far fewer pages than Caesar's famous commentary.

Although the monograph lacks a preface, Tacitus twice uses a first-person verb in the second paragraph:

> The Germani themselves I should believe are indigenous and not at all mixed with other nations through immigration or obligations, because those who sought to migrate did so not across land as in earlier times but were conveyed by ship; and the Ocean huge and, if I may say, hostile, is attempted by few ships from our part of the world.[29]

'I should believe' (in Latin, *crediderim*) merely conveys that Tacitus agrees with his sources; the first person can be handily discounted as a standard trope of historiography. However, the potential subjunctive in the somewhat rare perfect tense in Latin colours this assertion. Instead of an indicative statement of fact, *crediderim* expresses either caution or modesty; either the sources are wrong, or Tacitus is unable (or unwilling) to validate them, which calls attention to his role as mediator. Yet the origins of the Germani gain credibility when contrasted with the Romans, who were not at all indigenous. Their founder Aeneas, after a long journey by sea, immigrated to Italy and obligated himself to King Latinus, who promised his daughter's hand in marriage. And unlike Germania, Italy was a fertile land well worth fighting for.

The other first-person verb, 'if I may say', is also a negligible turn of phrase, merely qualifying the adjective. However, it also suggests that 'hostile' is hyperbolic, and Tacitus then pushes the reader to agree with him:

> Besides the danger of a fearsome and uncharted sea, who would leave behind Asia or Africa or Italy and seek out Germania, its untamed land and harsh climate as grim to inhabit as to behold, unless it were his native land?[30]

For Christopher Pelling, such uses of the first person have a 'buttonholing' effect that draws attention to the communicative process between Tacitus and his reader.[31]

Throughout the first part of the treatise, Tacitus' criticisms of Germania seem the reverse of Virgil's praises of Italy in the *Georgics* (2.136–76), a famous passage that celebrates Italy. For example, in Virgil's Italy spring is 'incessant' and summer so long that cattle can breed twice and fruit trees produce two harvests.[32] The climate of Germania, on the other hand, is so inhospitable as to lack a season: 'Winter and spring and summer have meaning and a designated word; the name and bounty of autumn are unknown.'[33] Virgil praises Italy's 'noble cities', while in Germania 'no cities do the people inhabit, a fact well enough known.'[34] Given that climate and urban planning are regular features of ethnography, these two examples may spring from a shared and somewhat narrowly circumscribed subject matter and nothing more. However, Tacitus' engagements with and adaptations of Virgilian language in the *Histories* and *Annals* are well documented.[35] Furthermore, while Virgil observed the generic expectations of ethnography in parts of the *Georgics*, Tacitus elevated the form as the only Latin author to devote an entire monograph to a group of people.[36] As Virgil created a way of talking about other peoples in the *Georgics*, 'Tacitus cheerfully puts himself into that literary tradition,' according to Richard Thomas.[37] Additionally, the *Germania* and the *Georgics* are didactic, in the sense that they are concerned with moral instruction by means of specialized topics. When Tacitus says, 'Now I shall set forth', he uses the Latin verb *expediam*, a common verb in Latin didactic poetry.[38] So it is worth looking at two more examples of his possible engagement with Virgil's praise of Italy. In both cases, Tacitus uses the first person.

As we have seen, with the first-person verb *crediderim*, Tacitus begins by emphasizing that the Germani are indigenous, whereas Virgil tacitly reminds the reader that the Romans are not. Alluding to the myth of Jason's quest for the Golden Fleece, Virgil reminds the reader that Italy never saw such creatures as sowed dragon's teeth, 'no crop of men bristling with helmets and spears'.[39] Virgil is referring to the dragon's teeth, some of which were sown by Cadmus, some as here by Jason, and which yielded in both cases a crop of *spartoi*, or 'sown men', sprung from the earth. With the help of Medea, Jason prevailed over this horrible army of giants. Italian soil never produced such a crop of autochthonous beasts.

When Tacitus affirms that the Germani did not intermarry, again he uses a first-person verb: 'I myself agree with the opinions of those who think that the peoples of Germania were untainted by marriages with foreign nations but that they existed as a race distinct, pure, and as such like only unto themselves.'[40] Tacitus does not say whether the Germani refrained from intermarriage by choice or by chance, nor does he say whether the practice was an advantage or disadvantage. Yet unlike the Romans, who perpetrated the rape of the Sabine women, the Germani could be considered morally superior because they did not trick their neighbours into intermarriage nor allow themselves to be tricked. However, the Romans were smarter because by adopting intermarriage they ensured their strength. So is Tacitus praising the Germani for their racial purity and by extension blaming the Romans, or is he criticising the Germani for their short-sightedness and praising the Romans for cleverly fortifying their ranks?

In asking who would even travel to Germania, Tacitus ranks it below three favourable places (Asia, Africa and Italy), whereas in the *Georgics*, Italy ranks above three favourable places:

> But neither the groves of Media, land most wealthy,
> nor the beautiful Ganges nor Hermus teeming with gold
> may contend with the praises of Italy.[41]

In Virgil's Italy rivers flow with silver, copper and gold.[42] When speaking of Germania's lack of mineral resources, Tacitus again uses the first person: 'The gods denied them silver and gold, whether out of kindness or anger I do not know. Yet I would not affirm that no vein of Germania produces silver or gold. For who has ever prospected?'[43] This is the second of only three times in the *Germania* that Tacitus will detain the reader from the proper subject matter and insist on an alignment of judgement.[44] As we have seen, the last word of the treatise is *reliquam*, 'I shall quit here on the grounds that such information is undiscoverable,' whether among the farthest tribes of Germania dwell creatures with the faces of men but the bodies and limbs of wild beasts.[45] Thus all three instances of the first person convey doubt and signal ignorance. The reader can be confident that he is in the hands of a sensible narrator who is prepared to admit the limits of his knowledge, but such admissions also raise the possibility that information not marked with such first-person qualifiers may be suspect. It would seem that Tacitus is most trustworthy at precisely these moments when he openly admits his ignorance. He thus ends his treatise with a first-person statement that situates his efforts at the outermost limits of the larger literary tradition about Germania. Coincidentally, Virgil ends his praise of Italy with a first-person statement that situates his efforts within the larger literary tradition going back to the didactic poet Hesiod: 'I embark on skill and matters of ancient renown, I who dared to unseal the sacred fonts of poetic inspiration, and I sing an Ascraean song throughout Roman towns.'[46]

From these similarities between the *Germania* and the *Georgics* we can discern the essence of a shared literary culture. While we dare not draw direct lines of influence from Virgil to Tacitus, we can observe the dynamic interplay between criticism and praise that drives the *Germania*.

Sometimes the difference between criticism and praise is indiscernible, so that the *Germania* appears to proceed harmlessly enough. Here are four examples of when Tacitus uses a first-person plural turn of phrase to illustrate a contrasting Germanic custom:

(1) Their horses are not noteworthy for beauty or speed, nor do they learn to vary manoeuvres *as is our custom*.[47]

(2) They reckon not the number of days, *as we do*, but of nights; so they make appointments and set dates; night seems to lead in the day.[48]

(3) They do not lay out their villages *as is our custom* with buildings connected and adjoining; each surrounds his own home with open space, either as a precaution against fire or because they do not know how to build.[49]

(4) They do not use the rest of the slaves *as is our custom* with specific tasks throughout the household.[50]

The phrases 'as is our custom' carry no value judgement; instead they merely assist the reader in comprehending the exotic by making recourse to the familiar. Of course, such statements also assume that the Roman custom is the standard against which all others are measured. The mores of the Germani are cast only in negative terms; as a result, they appear to be everything that the Romans are not. The identity of the Germani is so dependent on Roman ways that the monograph becomes a handbook for how to be a good Roman: (1) have beautiful, swift and agile horses; (2) reckon time by days, not nights; (3) build according to principles of urban planning; and (4) give household slaves specific tasks. In any case, the Germani and the Romans appear to be morally equivalent in these examples.

Sometimes, however, the Germani achieve the moral high ground. Instead of using overt language to signal the contrast ('as is our custom'), Tacitus can exploit well-known tropes of Roman moralizing discourse to highlight the difference between Germani and Romans, again in negative terms: 'So they live with chastity guarded, corrupted not by the enticements of the games nor the provocations of banquets. Men and women equally are ignorant of the secrets of letters.'[51] Images of chastity, games, banquets and love letters are deeply engrained in Roman elegiac poetry; the pages of Ovid are filled with provocative trysts.[52] Augustan marriage legislation and moral reform was founded on the principle that adultery and immorality had undermined the Roman republic. The Romans regarded the theatre and the games as vehicles for excessive indulgence and violence, and at banquets men and women could flirt in dangerous ways. Roman love elegy offers plenty of evidence that illicit affairs depended on secret love letters as a result. The Germani, by contrast, engage in none of these vices. They are explicitly praised for their chastity at the expense of the Romans, who are implicitly blamed for their immorality. Of course, the illiteracy that ensures moral purity also prevents the production of literature and is in fact Tacitus' warrant for assuming responsibility for transmitting the Germanic cultural heritage.

Tacitus next describes family structure and inheritance law. The Germani do not draw up wills, but they do value large families. Men with a great number of connections are honoured in old age, and 'there is no reward in childlessness.'[53] Here Tacitus alludes to legacy hunters, a particular menace in imperial Rome,[54] who attached themselves to wealthy childless individuals in hopes of becoming beneficiaries upon death. They were especially villainized because they exploited a shortcoming in the Roman legal system that allowed men of low-born status to acquire a fortune normally beyond their reach. Once again, Germanic purity elucidates Roman vice.

The next two examples of Germanic character prefigure themes that suffuse Tacitus' later works. Tacitus describes the daily habits of the Germani, who drink to excess and are not clever or cunning: 'the thoughts of all are exposed and laid bare.'[55] It is an ethnographic stereotype that barbarians are incapable of secrets (as evidenced already by their illiteracy), but for Tacitus the character trait takes on added significance. When Agricola died, 'in spirit and countenance he [Domitian] bore the guise of grief, since he was no longer worried about his hatred and he was the sort who could more easily conceal joy than fear.'[56] From the beginning of the *Annals*, Tacitus tells us, 'whether by natural inclination or by habit the words of Tiberius were always guarded and veiled, even in matters which he did not have to conceal.'[57] The Germani are incapable of such sinister and tyrannical dissimulation. While the inability to dissemble may protect the Germani from tyrants among themselves, it also exposes them to Romans who, if they do not scruple to lie to each other, will surely lie to the Germani.

Tacitus brings the first half of the *Germania* to a close with a description of their funeral practices: 'No pageantry attends their funerals [...] it is noble for women to mourn, men to remember.'[58] According to Rives, 'Tacitus' main purpose in this chapter is to contrast the simplicity of Germanic funerals with the extravagance of those among the Roman élite.'[59] For Germanicus extraordinary honours were decreed: his name was added to the song of the Salii; chairs for the priests of Augustus were garlanded; his ivory image was carried in the front of circus parades; triumphal arches were erected in Rome, on the Rhine and in Syria; a cenotaph was raised at Antioch where he died; and countless statues were dedicated. Lamentation was so protracted that Tacitus tells us Tiberius issued an edict calling for the conclusion of public mourning.[60] Of course, Germanicus was an exceptional person who died under exceptional circumstances and whose achievements merited such measures. In keeping with ethnographic stereotype, the Germani and Romans differ in terms of extravagance; however, they align in terms of gender roles. Women may express emotions, while men must be reticent. The family of Agricola are assigned precisely these roles upon his death: 'Call us your family from the depths of longing and womanly laments to the contemplation of your virtues for which it is not right to mourn or beat the breast.'[61]

Tacitus closes *Annals* Book 3 with the funeral of the noble Junia, niece of Cato, wife of Cassius and sister of Marcus Brutus. She was connected therefore most intimately with the assassins of Julius Caesar. Junia was publicly eulogized and her funeral procession included the *imagines* (waxen likenesses in the form of masks) of members of her family of long-standing nobility. However, the masks of two men were deliberately excluded from the procession: 'But outstripping them all were Cassius and Brutus all the more so because their *imagines* were not to be seen.'[62] As we can credit

Tacitus as the first to refuse to call a spade a spade, so here we find the origin of the modern expression, 'conspicuous by its absence'.[63] Presumably any physical indications of Brutus and Cassius, assassins of Julius Caesar, would have offended Tiberius; yet Junia's funeral procession bears witness to the power of memory, for Brutus and Cassius were remembered all the more vividly because their *imagines* were absent. Thus unlike Germanic funerals, Roman funerals carry political risks. No doubt the *Germania* forges Roman identity by contrasting Roman with German mores. But it also illuminates moral ambiguities by pausing on some of the more problematic aspects of Roman social and political practice.

Historical Content

Tacitus begins the second half by attempting to sort the Germani from the Gauls, for the Rhine is a more permeable boundary than originally suggested in the first sentence of the *Germania*. Of these tribes, the Batavi merit further explanation:

> Above all of these tribes in virtue are the Batavians, who dwell not so much on the bank but on an island in the Rhine. Once they belonged to the Chatti, but due to internal strife they migrated to the settlements in which they became part of the Roman Empire. The honour and indication of their ancient alliance remains, for they are not burdened with tribute nor does the tax collector wear them down. They are exempt from tax burdens and levies; set apart for use in battles, they are reserved for war, like weapons and armour.[64]

Information is provided rapidly and succinctly: the Batavians dwelled on an island in the Rhine; they migrated from the Chatti; they were subject to Roman rule but enjoyed special exemptions. Tacitus' reader would have heard of the Batavians and would surely have brought to the text more information than provided here. During the civil wars of 69 they served Vitellius, but when pressed for additional troops they rebelled under the leadership of the chieftain Julius Civilis, a name 'almost too good to be true', in the words of Holly Haynes,[65] for it is a reminder of the hybrid status of a Batavian chieftain among the many to receive Roman citizenship from a patron of the Julian *gens*.

In the *Histories*, Tacitus gives a much fuller description of the Batavians that includes information we might have expected in the *Germania*. He introduces this digression with the didactic verb *expediam*, 'I shall set forth more thoroughly':

> The Batavians, while they lived across the Rhine, were part of the Chatti, until driven by internal strife they occupied empty lands on the far shore of Gaul and a nearby island, which ocean surrounded in the front, the Rhine river to the back and side. Their wealth was not wasted, rarely did they enter alliances with stronger tribes; they supplied men and weapons to the Roman Empire. They were used for a long time in the German wars. Then their reputation increased because of service in Britannia, when their cohorts were transferred there, which their most noble commanded according to ancient custom. Still at home there was a select cavalry, especially good at swimming, which could cut through the Rhine carrying their weapons on horseback still keeping the formation intact.[66]

Some of the information is repeated from the *Germania*: the Batavians were originally affiliated with the Chatti; they were driven from their homeland because of internal strife (the same Latin phrase, *seditione domestica*, is used); they inhabited an island in the middle of the Rhine; their chief contribution to Rome was in weapons and manpower. In the *Histories*, however, Tacitus adds the Batavians' service in Britannia. Agricola had four cohorts of Batavians with him at the Battle of Mons Graupius;[67] although they were withdrawn from Britannia shortly afterwards, this aid was significant enough in Tacitus' eyes to merit mention in the *Agricola*. The Batavians' exceptional skills at swimming are attested in an inscription from the age of Hadrian, in which a Batavian boasts of his ability to shoot one arrow and hit it with another while swimming across the Danube.[68]

Clearly the Romans relied on the provinces for manpower; the Batavians assisted in Britannia and allowed themselves to get entangled in Rome's civil war. Long before this, however, Batavian horsemen were recruited by Julius Caesar and sided with Octavian, eventually becoming Augustus' guard and serving the Julio-Claudians in succession, and they later rode with Domitian against the Marcomani. Nerva adopted Trajan, whose guard, also called Batavi, was still used by the Severan emperors 100 years later.[69] Given this extraordinary record of loyal service to the Romans from the time of Julius Caesar to Tacitus' own time and beyond, the paragraph in the *Germania* (shorter and less detailed than any in the *Histories* or *Annals*) amid a catalogue of tribes of lesser distinction effectively downplays their importance and minimizes their contributions.

Tacitus returns to the Batavians once more in the *Annals,* where he attempts to map precisely the so-called island of the Batavians:

> The island of the Batavians was designated for the rendezvous because of its easy approach for receiving troops and its opportunities for transporting war. The Rhine continues in one channel or flows around islands of modest size; at the head of the Batavian lands it splits as if into two rivers. It keeps its name and the swiftness of its course where it runs past Germania until it flows into the ocean. On the Gallic bank it flows more broadly and calmly, and the inhabitants change its name, calling it the Vahal. Soon it changes name again to the Mosa and with a huge mouth it pours into the ocean as well.[70]

Although modern engineering has altered the estuaries and canals of the Rhine delta in the Netherlands so that it is no longer possible to trace Tacitus' route, the island is identified with modern Betuwe in the Dutch province of Gelderland. It lies between the rivers Waal (ancient Vahal) and Lek, a major branch of the Rhine delta. Judging from the details given in the *Histories* and in this physical description of the island of the Batavians, Tacitus truncates his discussion of the Batavians in the *Germania*, even though such information would not have been out of place. In her case study of Julius Civilis and the Batavians, Rhiannon Ash asserts that 'Tacitus clearly expects his readers to be familiar with his own earlier representations of Germans and individual tribes from the *Germania*, particularly the Batavians.[71] She is surely right that in the narrative of the Batavian revolt in the *Histories*, Tacitus cashes in on the stereotypes of Germanic behaviour that he outlined especially in the first part of the *Germania*. The *Germania* enriches the *Histories*, but Syme reminds us that it is also independent of the later historical works in inspiration and agenda,[72] as there were unique pressures exerted on the *Germania*.

In the year 98, Germania was a timely topic. Trajan was proclaimed emperor in 96 while on the Rhine, where whatever settlement Domitian had reached needed attention. Syme points out the irony that the last legate proclaimed emperor while campaigning on the Rhine had been Vitellius in 69.[73] Exactly 20 years later, the legate Saturninus led a revolt – brief and miscarried – against Domitian, and according to Pliny the Younger, Trajan came to his rescue.[74] Domitian went to Gaul in 82 or 83 ostensibly to conduct a census; however, he attacked the Chatti and in 83 took the name Germanicus, 'victor over Germania', and celebrated a triumph mocked for its obvious pretence: Domitian paid people to dye their hair and dress like captives.[75] Tacitus alludes to this triumph in a *sententia* at the end of his digression on the history of Roman interaction with the Germani: 'Nowadays we celebrate triumphs more than victories.'[76] The sentiment is pointed enough to throw the omissions of the exploits of Domitian and Trajan from the *Germania* into sharp relief. For Ash, therefore, 'The *Germania* in its own way reinforces and underpins the anti-Domitianic stance of Tacitus' other works.'[77] No doubt the received tradition was hostile towards Domitian, making it difficult to assess his character and achievements. However, we do well to remember that in 85 CE, the military zones known as Germania Superior and Germania Inferior became formal provinces, and a new frontier system was established that ensured peaceful Roman control of the left bank of the Rhine (modern Netherlands and Belgium) until the third century CE. Beyond this, Rome would never advance.

Domitian is consistently maligned in the sources; attitudes towards Trajan, however, are not so easily discerned. Syme asserts that except for a few roads and forts, 'Trajan quickly made it clear that the Roman public must expect no conquests in Germany.'[78] Trajan's substantial contribution to the Roman Empire would be the annexation of Dacia (modern Romania), but this was still a decade away and would be the subject of an epic poem by Caninius Rufus, who is encouraged by Pliny the Younger in a letter that dates to 107 CE:

> You do quite well to embark on writing *The Dacian War*. For what topic is so recent, so fulsome, so lofty, what else so ultimately poetic and so legendary although its events are verifiable? You will describe new rivers flowing into lands and the new bridges cast over them, camps on the sheer cliffs of mountains, a king driven from his kingdom and driven from life though not hopeless. Then after all this, two triumphs: the first over an unconquered people, the second quite extraordinary.[79]

Statius' poem on Domitian's German wars would have provided a model for Caninius to follow. But for Tacitus, there were no guarantees that Trajan would accomplish anything worth celebrating on the Rhine.

In part then, the digression on the history of Roman engagement with Germania is a catalogue of risks associated with imperial expansion. He is led into the topic by the mention of the Cimbri:

> Our city was in its 640th year when in the consulship of Caecilius Metellus and Papirius Carbo news of an army of Cimbrians was heard. From that time, if we reckon to the second consulship of the Emperor Trajan, almost 210 years have passed: so long has the subjugation of Germania been going on.[80]

Tacitus first calculates from the founding of the city before deploying the annalistic formula of eponymous consuls. The year was 113 BCE, and Trajan's second consulship was in 98 CE. Such overdetermined temporal markers interrupt the narrative of the Germani in their otherwise timeless, eternal existence; note, too, that Tacitus has slipped from the Cimbri in particular to the Germani more generally. Then Tacitus compares the Germani to other Roman foes:

> Within this period of so long an age, many losses were sustained on both sides. Not Samnites, not Carthaginians, neither Spain nor Gaul, not even Parthia ever threatened us more regularly. Surely the freedom of the Germani is more fierce than the kingdom of Arsacis. For what else can the East throw in our faces besides the slaughter of Crassus, itself crushed under Ventidius upon the loss of Pacorus?[81]

Tacitus sketches in rough outline the expansion of Roman hegemony first on the Italian peninsula, next in the Mediterranean, then into western Europe, and finally to the East. However, these enemies were a bit more formidable than this brief account implies. The Samnites fought three wars against the Romans for most of the fourth century BCE, supporting Pyrrhus against the Romans and still opposing Rome during the Social Wars of 91–87 BCE. Likewise, the Carthaginians were not annihilated until they had invaded Italy and fought three wars with the Romans. Spain was not fully subjugated until Augustus, and although Caesar pacified Gaul, the Romans never forgot that the Gauls had sacked the city in 386 BCE. As we saw in the previous chapter, even during the reign of Claudius the Gauls were still known for their long history of aggression towards Rome. The staggering defeat of Crassus by the Parthians in 53 BCE was one of the greatest disasters in Roman history. Despite Ventidius' invasion and Octavian's diplomacy, the Parthians continued to confront the Romans over control of Armenia even in the reign of Nero. This passage gives the impression that the Romans were defending themselves and their borders against foreign threats; however, recent scholarship has rejected the notion of 'defensive imperialism'. Careful scrutiny of the evidence for Parthia, for example, reveals that in fact the Romans were the aggressors. As Tim Cornell puts it, 'In a political sense Rome did not have a Parthian problem; but it is abundantly clear that Parthia had a Roman problem.'[82]

The comparative adverb and adjective (*saepius*, 'more regularly', and *acrior*, 'more fierce') express that the Germani pose the more serious threat: the bigger they come, the harder they fall. But is the comparison reasonable, or has Tacitus underplayed centuries of foreign conflict so as to exaggerate the Germanic threat? Such exaggeration obviously aggrandizes any Roman attempts against such a formidable enemy; but could it not also excuse the Roman inability to subdue the Germani, or even mock the Romans for their inability, precisely since more formidable opponents had been overcome – and by more capable men? So while Tacitus presents a robust argument for Roman imperialism, it does not mean that he is blind to the chinks in their armour.

Tacitus goes on to describe the losses to the Romans: 'When Carbo, Cassius, Aurelius Scaurus, Servilius Caepio and Mallius Maximus were routed or captured, the Germani stripped the Roman people of five consular armies at the same time, Augustus of Varus and the three legions with him.'[83] Carbo was the first to meet the Cimbri in 113 BCE. In 106 and 105, consular armies were led by Servilius Caepio and Mallius Maximus with legates Aurelius Scarus and Cassius.[84] As for Varus, his ghost still haunts the Teutoburg Forest, where he was ambushed by Arminius and the Cheruscans in 9 CE. As Tacitus expands upon his brief description of the Batavi with fuller accounts and more detailed descriptions in the *Histories* and *Annals*, so he turns this elliptical mention of Varus into one of the most poignant episodes in the *Annals*. Tacitus' rendition of Germanicus' return to the Teutoburg Forest six years after Varus' defeat will be a source of artistic inspiration even in the twentieth century, as we shall see in our final chapter.

The catalogue of Roman losses ends with the infamous defeat of Varus that effectively put an end to imperial expansion under Augustus. However, when compared to the sack of Rome by the Gauls or the invasion of the peninsula by Hannibal, the loss of three legions in a swamp nearly a thousand miles from the city of Rome seems rather small. Do our sources exaggerate the severity of the Varian disaster in order to exculpate Augustus for overstepping his limits, or perhaps to demonstrate that assimilated barbarians pose the more significant danger, since Arminius had access to intelligence that made him more of a threat? Eventually the Romans abandoned the annexation of Germania because the terrain beyond the Rhine proved intractable, and its permanent occupation would not have been worth the effort. Furthermore, expansion of the empire would have contravened Augustus' last wishes, as recorded by Tacitus: 'Augustus had written in his own hand and added the advice against extending the boundaries of the empire; whether he did so out of fear or envy is uncertain.'[85] Nevertheless, it was necessary to persevere in Germania, for imperial heirs like Drusus, Tiberius and Germanicus needed military experience to validate their credentials and set them on a par with the founder of the dynasty: 'Marius assaulted [the Germani] in Italy, Divine Julius in Gaul, Drusus and Tiberius and Germanicus within their own territories.'[86]

The losses to the Germani are concise and eventually meaningless. In the *Agricola*, Domitian at least knew that his triumph was openly mocked; here, Caligula is clueless:

> After this the gigantic threats of Caligula were rendered a laughing stock. Then there was a lull, until given the opportunity provided by our strife and civil wars they stormed the winter camps of our legions and even made inroads into Gaul, though driven back again. For nowadays we celebrate triumphs more than victories.[87]

The *sententia* effectively draws the digression to a close. This digression is especially conspicuous in a monograph without a preface or speeches, and clearly intrudes upon the narrative and halts the progress of the guided tour. It is removable; without it, the *Germania* would still be comprehensible. No new information is transmitted either about the Germani generally, or about particular tribes. The digression presupposes prior knowledge about Roman history on the part of the reader, who is expected to supply the missing details about each of the historical events mentioned. So what does this seemingly useless digression achieve?

First of all, in form this detachable paragraph embodies the tension between the particular and general, the part and the whole – the very principle of design that underwrites the *Germania*. Secondly, in a tour de force Tacitus condenses into a single paragraph the volumes written by Aufidius Bassus and Pliny the Elder (20 books!) on the wars with the Germani. Such condensation not only showcases Tacitus' skill but minimizes the import of the historical tradition by rendering hundreds of years in a mere epitome. Third, as a pause inserted to explain the history of Roman–Germanic interaction, the digression can be interpreted to represent in a microcosm the ideology of the entire *Germania* writ large. So in content, the digression is laden with thematic overtones that convey a Tacitean view of Roman imperialism and its discontent, most obviously expressed in the jab at Caligula's uselessness and the grandiloquent *sententia*. Furthermore, the losses sustained on both sides not only substantiate the earlier claim that the Romans have been attempting to conquer Germania for more than two hundred years, but this also demonstrates that the disadvantages to empire are mutual. At the core of the problem is the overweening freedom of the Germani, a recurring theme of the monograph. Finally, Tacitus names the three great commanders of the first century: Drusus, Tiberius and Germanicus, three men whose relationships were a complicated tangle of rivalry and devotion (Tiberius loved his brother Drusus but resented having to adopt his son Germanicus). In short, the digression contains as much to criticize as to praise, in both the Romans and the Germani.

In the *Germania*, any praise or blame ascribed to the Romans or the Germani derives from our author. Likewise, in the *Agricola* and the *Annals*, Tacitus struggles with the advantages and disadvantages of imperial expansion. Usually criticism of the Roman Empire is couched in speeches delivered by non-Romans to their compatriots, in which freedom is a recurring theme. Among the Britons, the chieftains Calgacus and Caratacus rouse their men by referring to the day of battle as 'the beginning of liberty', and Boudicca fights not just for herself but for the lost freedom of her people.[88] Arminius, furious that his father-in-law Segestes surrendered to the Romans, rouses the Cherusci: 'If you prefer your fatherland, your ancestors, your ancient ways to overlords and to new colonies, follow as your leader Arminius to glory and freedom rather than Segestes to ignominious slavery.'[89] Calgacus, Caratacus, Boudicca and Arminius (we can also add Civilis, leader of the Batavian revolt in the *Histories*) are 'distant voices of freedom'.[90] Although their opposition to Roman rule is bold, their causes are always lost; if anything, they demonstrate that revolt is no solution. And the uniformity of criticism – spoken by non-Romans to non-Romans far from the capital – attenuates its forcefulness. Hence these passages are often interpreted as meta-critical commentary on the taxed relationship between a servile Senate enslaved to a *princeps*. On the other hand, when the defeated Caratacus is paraded through Rome with his wife, daughters and brothers, he does not stoop in fear like the other captives but pleads for his life before the emperor's tribunal, and he succeeds in being pardoned. In the heart of Rome, he criticizes Claudius to his face: 'Just because you wish to dominate the world, does it follow that the world will accept your slavery?'[91]

Judging from the *Agricola*, the answer would be, in fact, yes. In his second winter as governor, Agricola undertook some 'highly beneficial measures', a phrase that quickly took on sinister overtones:

> In order that men isolated and rustic and for these reasons inclined to war might become habituated to peace and leisure through physical pleasures, Agricola gave private encouragement and public aid to build temples, fora and homes. He praised the eager and criticized the lazy. Thus a rivalry for honour took the place of necessity. He educated the sons of chieftains in the liberal arts, and preferred the character of the Britons to the eagerness of the Gauls, so that those who recently refused to learn Latin now coveted its eloquence. Then came the honour bestowed by our manner of dress, and togas were everywhere. Little by little they sunk to the enticements of vices, namely porticoes, baths and the elegance of dinner parties. And in their inexperience they called this culture, when it was merely part of their slavery.[92]

Here then is the list of ingredients for making a Roman: architecture, liberal arts, the Latin language, togas, and entertainment that inevitably leads to moral degeneration. In this sense, the paragraph is a digression on the ethnography of Rome. It is also an instruction manual for domination. The Italian Renaissance scholar Scipione Ammirato praises this passage because it demonstrates the best means of governing the people.[93] To the modern mind, however, the passage is disturbing for its brutal honesty, its glimpse of the dark side of civilization and the reminder that cultural advancements always come at a price, usually the annihilation of a way of life. There are no alternatives to imperialism: either the Britons refuse the Roman way of life but retain their glorious freedom, or they accept the Roman way of life and all of its comforts and benefits (as well as its drawbacks) but lose their freedom. In this paragraph we may also detect Tacitus' own cynicism towards the active role played by his father-in-law. One could excuse Agricola, since the alternative (endless warfare with the natives) is even less desirable.[94] Indeed, when things were falling apart in Moesia, Dacia, Germania and Pannonia, the people clamoured for Agricola to take command[95] – and why not, when his methods in Britannia had proven so effective? Instead, Domitian machinated his downfall. The *Germania* thus demonstrates what happens when 'highly beneficial measures' are not taken.

I hope to have shown that far from being an anomaly, the *Germania* contains themes and concerns that are central to Tacitus' way of thinking. In the treatise Tacitus exhibits an overt discomfort with hybridity and an unease with the permeability of the boundaries between Romans and Others. More than just a technical treatise, the *Germania* engages artfully with its literary precedents, especially Caesar's *Gallic Wars* and Virgil's *Georgics*. The theme of dissimulation that occupies Tacitus in the *Agricola*, *Histories* and *Annals* already begins to surface in the *Germania*. The ethnography is a formulation of Roman identity constructed along lines of praise and criticism that make it a far more complex text than initially meets the eye. Furthermore, the *Germania* bears the imprint of its context of production. Through its descriptions of barbarian tribes with their customs frozen in time on the periphery of the known world, Tacitus filters the never-ending narrative of Roman conquest, in all of its imperfections.

V

THEN AND NOW

UNTIL 1425, NOBODY had ever heard of the *Dialogue on Orators*; once it was published, its authorship by Tacitus was soon rejected. A lacuna of indeterminate length further plagues interpretation, and proposed dates of composition span 25 years, ranging from 81 to 109 CE. We are going to have to roll up our sleeves, but our efforts will repay themselves, for in the *Dialogue on Orators*, rhetoric is a weapon and a shield for managing asymmetrical relations of power, as interlocutors wield and react to the power placed in their hands and over their heads. Furthermore, certain historical persons mentioned in the *Dialogue* are also present in the *Agricola* and *Histories*, while particular themes resurface in the *Annals* that demonstrate how Tacitus rethinks, remembers and reassembles ideas.

Thanks to Stephen Greenblatt's 2011 Pulitzer Prize-winning book, *The Swerve: How the World Became Modern,* the Italian humanist Gian Francesco Poggio Bracciolini is no longer a stranger to modern readers. In January 1417, he discovered the only surviving manuscript of Lucretius' poem, *On the Nature of Things,* a book which would change the course of scientific thinking in the Renaissance and beyond.[1] Not all of Poggio Bracciolini's discoveries were so splashy or so definitive. Eight years later, he learnt of a ninth-century manuscript in Hersfeld Abbey in Germany that contained (among other texts) the *Agricola*, *Germania* and the *Dialogue on Orators* attributed to Tacitus but hitherto unknown and unattested. A copy of the Hersfeld codex did not reach Rome until some 30 years later, and the subsequent copies of the *Dialogue* that derived from it formed the basis of the first printed edition of Tacitus' known works in 1472.[2]

Before the mention of the minor works in the catalogue of the Hersfeld codex, Tacitus was known solely as a historian. The distinctly Ciceronian style of the *Dialogue* was such a radical departure from the terse prose of the *Histories* and *Annals* that Beatus Rhenanus questioned its authorship in his edition of 1533 and Justus Lipsius ascribed it to Quintilian in 1574. Later scholars proposed an anonymous or unknown author; some went so far as to cajole the evidence into supporting authorship by Pliny the Younger. Such endeavours are especially remarkable since a dozen manuscripts uniformly ascribe the work to Tacitus.[3]

Our eighteenth-century adversaries Thomas Gordon and Reverend Thomas Hunter have nothing to say about the *Dialogue* because it was not until 1814 that authorship was secured. A. G. Lange detected a verbal correspondence between Pliny and Tacitus in a letter to Tacitus dated to 107 or 108. Pliny confesses to his friend that his 'efforts at poetry, which you think is best achieved "amid glades and groves", are at a standstill'.[4] The phrase 'glades and groves' occurs twice in the *Dialogue*: Aper criticizes poets because they must quit society and retire 'to glades and groves', and Maternus responds directly to the criticism: 'As for the glades and groves and seclusion that Aper chastises...'[5] Although it is impossible to ascertain the direction of influence, whether Pliny echoes the *Dialogue*, Tacitus uses Pliny's turn of phrase or one revised his writings in light of the other's, the verbal correspondence between contemporary authors has been enough, when taken with the manuscript evidence, to dispel doubt and confirm Tacitus as author.[6]

The oldest manuscripts derived from the Hersfeld codex state in the margin that six pages are missing after chapter 35; however, we do not know the dimensions of these six pages – if indeed as many as six pages were lost.[7] The lacuna may have been long enough to have included an entire speech by Secundus, although it is unlikely since no reference is made to him in the closing scene, and the traditional form of a dialogue admits usually three, not four interlocutors. Most assume that the lacuna contained the end of Messalla's speech and the beginning of Maternus', with a brief interlude.[8]

As for the date of composition, if, based on the preface of the *Agricola*, we rule out the so-called silent years under Domitian, then the *Dialogue* was composed either before 81 or after 96. To account for its pervasive Ciceronian style, some have proposed it was written under Titus, giving Tacitus a good 15 years to abandon Cicero and develop his own voice. Yet when Tacitus says in the preface of the *Agricola* that he would have forgotten the dark years under Domitian if forgetting were as easy as keeping silent, and he announces that 'Now at last our spirit is returning,'[9] the distinct impression is that the *Agricola* is his first work. Therefore, the *Dialogue* could only have been written as early as 96. However, the dedicatee Justus Fabius was consul in 102 and governor of Syria in 109; if the *Dialogue* was intended to commemorate one of these events, then allusion to glades and groves in Pliny's letter of 107 or 108 pushes the date towards 102. Consequently it was likely composed while Tacitus was also working on the *Histories*. For our purposes, then, we can assume that the *Dialogue* is the third and final of the minor works, written after the fall of Domitian, perhaps dedicated in 102 and therefore concomitant with some portion of the *Histories*. It certainly precedes the *Annals*.[10]

After surveying Tacitus' attitudes about the value of the past versus the present, the first part of this chapter ('Past and Present') introduces the three main interlocutors, Maternus, Aper and Messalla, and then offers a close reading of the *Dialogue* from prologue to exeunt. The second part of the chapter ('Revisiting the Future') explores thematic correspondences between the *Dialogue* and the beginning of *Annals* Book 13, the eulogy that Nero delivered at the state funeral for Claudius in 54 CE. In this passage Tacitus revisits the comparison of past to present, the decline of oratory, the periodization of the genre according to political regime, and the influence of politics on the art of persuasion. While the events of the *Annals* predate the dramatic date of the *Dialogue*, in point of fact the *Dialogue* was composed first, such that Tacitus, once protégé of the best of his day, returns to the subject of the *Dialogue* as a mature historian.

Past and Present

Let us begin with two quotations from the *Annals*. The first is from the obituary of Arminius, the Cheruscan freedom fighter who fell by the treachery of his own people. Tacitus is surprised that Arminius is wholly unknown to Greek historians and not duly celebrated by Romans, 'since we extol the past and are uninterested in recent times'.[11] The second is from a digression on the origins of luxury in *Annals* Book 3: 'Not everything in our ancestors' time was better, but our age too offers to posterity many examples of praise and skill to imitate.'[12]

Clearly Tacitus is ambivalent about the value of the past. He refers to the decisions, institutions and actions of the *maiores*, the Roman forebears, for a variety of reasons and in a variety of contexts that do not map easily onto favourable or unfavourable moral judgements. Character is revealed by adherence to or departure from ancestral traditions, which can be invoked either as precedents to be retained or as justification for change. For example, Agricola, Germanicus and Corbulo, generals on the edges of the Roman Empire in Britannia, Germania and Parthia, are 'anachronistic figures' whose traditional virtues and integrity are out of sync with progressive trends back in Rome.[13] Yet, while these men embody the ideals of the Roman past, they also challenge the status quo. Such syncopation occludes their successes and failures, yet the past is not an absolute standard; senators, generals and especially informants could subvert it for their own purposes.[14] In the *Annals*, Tacitus follows the Tiberian debate over the laws against luxury that took place in the Senate in 22 CE with a digression that allows him to venture beyond the temporal scope of the *Annals* and speak of Galba and Vespasian. It is worth quoting the paragraph in full because it is a rare moment when, according to Ronald Syme, 'Tacitus speaks in his own person for his own epoch of imperial Rome.'[15] I have retained the sentence numbers for easy reference:

(1) Gradually discontinued was the table luxury which had been practised for 100 years through profuse expenditure from the end of the war of Actium to the civil war in which Servius Galba obtained power. I should like to investigate the causes for this change.

(2) In days of old, rich families that were noble or distinguished for their renown kept declining because of their eagerness for luxury, for even then it was permitted to cultivate and be cultivated by plebeians, allies and kingdoms. As each increased his wealth, house and furnishings, he was considered more famous because of his name and his list of clients.

(3) After savagery due to slaughter and greatness of fame meant destruction, the rest turned their attention to wiser ways. At the same time, new men from municipalities and colonies and even provinces who gained admission to the Senate brought their native thriftiness, and although several reached a well-financed old age whether by luck or hard work, still their earlier character remained.

(4) But the chief instigator of strict morality was Vespasian, himself a man of old-fashioned attire and diet. From then on, obedience towards the *princeps* and a desire to imitate him was stronger than any punishment or fear of laws –

(5) unless perchance in all things there is a regular succession such that as seasons change so does morality. Not everything in our ancestors' time was better, but our age too offers to posterity many examples of praise and skill to imitate. Thus may these contests for integrity with our ancestors persist.[16]

In the first sentence Tacitus delineates the period of the Julio-Claudian principate, from the ascension of Augustus after Actium to the end of Nero with the civil wars of 69, as especially noteworthy for its extreme luxury. In the second sentence, Tacitus begins his investigation by describing the origins of luxury in the Republic, a common theme in Roman historiography. According to Livy, luxury first arrived in Rome when the soldiers of Manlius, who triumphed over the Gauls in 187 BCE, brought bronze couches, expensive tapestries, single-footed tables and other items of furniture, along with female musicians and entertainers who performed at banquets that were prepared with increasing care and expense.[17] Polybius attributes the influx of luxury much earlier, to the sack of Syracuse in 211 BCE, while Sallust dates it much later, to the conquests of Sulla in 87–83 BCE. All three historians blame Rome's moral decline on the importation of foreign luxuries and implicate the generals who sack the cities, the soldiers who bring home the goods and the citizens who allow themselves to be smitten with these novel objects. Thus foreigners as well as Romans are criticized, the one for inventing luxuries, the other for pillaging and prizing them, and neither is held accountable. What Livy calls 'the seeds of further luxury' were sown by warfare and imperial expansion in the Mediterranean; for Tacitus, on the other hand, provincial senators and the warfare of the year 69 – the result of imperialism – eventually curbed luxury.

Although the third sentence is introduced with the temporal conjunction 'after' (in Latin, *postquam*), the sense is difficult to ascertain. According to Tony Woodman, 'savagery due to slaughter' refers to the civil wars, while 'greatness of fame meant destruction' refers to the reign of Domitian; others suppose that the clause refers to the reigns of Caligula, Claudius and Nero.[18] And while the frugality of provincials was a stereotype, it is not clear which specific provinces Tacitus is referring to. Nevertheless, the role of Vespasian is unequivocal, and his influence could only be undermined by a cycle of history in which trends are eventually repeated. Tacitus would seem to subscribe to this theory, although he is not so simple-minded as to believe that history merely repeats itself. Rather, the usefulness of history is in recognizing patterns of behaviour that are likely to be repeated in different circumstances. This happens even at the level of language, as for example in the opening sentence of the reign of Nero ('the first death of the new principate...') that deliberately echoes the beginning of the reign of Tiberius ('the first crime of the new principate...').[19] Yet in this digression on luxury, Tacitus believes that the influence of Vespasian was stronger than any natural cycle of history. The result is that 'not all things in the past were better.' Less important than a cohesive stance towards the past is Tacitus' continual questioning of its value – and its malleability. Such 'contests for integrity with our ancestors' are at the core of the *Dialogue*.

Neatly poised between then ('earlier ages') and now ('our age'), the question that drives the *Dialogue on Orators* pits a degenerate present against an honourable past:

> Often you ask me, Justus Fabius, why, when earlier ages abounded with the talents and glory of so many outstanding orators, our age is particularly

empty and bereft of the praise of eloquence, such that scarcely even the very name orator remains.[20]

The theme of past versus present guides the form and structure of the dialogue, in which the Latin word *tempus*, meaning 'time', is used 40 times in the course of the 41-chapter treatise. Beginning with the temporal adverb 'often', the *Dialogue* presents itself as an ongoing, never-ending discussion. The adverb also indicates the long-standing experience, equivalent status and mutual respect of Tacitus and Justus Fabius. 'Often' denotes that the action has already taken place many times, frequently, at least more than once: there is nothing new or special here. In effect, the initial adverb dissolves the difference between past and present, so that the relationship is not adversarial (i.e. then versus now) but equivalent: then equals now. Since Justus Fabius has asked before and is asking the same question again, he must not have received a satisfactory answer from Tacitus, nor will he on this occasion either, since nowhere in the *Dialogue* does Tacitus state his own opinions in the first person; on the contrary, he outright abjures any opinions of his own: 'By God I would scarcely dare [answer the question] if I had to offer my own opinion and not repeat a conversation among the most learned men of our time.'[21]

In order to repeat the conversation, Tacitus says he needs not so much talent (the Latin word is *ingenium*, a term applied to literary talent in particular) as 'memory and recollection'.[22] More than just a common strategy of putting off responsibility for the answer onto others, and more than adhering to the classic structure of a literary dialogue as established by Plato, this method demonstrates the timelessness of the discussion. Not only has Justus Fabius asked often, but the answer derives from a conversation that has already been held. The *Dialogue* is dependent on memory; yet more than a mechanism for retrieving an answer to Fabius' question, Tacitus' appeal to memory also obfuscates the authorial voice of the dialogue and may have even contributed to the doubts about Tacitean authorship. Memory brings the past into the present and dissolves the distance between 'then', when the conversation was held, and 'now', when it is being recited. By sharing his individual memory, Tacitus thus brings Fabius into the company of the interlocutors and indeed makes listeners of us all. Finally, memory was one of the five canons of classical rhetoric (together with invention, arrangement, style and delivery). An orator must recall in order to perform, and Tacitus is about to perform a tour de force that will make him a man worth remembering.[23]

The dramatic date of the *Dialogue* is indicated in the text as the sixth year of Vespasian's reign (17.3), that is, 75 CE. While one might quibble over when precisely Vespasian's reign began (either July 69, when he was first acclaimed emperor in Egypt, or January 70, after the defeat and death of Vitellius and the inauguration of peace), the six-month margin is negligible. Tacitus would have been in his late teens, maybe 19 years old. The *Dialogue* as we have it (notwithstanding the lacuna) recounts three pairs of speeches that debate the relative value of oratory versus poetry, the preference for contemporary over old-fashioned literary styles, and whether the causes for the decline of oratory are due to cultural or political factors (see Figure 5.1). The three pairs of speeches are distributed among three historical persons, with a fourth serving as arbiter: Julius Secundus served as Otho's minister of correspondence and was noticed by Quintilian for his elegance.[24]

1–5.2: Preface and Setting.

    {   5.3–10.8:   Aper prefers oratory.
        11–13.6:   Maternus prefers poetry.

14–16.3: Messalla enters.

    { 16.4–23.6:   Aper prefers modern oratory.
           24:   Maternus mediates between Aper and Messalla.
        25–26:   Messalla prefers oratory of the past.

27: Maternus interrupts and redirects inquiry to the causes of decline.

       28–32:   Messalla attributes decline to cultural changes.
    {   33.1–3:   Maternus asks for specifics.
     33.4–35.5:   Messalla describes decline in education.
        LACUNA
       36–41:   Maternus attributes decline to political changes.

42: Closing Tableau.

5.1   Outline of the contents of the *Dialogue on Orators*.

The historicity of the speakers invites what Christopher van den Berg calls 'character-oriented readings' either to gauge the sincerity of the speakers' opinions against what we know about them in real life, or to use speakers' opinions in the *Dialogue* to supplement our limited knowledge of the historical figures.[25] Speakers are identified with distinct ideological positions or even with Tacitus himself. It is easy, therefore, to assume that as a practitioner of oratory Tacitus must have been invested in the arguments, and so it seems natural to equate his opinions with those expressed by an otherwise unattested Maternus, the only interlocutor available for such ventriloquism (since Aper and Secundus were Tacitus' teachers and Messalla was so well known that he could not be easily co-opted without obvious departure from fact). Yet Maternus argues in favour of poetry; is this really a position we can imagine Tacitus espousing? Such a contradiction would fuel doubts of Tacitean authorship. Clearly it is better to resist equating Tacitus with any one character, and such a method for reading the *Dialogue* should be avoided, since it imposes assumptions on the *Dialogue* that cannot be sustained. Rather, there is a little bit of Tacitus in each of the six speeches of the *Dialogue*, and this fact more than any other contributes to its artistic unity.[26]

Curiatius Maternus is the most important speaker in the dialogue, but also the most problematic, since we only know what he (that is, Tacitus) tells us about himself: 'I set out on my career when during the reign of Nero I broke Vatinius' wicked power that destroyed the sanctities of culture.'[27] Vatinius had been dead seven months when Otho mentions him in the *Histories* in the same breath as Polyclitus and Aegialus, two other henchmen of Nero.[28] In the year 64, Vatinius produced gladiatorial games at Beneventum. Tacitus describes him in some detail in the *Annals*:

> Vatinius was among the foulest monstrosities of the court. Raised in a shoemaker's shop, he was a facetious buffoon with a deformed body. He was originally enlisted as a laughing stock, but when he informed against the most noble men his influence increased to such a degree that he outstripped even evil men in terms of favour, money and the ability to harm.[29]

Surely this is the same Vatinius whom Maternus would have prosecuted sometime between 64 and 69. It is tempting to identify Maternus with a Maternus whom Domitian executed in 91 or 92 for speaking against tyrants, or with the Maternus recorded in an inscription from Spain, or with both, but no evidence yet has confirmed these hypotheses.[30] It is safer to assume that since Vatinius is a historical person, it is unlikely that Tacitus would fabricate his prosecutor. It is to Maternus' credit that he brought down Vatinius, although as we have seen in the case of Fulcinius Trio, prosecutors do not always occupy the moral high ground. Maternus resists easy interpretation.

Marcus Aper is otherwise unknown to us apart from his appearance in the *Dialogue* which provides us scant details, and again we do well to remember that all are under Tacitus' authorial control. Aper was Tacitus' teacher, therefore at a certain level he was someone Tacitus esteemed and may have even aspired to emulate. He was a 'new man' in the Senate, that is, the first in his family to achieve senatorial status, and was from a province, perhaps Gaul. He was in Britannia probably with the invading army of Claudius in 43. Since a Flavius Aper is attested in the Senate in 105 and a Marcus Flavius Aper consul in 130, Syme conjectured the full name Marcus Flavius Aper.[31]

Yet perhaps thornier than Aper's identity is his persona in the *Dialogue*. Because all of the interlocutors speak in the first person (as constructed by Tacitus), it raises the question of whether the 'I' is the actual historical person (Aper, Maternus, Messalla, Secundus – even Tacitus himself in the opening and closing paragraphs), a persona fabricated by Tacitus or a voice through which Tacitus speaks for himself. The interlocutors reveal biographical details about their lives, but Aper must be a 'devil's advocate' whose challenges to the speakers are merely required by the exercise; otherwise, he would be too irksome a personality to qualify as one of Tacitus' teachers.[32] He has been described as 'objectionable', and because of his social status as an *arriviste* it is easy to label him brash and vulgar.[33] Of course it is possible that Tacitus deliberately portrays Aper as boorish in order to undermine his position in the dialogue. Recently, however, Aper has been reassessed for his 'shrewd, progressive, and fundamentally receptive analysis of contemporary literature'.[34] One thing everyone can agree on is that Aper represents modernism.[35] And as Roland Mayer reminds us, the speakers of the dialogue begin and end as friends.[36]

Of the three speakers of the *Dialogue*, the identity of Vipstanus Messalla is most secure. He is descended from the Vipstani, a family that rose under Tiberius and was connected to the Messallae.[37] In the *Histories*, Tacitus introduces him as a man of 'noble ancestry, outstanding on his own merits and who alone achieved an honourable career in this war'[38] – of course not everyone knew which horse to back in all the turmoil. Messalla served the Flavian cause under Antonius Primus as a military tribune in 69 and was his unit's acting commander by the end of the year.[39] And since history is written by the victors, Tacitus consulted his memoirs for his account of the battle of Cremona.[40] Beyond his military service, Messalla was also known for boldly opposing at the beginning of Vespasian's reign the prosecution of his stepbrother Aquilius Regulus for a lingering grievance under Nero. Apparently the power-hungry Regulus was responsible for the downfall of two families, and the survivors were seeking retribution. In Tacitus' eyes, a greedy prosecutor like Regulus was a bad man with bad motives; however, his prosecutor Curtius Montanus was even worse. Not only did he implicate Regulus in the murder of Galba's adopted son Calpurnius Piso, but he accused him of biting the head of Piso's corpse. Although Messalla did not attempt to defend the case or his stepbrother, nevertheless 'he cast himself in the face of his stepbrother's accusations and caused some senators to relent,' whatever that means.[41] The prosecution of Regulus revived several more leftover animosities, and Vespasian eventually recommended amnesty even if it meant excusing vicious informants.[42] Furthermore, after Nero, Regulus no longer prosecuted actively but spoke only in defence cases until his death in 105.[43] Such ambivalent behaviour and ambivalence over the morality of prosecutors and defendants forms a critical background to the debates over the efficacy of rhetoric in the *Dialogue on Orators*.

Tacitus sets the stage in the first five paragraphs. The conversation took place on the day after Curiatius Maternus had given a reading of his tragedy *Cato*, which had offended some powerful men in the audience, presumably because of its political overtones. Cato was the arch-enemy of Julius Caesar in a rivalry that began in 63 BCE when the two disagreed over the punishment of the Catilinarian conspirators and ended in 46 with Caesar's victory at Thapsus and Cato's suicide in Utica. As a notable Stoic in the late

Republic, Cato became a hero and a symbol of freedom in the Neronian age, when Thrasea Paetus wrote a *Life of Cato* that probably shared affinities with Lucan's portrayal of Cato in his epic poem *The Civil War*; neither could have pleased Nero, and both probably exacerbated the tyrant's ire and hastened the authors' untimely deaths.[44] The *Dialogue* takes place on the heels of the execution of Thrasea Paetus' son-in-law Helvidius Priscus, persistent critic of the Neronian regime and biographer of Herennius Senecio. With his *Cato*, Maternus is thus courting the kind of danger (capital punishment, book burning, exile) that Tacitus describes at the beginning of the *Agricola* and the end of the *Annals*.

Tacitus went with his mentors Marcus Aper and Julius Secundus to the home of Maternus, where they found him with the troublesome book in his hands. Secundus asked Maternus whether he intended to revise the play in light of the unfavourable response and to 'publish, if not a better, at least a safer *Cato*'. Maternus replied: 'You shall read what Maternus owed it to himself to write, and you will recognize what you have heard. And if anything was omitted from the *Cato*, it shall be supplied by the upcoming recitation of the *Thyestes*.'[45] It sounds somewhat odd that Maternus would refer to himself in the third person, although such self-reference was an accepted trope of emphasis among ancient writers.[46] Maternus champions the cause of free speech and will not be deterred from writing what he intends. As for the *Thyestes*, mythology could be just as dangerous as history, for the younger Helvidius was executed by Domitian for writing a play about Paris and Oenone that was perceived as critical of Domitian's recent divorce.[47]

Aper criticizes Maternus for spending his time and talent on poetry when his friends and clients need his help and his eloquence in court. Apparently, this is an argument they have had before: 'Your severity would trouble me except that this frequent and persistent argument of ours has practically developed into a habit.' Aper is always harassing poets, and Maternus must repeatedly defend them (the Latin adjective is *cotidianum*, 'daily').[48] Once again, the reader is reminded that this ground has been covered before.

The first of the three debates ensues. Aper argues for the value of oratory over poetry on the grounds that oratory is useful for creating and maintaining friendships, acquiring connections and gaining fame and celebrity at home and abroad. As an aid to friends and a help to strangers, oratory strikes fear into foes and is therefore both a shield and a weapon. In addition, oratory brings pleasure, since speakers like Eprius Marcellus and Vibius Crispus are admired for their abilities and not for their birth or wealth (8.1). Of course, these examples are problematic, since they represent two of the most vicious informants of the day. Eprius Marcellus was born around 18 CE in Capua to a poor family. He was one of the prosecutors of Thrasea Paetus in 66 and was probably more responsible than anyone for the destruction of victims of Nero, for which he received such ample payment for his services that he amassed one of the largest private fortunes in the Roman Empire.[49] He was consul in 74 (just a year before the dramatic date of the *Dialogue*) and may have been partly responsible for the downfall of the younger Helvidius.

Vibius Crispus likewise rose from humble origins to become one of the richest men of the empire. In an epigram of Martial, Crispus' wealth was proverbial: 'Though richer than Crispus', still you cannot escape death.' The imperial biographer Suetonius credits Vibius Crispus with an amusing retort. At the beginning of his reign Domitian was said to spend hours in seclusion stabbing flies with a sharp stylus, so that when someone asked whether anyone was with the emperor, Vibius Crispus replied, 'Not even a fly.'[50] Vibius Crispus was not only witty, but also exceedingly savvy: he was able to be consul under Nero, Vespasian and Domitian. Under Nero he was governor of Africa and curator of the aqueducts; under Vespasian, legate of Hispania Tarraconensis.[51] After the fall of Nero, Crispus used his wealth and power to strong-arm the Senate into prosecuting a personal enemy (Annius Faustus) on the grounds that Annius had been a vicious informant under Nero.[52] Crispus eventually became one of Domitian's most trusted advisors. In a satirical send-up of Domitian's privy council, the poet Juvenal describes Crispus thus:

> Amiable old Crispus also arrived, a gentle soul, with a character resembling his eloquence. Who would have been a more useful companion to the ruler of seas, lands, and peoples, had he only been allowed, under

that plague and disaster, to condemn his cruelty and offer honourable advice? But what's more savage than a tyrant's ear? On his whim the fate of a friend simply intending to talk about the rain, or the heat, or the showery spring, hangs in the balance. So Crispus never swam against the flood; he was not the kind of patriot who could speak his mind's thoughts freely and risk his life for the truth. That's how he managed to see many winters and his eightieth summer. He was protected by this armour even in that court.[53]

Juvenal thus gives us the picture of a shrewd man who, unlike Agricola, sacrificed integrity for survival. In short, Eprius Marcellus and Vibius Crispus are not innocent examples. They are some of the most controversial men of the day.

Aper's speech is followed by a brief but important sentence in which Tacitus sets up Maternus' reply: 'When Aper had said these things rather forcefully as usual and with a serious expression, Maternus, relaxed and smiling, said...'[54] The phrase 'as usual' not only alerts us to the constancy of Aper's character but also reminds us of the ongoing nature of the debate: this material has been covered before. The participle 'smiling' (the Latin word is *subridens*) is curious. Perhaps Tacitus intends for the reader to recall the *De Oratore*, Cicero's dialogue on the ideal orator in which one of the interlocutors, Quintus Mucius Scaevola, is also 'smiling' as he delivers his reply to Lucius Licinius Crassus. However, Cicero uses the Latin word *ridens*, that is, without the prefix. *Subridens*, on the other hand, is used in the *Aeneid* of Jupiter after he hears the impassioned plea of his daughter Venus on behalf of the shipwrecked Aeneas.[55] So while the gesture of smiling gives the moment a Ciceronian feel, the Virgilian echo of *subridens* positions Maternus above Aper in wisdom if not power, or at least gives Maternus an air of divine self-possession.

The allusion to Virgil is confirmed in Maternus' defence. Maternus begins by citing his credentials as an orator but insists that his fame derives more from his poetry than his speeches. He prefers the solitude of poetry, the first of the literary arts. Poets like Orpheus and Linus enjoyed a privileged position among gods and kings; Homer is as much honoured as

Demosthenes, Euripides and Sophocles as much as Lysias and Hyperides. Then as if to answer for the Virgilian compound participle *subridens*, Tacitus has Maternus say: 'Today you will find more who criticize the glory of Cicero than of Virgil.'[56] Maternus goes on to argue that poets have good lives: Virgil enjoyed a serene, calm, peaceful retirement with Augustus' favour. He was famous throughout Rome, and a story still circulates that when an audience heard some of Virgil's poetry, they rose and paid him homage. The orators whom Aper extols, Vibius Crispus and Eprius Marcellus, were constrained, not liberated, by their occupation. They are not to be envied, since they are never considered servile enough by those who rule nor free enough by those who do not. Maternus wraps up his speech by quoting a passage of Virgil that also compares occupations: 'As Virgil says, "but as for me the muses are sweetest".'[57] Maternus is satisfied to possess no more than what he can leave to whom he pleases, and he will be happy if his tomb is decked with a laurel-crowned statue that needs no special resolutions in the Senate or petitions to the emperor.[58]

As soon as Maternus finishes his speech, Vipstanus Messalla, like Alcibiades in Plato's *Symposium*, arrives late to the gathering. Two further similarities suggest that Tacitus is engaging with Plato. Both hosts, Maternus and Agathon, are tragic poets; both conversations take place on the day after performances.[59] Judging from the serious expressions, Messalla asks whether he is interrupting some private deliberation or the preparation for some court case. Secundus assures him that he is welcome and would have been welcomed even earlier. Then in one neat sentence he summarizes all that has already transpired:

> For you would have enjoyed the very sharp-witted speech of our friend
> Aper in which he urged Maternus to turn all his talent and energy
> towards court cases, and then the glad speech of Maternus on behalf
> of his poetry; as is fitting for the defence of poets, it was rather bolder
> and more like poetry than oratory.[60]

This sentence is a form of interior duplication, or *mise en abyme*, whereby it mirrors the framework of the *Dialogue* itself: one man recounts a conversation to another. Messalla agrees that he would have enjoyed the discussion, and adds that he is glad that his friends are willing to spend their time in this way, noting Aper's preference to pursue modern rather than antiquated habits in his leisure time.

The remark leads to the second debate, this time between Aper and Messalla over modern versus ancient tastes, styles and practices of oratory. Aper begins by challenging the accepted definition of ancients (in Latin, *antiqui*). Maternus had mentioned the fourth-century Attic orators Demosthenes and Hyperides, but for Aper, they are not ancient when compared to Ulysses and Nestor, who lived 1,300 years before. According to Cicero's *Hortensius* (a dialogue that is unfortunately lost to us), the definition of a 'true year' encompasses 12,994 years, making Demosthenes and Hyperides practically contemporary.[61] As for Latin orators, Cicero lived only 120 years before – the span of one man's lifetime, for Aper himself had seen a man in Britannia who had heard Julius Caesar speak.

Having thus established his definition of antiquity, Aper proceeds to his main argument. The types and varieties of eloquence change with the times; as he says, 'eloquence does not have one face.' Thus oratory must change with the circumstances of the age and with altered tastes. Today's audiences do not tolerate the kinds of effects that audiences appreciated in the past, and nowadays people expect to hear quotes from Virgil, Horace and Lucan, and not the early Republican poets Accius or Pacuvius. Aper's speech is a valuable source of testimony for Latin orators and poets whose works have not survived. It is also a valuable reminder that our modern-day impressions of Latin oratory depend almost entirely on Cicero, who was just one among hundreds of orators and whose very style is under attack. According to Aper, Cicero's introductions are tedious, his narratives too long, his digressions careless and his conclusions indefinite. One quotes Cicero only for a laugh; he coined the phrase 'Wheel of Fortune', which even today has a tinny ring. Aper also pokes fun at Cicero's 'justice of Verres', which in Latin (*ius uerrinum*) sounds the same as a phrase that means 'boar gravy' (perhaps *porc au jus* helps capture the pun, since *jus* are the first three letters of justice). Even Quintilian mocked Cicero's pun, but Tacitus himself may be having a bit of fun, since the name Aper means boar.[62]

In response, Messalla embarks on his defence by complaining that while Aper mentioned plenty of ancient authors by name, he did not mention comparable modern orators, perhaps because he did not want to offend anyone whom he might have inadvertently overlooked. So Messalla promises to name individuals,[63] but naming contemporary individuals can be tricky. In a digression on historiography in *Annals* Book 4, Tacitus says that historians must be careful when naming specific people in their writings. Even if they are deceased, their descendants may infer that they are being blamed for their ancestors' wrongdoings.[64] The poet Juvenal went so far as to claim he would attack only the dead in his satires.[65] Furthermore, the digression in the *Annals* is followed by the prosecution of Cremutius Cordus, a historian charged under the law of treason with publishing a history that offended Tiberius. After defending himself before the Senate, Cremutius took his own life. Following his death, the Senate decreed that his books be burnt, in one of the most important episodes of freedom of speech in Roman history.[66] So perhaps Aper played it safe by not mentioning contemporaries, whereas Messalla is willing to take a risk in the name of freedom of speech.

Suspecting that Messalla is veering off-topic, Maternus interrupts and reminds him that the subject at hand is not a defence of the superiority of the ancients ('which as far as I'm concerned is admitted') but a discussion on the causes of decline, which Messalla told them he was 'in the habit of treating', before Aper's speech riled him up.[67] Thus like Aper, whose behaviour is described as frequent, persistent and habitual, so too Messalla treads familiar ground. Messalla believes that the rules of debate allow for frank convictions to be expressed without damaging friendships, and Maternus grants him leave to continue: 'Proceed, then, and when you speak of the ancients use that ancient freedom of speech from which we have degenerated more than from eloquence.'[68] In short, this interlude does more than merely maintain the fiction of the dialogue or introduce the third debate on the causes for the decline of oratory; it significantly expands the thematic development of the *Dialogue*.[69]

Messalla attributes decline to cultural changes: young men are lazy; parents are careless; teachers are ignorant; old discipline is neglected. What follows is a wellspring of valuable information about Roman social life,[70] an ethnography of sorts that pointedly resembles the descriptions of the customs and habits of the Germani. Messalla colonizes the past, as it were, by admiring the ancient Romans for their native ways. Just as German mothers breastfed their own children and did not hand them over to wet nurses or nannies, in the Republic noble mothers likewise personally saw to the rearing of their sons. Cornelia took charge of raising Gaius and Cornelius Gracchus, Aurelia raised Julius Caesar, and Atia Augustus.[71] 'By contrast, nowadays a newborn infant is handed off to some Greek nanny who herself has one or two of the worst slaves unsuited for any serious work.'[72] Moreover, we might detect in Messalla's idealized Romans something of Agricola's mother, who, as we saw in Chapter II, reared him in her care and kindness, set him on the path to respectable skill, turned him away from philosophy and protected him from troublemakers.[73]

Messalla paints a grim picture of Roman families, who do not appear to value virtue or modesty. His conservatism is hauntingly familiar. Nannies tell the children bad stories, and we might infer that the children pick up the nannies' undesirable accents. When Messalla criticizes parents who use baby talk and let their children indulge in the theatre and circus, we can easily imagine toddlers parked in front of televisions watching endless episodes of *Teletubbies*, or teenagers binge-watching season after season of *The Walking Dead*. In contrast, Messalla advocates the kind of education that produced Cicero – someone to be imitated, not ridiculed. He studied the liberal arts, not only rhetoric and philosophy, but also geometry, music, grammar, logic, earth science and physics, and he studied not only in Rome but throughout Greece and Asia Minor.[74] According to Messalla, education simply isn't what it used to be, and the genre of oratory has suffered because the curriculum, by popular demand, delivers skill sets and not critical thinking (a point of view that might be found in the *Chronicle of Higher Education*). Messalla describes the vast gulf between what oratory was then and what it is now:

> Into the smallest conceits and into mere *sententiae* they shoved eloquence
> as if expelled from her kingdom, so that she, who once mistress of all
> the arts filled hearts most beauteously attended, is now clipped and

pruned without embellishment, without honour, I daresay without breeding and is learned as if she were one of the most menial of tasks.[75]

The personification of the eloquence of the past as an exiled mistress puts current oratory in the position of lowly slave in a metaphor that fulfils the conservative mandate – and gently reminds the modern reader heartened by Messalla's robust defence of the liberal arts that his was a slave-based society.

Messalla closes by acknowledging that he may have omitted other causes for the decline of oratory, and he takes full responsibility if he has offended anyone. For the third time, Tacitus returns to this keystone. Offence is the result of unequal relations of power and asymmetries in social status, whether real or perceived. Reasoned intellectuals accept that others will hold different opinions, and social equals can criticize each other openly and without penalty. These are the terms by which the interlocutors of the *Dialogue* operate; however, these are not the terms by which Roman imperial society necessarily operated. Therefore, throughout the *Dialogue* Tacitus explores various configurations of giving and receiving offence. First, Maternus offends men in power with his play *Cato*, next Aper avoids giving offence by not naming contemporaries, then Messalla takes responsibility for possible offence given. None are oblivious to their actions; on the contrary, all three are fully cognizant of the consequences of giving and taking offence. Aper and Messalla engage in constructive offence among equals, yet the entire dialogue is cast in the shadow of Maternus' wilful risk.

Maternus asks for further clarification on the process of training the orator, and so Messalla describes the decline in education and contrasts past and present explicitly: 'Among our ancestors,'[76] students learned the art of persuasion not only in the classroom but also in the courtroom. Theoretical knowledge was complemented by practical experience in the forum, where students observed real cases as they were argued and adjudicated; '[b]ut nowadays our students are led to classrooms of those so-called professional rhetoricians,'[77] where instead of gaining first-hand experience, they merely recite dull homework exercises known as declamations. Beginners were assigned *suasoriae*, exercises in which the students composed speeches advising a course of action in a historical, pseudo-historical, or even mythological situation; for example, convincing Agamemnon that he should not sacrifice his daughter Iphigeneia. More advanced students were assigned *controversiae*, in which they composed speeches in character on both sides of a debate.[78] Messalla objects strenuously to the questionable subjects of these *controversiae* (e.g. the reward for killing a tyrant, the options available to a virgin who has been raped, or a mother's incest) that have nothing to do with real life. The rest of his speech is lost in the lacuna.

When the text resumes, Maternus is arguing that the decline in oratory is due to political changes. In the Republic there was constant strife, personal enmities, plundering of allies and social upheavals that demanded eloquence of all citizens. While it is better to live in a society free of such ills, when they occurred they nevertheless supplied great material for orators. A similar sentiment is expressed by Tacitus in that part of the digression on historiography in *Annals* Book 4, which we examined in Chapter III. The talents of historians of the distant past should not be compared with his own, since they had at their disposal plenty of violence and upheaval to record, while his work is circumscribed and boring. Like history-writing, eloquence feeds off conflict; hence our best orators are from Athens in the fourth century and Rome in the first. Maternus vividly describes the celebrated oratory of the past with a series of precisely calibrated phrases that culminate with the crux of the *Dialogue*:

> That great and famous eloquence is the nursling of licence, which
> stupid men call freedom; it is the companion of upheaval, the goad
> of an unbridled populace without obedience, without self-control,
> fierce, rash, arrogant, and which has no place in a well-governed state.[79]

The notion that oratory flourishes in conflict is contrary to the position of Cicero in the *Brutus* that oratory is the product of orderly governance. In fact, this climactic sentence is just one of Maternus' many allusions to Cicero even as he categorically rejects Cicero's premise that oratory thrives in a state of peace and leisure. According to Tom Keeline, the accumulation of allusions to Cicero results in 'a real criticism of the imperial system that has engineered the end of oratory and the end of freedom'.[80] No doubt highly idealized by the interlocutors, Cicero set the standard for excellence in Roman oratory not just for Messalla and Maternus, but also for Tacitus, who composed the entire *Dialogue* in Ciceronian style. The deliberate anachronism underscores the radical transformation of political culture from Republic to principate.

In the closing tableau the three interlocutors share a brief exchange:

> When Maternus had finished, Messalla said, 'There were some things which I would contradict and others about which I wish more were said, but now the day is spent.'
>
> Maternus said, 'It shall be as you wish later, and if anything from my speech seems unclear to you, we shall discuss these things again.' And as he stood up and embraced Aper, he said, 'We shall accuse you, Messalla on behalf of the ancients, I on behalf of the poets.'
>
> 'But I shall accuse you on behalf of rhetoricians and professors,' he said.
>
> When they had laughed, we left.[81]

They part as friends and tease that they will bring each other to court, but clearly the business is unfinished. The *Dialogue* thus records debates that reveal significant shifts in social, cultural and political dynamics, but we need not read it or any part of it as absolute. Rather, Tacitus has given us a snapshot of those changes as they were occurring one afternoon in the reign of Vespasian, at the end of a brutal civil war. The reader who picks up the *Dialogue on Orators* is like the visitor to Pompeii who walks into an ordinary moment that has been frozen in time by cataclysmic forces.

Revisiting the Future

Tacitus opens *Annals* Book 13 with Nero's accession in the year 54, the contents of his funeral oration for Claudius and a digression on the decline of oratory from Julius Caesar (an orator to rival the best) to Nero (so incapable as to need a speech-writer). This is my translation of *Annals* 13.3:

On the day of the funeral the *princeps* embarked on a eulogy of the man and was himself as earnest as everyone else while he enumerated the antiquity of Claudius' lineage and the consulships and triumphs of his ancestors; even the recollection of his liberal arts, and that nothing grim had befallen the state at the hands of foreigners during his rule, were listened to with favourable attention. But, after he turned to the man's foresight and wisdom, no one restrained his laughter, although the speech, composed as it was by Seneca, presented considerable refinement, given that the latter's was an attractive talent and one well adapted to contemporary ears. (The elders – whose retirement is spent comparing past and present – noted that, of those who had been in charge of affairs, Nero was the first to have needed someone else's fluency. For the dictator Caesar was the rival of the highest orators; and Augustus enjoyed a free and flowing eloquence such as becomes a *princeps*. Tiberius had skill too in a technique whereby he weighed his words, on such occasions being either effective in his sentiments or purposely ambiguous. Even Caligula's disturbed mind did not ruin his power of speech; nor in Claudius' case, whenever he held forth on prepared material, would you have wanted for elegance. But as for Nero, even in his boyhood years he diverted his lively mind to other things: engraving, painting, practising songs or his control of horses; and sometimes in the composing of poetry he showed that he had elements of learning).

Some 20 years after the death of Claudius and Nero's delivery of the eulogy, Tacitus was present at the discussion among friends about the decline of oratory. Thus Tacitus, once protégé of the best orators of his day, returns to the subject of the *Dialogue* as a mature historian, and in *Annals* 13.3 he revisits the comparison of past and present, the periodization of the genre and the influence of politics on the art of persuasion.[82]

We should begin with the most obvious point of comparison, the description of Seneca. His talent was 'adapted to the ears of his times', a phrase lifted from the *Dialogue*, when Aper refers to oratory that is 'adapted to the ears of the judges'.[83] According to Suetonius, after the death of Claudius, Nero first addressed the soldiers in the praetorian camp, then proceeded to address the Senate, and then delivered the eulogy, with no mention of Seneca's help in composition. According to Dio, Nero first read the soldiers a speech 'that Seneca had written for him', and then delivered a speech to the Senate, 'this one also written by Seneca'. It was so favourably received that the senators insisted it be inscribed on a silver tablet and read every time new consuls entered office.[84] Like Tacitus, Dio records twin speeches, the second a success before the Senate.[85] However, Dio omits the funeral oration and any interruption by the audience, and he is explicit about Seneca's composition of both speeches, whereas Tacitus leaves it to the reader to infer that the speech to the Senate was composed by Seneca.

The eruption of hilarity begs the question of whether Seneca intended to be funny. According to Ronald Mellor, 'We can well imagine Tacitus laughing at Seneca's parody of Claudius' deification.' Miriam Griffin disagrees: 'Tacitus is quite definite in his indication that the result was not intended by Seneca.' Christopher Star finds middle ground: for Tacitus the laughter was 'an unintended consequence' that was nonetheless 'intentionally ironic'. Paul Plass admits uncertainty:

> It is not clear whether the section was an ironic joke appreciated by everyone present, though perhaps missed by Tacitus who thought it was meant seriously, or whether it was serious flattery which immediately struck everyone except Seneca as a ridiculous lie.[86]

Although we cannot know whether Seneca scripted a joke nor whether Tacitus perceived it as such, the laughter disrupts the otherwise serious *Annals*. Ridicule requires speaker, audience and target, yet in *Annals* 13.3.1 these distinctions blur. Within the context of the *Annals*, Nero is of course the speaker; the audience is, well, everyone, since no one could keep from laughing; and Claudius is obviously the target. However, since the speech was written by Seneca, could he not also be considered the speaker? Or is he the target, ridiculed because he unwittingly transgressed the limits of the believable about Claudius' virtues? Or is Nero the target of the laughter, because his dependence on a ghostwriter backfired?

As the digression in the *Annals* begins with laughter, so the *Dialogue* ends with laughter, albeit more urbane than aggressive: 'When they had laughed, we left.'[87] There are eight instances of words connoting laughter or ridicule in the *Dialogue*, four of which are in contexts of the sparring between Aper and Messalla over the rivalry between ancient and modern style, as set forth first in the prologue: 'Nor indeed did the opposite side lack an advocate who after much criticism and ridicule of old times maintained the superiority of the eloquence of our own days to the great orators of the past.'[88] The same arguments are contested by the elders in *Annals* 13.3.2. In the second instance, when Messalla arrives, Aper notes his antiquated tastes: 'Messalla, you never stop marvelling at old and bygone things and mocking and scorning the practice of our times.' And so in opposing Messalla, Aper says, 'I will frankly admit that I can hardly keep from laughing at some of the ancients.' The third instance occurs later, when Aper says, 'I do not wish to ridicule phrases like "Wheel of Fortune" or "*porc au jus*".' In the last speech of the dialogue, Maternus makes his case that strife begets eloquence with concession to possible mockery: 'Perhaps what I am about to say will seem trifling and ridiculous, still I will say it even to be laughed at.'[89]

Perhaps what strikes the Neronian elders as ridiculous is the mismatch of form and content, a serious funeral oration full of preposterous statements about Claudius.[90] Such a mismatch is the essence of parody, in which a grand subject is treated in trivial form (or vice versa). According to Gérard Genette, parody modifies a prior text such that the second is self-consciously distinct from the first while maintaining resemblance; the gesture is recognizable. Parody is a genre of approximation. Thus *Annals* 13.3 is *like* the *Dialogue*, but is *not* the *Dialogue*. Furthermore, parody is always a reduction that transforms meaning.[91] In our instance, 42 paragraphs have been reduced to one. Finally, parody will signal its artistry; ours is a digression, separate but integral, as signalled by the parentheses.

Quotation marks are an even more graphic indication of a text's secondary status. In this sense, the *Dialogue* is itself a kind of parody of the conversation Tacitus heard and reports; the text is already an approximation that is dependent on memory and will lend itself to imitation. The *Dialogue* is a text already 'in the second degree', to use Genette's subtitle, making its reappearance in *Annals* 13.3 all the more conspicuous.

In composing *Annals* 13.3, Tacitus tinkered with three elements of the *Dialogue*: the physical setting, the promise to return to a topic, and the cast of characters. So Maternus bemoans that scope for greatness is limited because most cases are argued in small spaces, little rooms: ironic, since his friends have gathered in his *cubiculum*, a Latin word that originally denoted a bedroom but more generally any room.[92] For Olivier Devillers *cubiculum* conveys the political reality that private space becomes the arena for public affairs, and 'for trials in particular, as is the case under Claudius'.[93] This is precisely the practice Nero disavows in his inaugural address to the Senate, complete with wordplay on Claudius' name:

> He would not, he said, be the judge of every business, so that, with accusers and defendants shut together [*ut clausis ... accusatoribus*] in the same house, the powerfulness of a few might spread; nothing in his home would be open to bribery or canvassing: house and state were separate.[94]

Indeed, the settings are transposed: in Nero's day, men could discuss the decline of oratory in public settings, such as at state funerals; in Vespasian's day, such discussions took place in the private *cubiculum*. This unsatisfying inversion underscores an unresolved tension between public and private that persists under the principate. The *cubiculum* remains a vexed space.[95]

None of Tacitus' three extant promises to compose works about Nerva, Trajan or Augustus came to fruition, as far as we know. For Tony Woodman, promises of future works are so conventional in ancient historiography as to be negligible,[96] yet such promises frame the *Dialogue*. At the beginning, Maternus announces plans to write a *Thyestes* and Aper chides him for planning a *Domitius*, a play that would have honoured an ancestor of Nero (either Ahenobarbus, enemy of Caesar who fell at Pharsalus, or his son who defected to Octavian and then committed suicide).[97] Then at the end, Maternus makes a promise to return to the subject matter on a future occasion: 'and if anything from my speech seems unclear to you, we shall discuss these things again.' Of course, this phrase may simply invite what

Mayer calls a 'rematch', a closural device typical of philosophical dialogue;[98] for Tacitus, however, the accession of Nero – descendant of Domitius – seems to be a suitable occasion on which to return to Maternus' topic, for Maternus began his career as an advocate by fearlessly prosecuting Vatinius, among the foulest of Nero's court.

Maternus is not the only character from the *Dialogue* to lurk in the background of *Annals* 13.3. Messalla would not have been one of the *seniores* of *Annals* 13.3, but he might have been one of those students who would hang around and listen to the banter of the elders, like the young Tacitus, who 'would follow them [...] when they appeared in public [...] and [...] listen diligently to their trivial talk, their more serious debates and their private and esoteric discourse'.[99]

Furthermore, Messalla has not a kind word for actors. Enthusiasm for the stage is incompatible with the training of a decent orator, and while acting is not singled out in *Annals* 13.3.3, it will of course become Nero's obsession, an indicator of his lack of engagement with politics, and eventually a cause of his downfall.[100]

Then there is Aper, for whom oratory is preferred to poetry. Poems 'bring no dignity to the author, nor do they improve his circumstances', and even if a poet is successful, 'all the glory is, so to say, cut short [...] and does not come to any real and substantial fruit'.[101] This morality is reaffirmed in *Annals* 13.3.3, when Nero's attempts at composing poems had no intrinsic value except to demonstrate his ability to learn. The moral indignation is born in the divide between the social hierarchy as it was and as it ought to be, that is, in the ever-growing divide between a political leader whose rhetorical skills rivalled the best and a political leader whose rhetorical skills were non-existent.[102] Furthermore, this decline and its morality correspond directly to the structure of the *Annals*, composed of hexads devoted to individual *principes*, a principle of periodization anticipated in *Dialogue* 17.3 in which Aper reckons the years from Octavian's first consulship to the present reign of Vespasian.[103] Aper's robust point of view underwrites *Annals* 13.3.

According to Olivier Devillers, the question underpinning any analysis of the *Agricola*, *Germania* and *Dialogue* (the so-called *opera minora*) vis-à-vis the historical works is whether Tacitus' corpus is a random succession of independent compositions whose coherence appears only in retrospect, or whether we can identify a planned consistency.[104] We have been exploring the intricate relationship between who Tacitus was and what he wrote, and the repetition of themes and content offers a window on the thoughts that occupied him over the course of decades. The Ligurian woman in the *Histories* recalls the story of Agricola's mother; the revolt of Boudicca is told in both the *Agricola* and the *Annals*; the Batavians briefly introduced in the *Germania* are significant in the *Histories*; the Stoic martyrs mentioned at the beginning of the *Agricola* occupy the end of the *Annals* as we have them. Therefore, it is reasonable to regard *Annals* 13.3 as a self-conscious parody of the *Dialogue* that in mocking the theme of the decline of oratory simultaneously declares it as a central tenet across Tacitus' literary career, from the early works to the last hexad of the *Annals*. The parody amplifies the themes of freedom, outspokenness and licence that pervade the *Dialogue*. In Nero's day, there was no healthy debate among friends, only the sterile observations of old men, and only emperors engaged in oratory. Of course we now know that for the Neronians, that rare happiness of the times (when one can think what one pleases and write what one thinks) would eventually come. For Tacitus, free to mock himself, it already had.

VI

YESTERDAY
AND TODAY

IF THE FEUD BETWEEN Whig Thomas Gordon and Tory Reverend Thomas Hunter has taught us anything over the course of the last five chapters, it is that Tacitus can be pressed into the service of radically divergent ideologies. The Italian Renaissance philosopher Francesco Guicciardini put it best: 'Cornelius Tacitus teaches those who live under tyrants quite well the way of living and governing themselves prudently, just as he teaches tyrants the ways of founding tyranny.'[1]

The so-called 'black' Tacitus supports monarchy and the status quo; 'red' Tacitus instigates revolution and menaces the establishment.[2] In every age, Tacitus has had detractors and supporters, those who thought his works championed monarchy and those who found in him an advocate of the people, those who could not put him down and those who threw him away with both hands. It is as if the afterlife and reception of Tacitus recapitulate his own verdict on the emperor Augustus given at the outset of the *Annals*. Wise men spoke of his life with praise and censure in equal measure: some said he had no choice but to avenge the assassination of Julius Caesar and that there was no other remedy for a land ravaged by civil war but that it be ruled by one man; on the other hand, there were those who said that all was pretence and whatever peace he achieved was tainted with the blood of citizens. *Annals* 1.9–10 is framed in diametrically opposed categories of praise and blame inherited from the rhetorical tradition of epideictic oratory that sought to demonstrate or deny the value of a person or thing, and this dichotomy has been reinscribed in the modern pro- and anti-Augustan debates. We would prefer it if men like Augustus would readily submit to classification, but his enduring fascination derives not least from his intractable character. So too with Tacitus: for centuries across Europe he has captivated the imagination precisely because he defied labels.

Of course among Counter-Reformation Christian writers the verdict was straightforward: Tacitus was, as we have seen, 'a pagan, idolator [*sic*] and enemy of Christ our Redeemer and of the Christians'.[3] Tacitus was unpopular because he chose to write about vices rather than virtue, because he was deliberately mendacious and because he was overtly hostile to Christianity.[4] For these reasons it is easy to envision a pious Christian monk refusing to transcribe the now missing books of the *Annals* containing the scandalous deeds of Caligula, who murdered Tiberius and habitually engaged in incest with not one but all of his sisters – a juicy detail courtesy of Suetonius.[5] Yet even in antiquity, the theologian Tertullian (c. 155–240 CE) criticized Tacitus for his biased depiction of the Jews in the *Histories* and called him 'that most verbose of liars' (*ille mendaciorum loquacissimus*).[6] For their own purposes, Orosius (385–420 CE) quotes Tacitus extensively, and his contemporary Sulpicius Severus of Aquitaine (*c.*363–424 CE) draws on Tacitus' account of Nero's grisly punishment of the Christians who were blamed for causing the Great Fire of Rome in 64 CE. Tacitus writes:

> It was believed that the fire was ordered by Nero. So to abolish the rumour Nero fastened guilt and afflicted with the most exquisite punishments those whom the vulgar crowd calls Christians, hated for their crimes. The founder of this sect, Christ, had been put to death during the reign of Tiberius by the procurator Pontius Pilate; the unspeakable practices checked for the present broke out again not only in Judea, the original site of this evil, but even in Rome where all atrocities and

shameless acts pour in on all sides and are celebrated. Therefore at first they were arrested who confessed; then on their information a huge host was added hardly so much on the crime of arson as for hatred of humankind. Mockery was added to their deaths, as covered by pelts of beasts they died at the jaws of dogs or fixed to crosses like torches so that when daylight faded they burned for use as night lights. Nero offered his own gardens for the spectacle and put on a show in the circus, mingling with the common folk dressed like a charioteer or perched on his car. Then pity was aroused, albeit against the guilty and men deserving of the most exemplary punishment, as though not for public good but for the savagery of one man they were being destroyed.[7]

This passage presents significant interpretive obstacles. Does Tacitus transmit Roman attitudes towards Christians under Nero, or does he import the attitudes of his own time into his account of the fire and its aftermath? What exactly were the Christians charged with, since the crime of arson was fabricated and 'hatred of humankind' is not a legal offence? Then there is the lack of evidence for any systematic, widespread, state-mandated persecution of Christians under Nero (or Trajan for that matter). Tacitus' narrative of an exceptional event under Nero is applied anachronistically as normative evidence for the persecutions that would take place in the second half of the third century.[8]

The anachronism persisted into the twentieth century. Tacitus' vivid description of the persecution of the Christians motivated the centrepiece of the epic film *Quo Vadis*, based on the 1895 novel *Quo Vadis: A Narrative of the Time of Nero* by Henryk Sienkiewicz. The film was produced in 1951 and stars Robert Taylor as the virtuous Roman military commander Marcus Vinicius and Peter Ustinov as the vain, decadent and ultimately mad emperor Nero, fiddling his lyre while Rome burned, just as Tacitus insinuates in the *Annals*: 'A rumour went about at the very time when the city was burning that he entered his private stage to sing "The Fall of Troy", in which he compared the present malady to disasters of old.'[9]

The special effects that reproduced the conflagration of the city in the film are reported to have cost $100,000. The martyrdom scenes adhere closely to Tacitus. Christians are mauled by lions and tied to crosses and set on fire in a 60,000-seat arena built for the set. Yet in postwar America, the pervasive conflict that menaced society was not between Christians and pagans but between democracy and communism. Monica Cyrino goes so far as to suggest that the persecution of the Christians is emblematic of the Second Red Scare and the McCarthyism that persecuted Hollywood actors and filmmakers as communist sympathizers.[10]

But we have jumped the queue in the reception of Tacitus. With the exception of the seventh and eighth centuries, he is attested continuously, if sparsely, from his publication until his rediscovery in the fourteenth century. Pliny the Younger is the only contemporary author to mention Tacitus by name, although there is good reason to believe that Juvenal's satires were shaped in part by the writer.[11] The geographer Ptolemy (*c.*150 CE) and the historian Dio Cassius (*c.*220 CE) also used Tacitus as a source.[12] In the fourth century, the biographer Flavius Vopiscus records that the emperor Tacitus 'ordered that Cornelius Tacitus, author of an Augustan history, be acquired by every library because he claimed him as an ancestor.'[13] In 1896, Friedrich Leo concluded his essay on Tacitus with the observation that 'The work of Tacitus had to wait nearly 300 years for something to succeed and continue it. And the first Roman historian after Tacitus was a Greek from Antioch.'[14] Indeed, in the fourth century, Ammianus Marcellinus wrote a history that commenced with the accession of Nerva in 96. His *Res Gestae* is in effect a continuation of the work of Tacitus, picking up where the *Histories* left off. Thanks to Jerome (*c.*347–420 CE), we know that the *Histories* and the *Annals* together comprised 30 volumes.[15] At the end of the fourth century, Servius mentions Tacitus in his commentary on the *Aeneid*, while in the fifth century Sidonius Apollinaris clearly consulted Tacitus and also makes a pun on his name that means 'the silent one.'[16] The last Latin author to use Tacitus appears to be Cassiodorus in the sixth century. He cites 'a certain Cornelius' (has the name Tacitus been forgotten?) who writes about the origin of amber, clearly a reference to the penultimate paragraph of the *Germania*.[17]

Nothing is heard of Tacitus again until the ninth century, when quotations from the *Germania* are recognizable in a history written by Rudolf of

Fulda in 863. Furthermore, Rudolf cites Tacitus on the name of the Visurgis river, a reference specific to *Annals* Book 2.[18] Tacitus was still available, if somewhat neglected. As we saw in Chapter V, the Hersfeld codex containing the minor works dates to the ninth century, although it was not brought to light until 1455. Thus we can be confident that the manuscripts of Tacitus were read and copied, if only by a few, in monasteries in Germany and also in Italy during the Middle Ages.

The discovery of Tacitus dates to the Italian Renaissance, when Boccaccio is credited with bringing an eleventh-century manuscript from Monte Cassino to Florence in 1360. The manuscript now known as the Second Medicean (commonly abbreviated M2) was written in a Beneventan script and contained *Annals* Books 11–16 and *Histories* Books 1–5. Niccolò Niccoli acquired the manuscript by 1427, and when he died it was transferred to the Laurentian Library in Florence. The discovery of the Second Medicean together with the minor works warranted the first printed edition of Tacitus' *Annals* Books 11–16, *Histories* Books 1–5, the *Germania* and the *Dialogue on Orators* in Venice by Vindelin de Spira sometime between 1470 and 1473. The next edition in 1476 was edited by Puteolanus in Milan, who added the *Agricola*. Puteolanus issued a second edition which for the first time carried the date, 1497.[19]

The last of Tacitus' works to be discovered were his *Annals* Books 1–6, which survive in a single manuscript known as the First Medicean (M1). It was written in the middle of the ninth century in the monastery in Fulda and moved to Corvey in Saxony. Its Carolingian minuscule script is easier to read than the Beneventan of M2. In 1508, the manuscript came into the possession of Pope Leo X; whether he borrowed or stole it is not clear, but in any event it was never returned to Corvey. Instead, the monastery received a bound volume of the first printed edition that included *Annals* Books 1–6 by Filippo Beroaldo in 1515, while the manuscript was eventually transferred to Florence.[20]

All the discovered works of Tacitus were printed continuously between 1515 and 1527; however, the year 1533 was a milestone. Beatus Rhenanus, the German scholar and student of Erasmus, was the first to publish an edition with an extensive body of critical notes on passages that were corrupted by the transmission of the text. Rhenanus also included a study of word usage that led him to question the authorship of the *Dialogue*, as we saw in Chapter V. In 1574, in the middle of the turbulent Counter-Reformation, Justus Lipsius produced the definitive edition of Tacitus that was unsurpassed for 100 years because of its substantial improvement of the text and because it included the first complete commentary on Tacitus. Finally, the 1607 print edition of Tacitus by Curtius Pichena is noteworthy because it is the earliest edition to include our modern chapter divisions.[21]

Given the tenuous transmission of classical literature through the period when European centres of learning were in decline and manuscripts languished unread, uncopied and unknown, it is a miracle that we have as much of Tacitus as we do. The saga of the most recent discovery of Tacitus in the twentieth century further demonstrates just how precarious the fate of a single book can be. In 1902 a fifteenth-century manuscript was discovered in a private library in Jesi in central Italy. Known as the Codex Aesinas (*Aesis* is Jesi in Latin), it contains a poem about the legendary Dictys of Crete who fought at Troy, the *Agricola* and the *Germania*. The pages of the *Agricola* may have been lifted from the ninth-century Hersfeld codex; however, the *Germania* is copied in a fifteenth-century hand, and its variances with the Hersfeld codex are significant enough to suggest that it may have been copied from yet another, earlier source. The Codex Aesinas eventually passed into the possession of the Balleani family, who inherited the library in which it was shelved. When it was discovered in 1902, it was proclaimed the oldest manuscript of the *Germania*, so in 1936 Hitler asked Mussolini if the Codex Aesinas might be returned to Germany. Mussolini agreed at first, while visiting Germany, but once he returned to Italy to face the resistance of Italian scholars, he went back on his word. Heinrich Himmler, in his capacity as Reich Commissioner for the Consolidation of German Nationhood (*Reichskommissar für die Festigung deutschen Volkstums*), regarded the possession of the Codex Aesinas – the oldest surviving manuscript of the most important document of German nationalism – as a matter of national importance. Perhaps no other paragraph of Tacitus has had such a profound impact on the history of modern Europe than *Germania* 4:

I myself agree with the opinions of those who think that the peoples of
Germania were untainted by marriages with foreign nations but that
they existed as a race distinct, pure and as such like only unto themselves.
Whence too the same physical appearance for all in such a vast number
of peoples: fierce blue eyes, red hair, sturdy physiques fit for attack.[22]

No wonder Himmler insisted on possessing the oldest and most important
manuscript of the *Germania*. So in the autumn of 1943, when Italy was
under German occupation, an SS detachment stormed the Villa Fontedamo
belonging to the Balleani family, who were hiding in another of their homes
in Osimo, while in Jesi, 'deep in a little kitchen cellar, inside a tin-lined trunk,
was the manuscript that began in capitals of red and black DE ORIGINE
ET SITU GERMANORUM.'[23] Eventually the Codex Aesinas was moved to
Florence, where it was damaged by the flooding of the Arno River in 1966
(damage which ironically would have been avoided had the manuscript
been enshrined in Germany as Himmler envisioned). In 1988 the codex was
brought to the Liceo Classico Vittorio Emanuele II di Jesi, where some very
fortunate secondary school pupils were able to examine and handle it. Since
1994 it has been safely catalogued in the Biblioteca Nazionale in Rome.[24]

Such is the history of the text and transmission of Tacitus from antiquity
to print. In the first part of this chapter, we shall review briefly his influence
on political theory from the Italian Renaissance to the nineteenth century;
in this section I am particularly indebted to Ronald Mellor's volume on
Tacitus in the classical tradition. Then we will turn to Tacitus in the twentieth
and twenty-first centuries, when he is mainly consulted either by scholars
or by novelists. Among playwrights, painters and poets, however, Tacitus
has always been a rich source of inspiration. Therefore, we shall conclude
with an examination of a play, a painting and a poem inspired by Tacitus'
extended narrative of the campaigns and death of Germanicus in the first
two books of the *Annals*. 'North Woods' by American composer Scott
Ordway premiered in January 2016. The lyrics are derived from the *Agricola*
and *Germania* and confirm the observation made by Friedrich Leo more
than a century ago: 'Tacitus was a poet, one of the few great poets that the
Roman world possessed.'[25]

Yesterday

Although in the Renaissance and Reformation eras Tacitus would be appropriated for the competing and conflicting aims of monarchic absolutism and religious reform, everyone, regardless of his ideological purpose, finds in Tacitus important and abiding lessons about human nature and especially about how people manage their authorities. Indeed, we have explored throughout this book how different members of society wield and react to the power placed in their hands and over their heads. In this regard, Niccolò Machiavelli may well be one of Tacitus' best readers. Born in Florence in 1469, Machiavelli received an excellent humanist education and embarked on a successful career as a diplomat. When the Medici returned to power in 1512 and defeated the republic's armed forces, Machiavelli was put under house arrest and then tortured for several weeks for information regarding a conspiracy. Machiavelli was forced to retire from public service to a life of literary pursuits. His first work and the one for which he is best known, *The Prince*, was dedicated to Lorenzo de' Medici, but it did nothing to restore Machiavelli to favour; little wonder, since *The Prince* challenges and criticizes the prevailing moralistic view of authority. For Machiavelli, legitimate authority derives not from moral goodness but from power, and the legitimacy of law relies on the threat of coercive force (a tenet drawn, perhaps, from personal experience).[26]

Although the ruler in *The Prince* resembles Tiberius (especially as a great pretender and dissembler), the first hexad of the *Annals* was not published until 1515. *The Prince* was written at the end of 1513 and beginning of 1514 and published posthumously in 1532. So either Machiavelli had early access to the contents of the First Medicean manuscript, or he revised the treatise once it became accessible. He surely consulted the later books of the *Annals*. In chapter 13, 'Of Auxiliaries, Mixed Soldiery, and One's Own', he quotes *Annals* Book 13: 'Nothing can be so uncertain or unstable as fame of power not founded on its own strength.'[27] Machiavelli's engagement with Tacitus is more sustained in his *Discourses on Livy* (begun in 1514, completed by 1519, and published posthumously in 1531), in which he names Tacitus as a source and draws from the contents of the Second Medicean, including the Pisonian conspiracy in *Annals* Book 15 as well as the *Histories*. For example, in Book 1 of the *Discourses*, Machiavelli quotes a *sententia* drawn from the beginning of *Histories* Book 4: 'So much more inclined are we to repay injury than kindness, because gratitude is considered a burden, while revenge can be turned into gain.'[28] Less important than Machiavelli's quotations is his sympathy for Tacitus, who was able to explain how a grand republic like Rome, for all its political and imperial strength, eventually fell into the clutches of monarchs.[29]

Although *The Prince* was listed on the papal Index of Prohibited Books in 1559 for its perceived atheist, even anti-Christian content, the Protestants liked it no better for its grim take on human nature. As a result, the reputations of Machiavelli and Tacitus slowly began to merge. In the dedication of *The Reason of State* Giovanni Botero credits them with instigating his work: 'Provoked by indignation or zeal, I have often been emboldened to write of the corruption fostered by these two men in the policy and counsel of princes.'[30] Traiano Boccalini, a contemporary of Botero, followed suit: 'It is the teaching of Tacitus that has produced Machiavelli and other bad authors, who would destroy public virtue.'[31] According to Ronald Mellor, these scholars 'ushered in an eclipse of Machiavelli in Italy for almost 150 years'.[32] The golden age for Tacitus, however, was still on the horizon.

While Machiavelli was composing his political works in forced retirement, Martin Luther was nailing to the door of a church in Wittenberg a piece of paper that would change the course of history, and here too Tacitus was claimed by both sides. Enea Silvio Bartolomeo Piccolomini (later Pope Pius II, the Latin adjective *pius* to complement his given name, *Aeneas*) was the first to bring the *Germania* to the attention of the German people in 1496. In his capacity as cardinal, he received protests about the treatment of the Germans by the papal court in Rome. In response, Piccolomini composed a letter – a three-volume treatise, in fact – drawing widely on Tacitus to describe a beastly Germany without towns, settlements, gold, silver, literacy or any of the trappings of civilization. The inhabitants even practised human sacrifice! But at present of course Germany was the pinnacle of Europe, replete with cities, martial prowess and liberal arts. This radical change could only have come about thanks to the Roman Catholic Church.

Of course, instead of convincing the Germans of the great benefits of the papacy, the treatise only goaded them to take up Tacitus for themselves.[33] Piccolomini could not have known what he had unleashed.

In 1487 Conrad Celtes was crowned the Holy Roman Empire's first poet laureate of German descent (the only other poet laureates before him had been Petrarch and Piccolomini). Celtes published his own *Germania* in 1500 in which he argued against Piccolomini, who had used Tacitus to claim that modern Germans owed a debt to the Roman papacy for their present state of civilization. Instead, Celtes emphasized Rome's corruption of the bravery and freedom of the Germani, as described by Tacitus. Throughout his travels across Europe and his career as a professor in Heidelberg, Celtes continued to publish on the origins of Germany for the remainder of his life, and when he died, according to Herbert Benario, 'his reputation was secure as the leading spokesman of German national aspirations.'[34]

In this cultural climate the German poet Ulrich von Hutten gave voice to Arminius, the Cheruscan freedom fighter. Immediately upon the dissemination of the Tiberian hexad in 1515, Hutten composed the *Arminius*, a dialogue in Latin that was published posthumously in 1529. The *Arminius* was modelled on the *Dialogues of the Dead* by Second Sophistic writer Lucian, in which King Minos, one of the judges of the Underworld, had ranked the greatest generals who ever lived: Alexander the Great took first place, Scipio second and Hannibal third. In Hutten's poem, Arminius asks for a reconsideration. Mercury then summons Tacitus from the Elysian fields to testify before Minos that Arminius surpassed all others. *Annals* 2.88 is convincing:

> But Arminius, roused by the fact that the Romans were retreating and King Maroboduus was driven out, held sway heedless of popular liberty. He attacked with force of arms, fought with mixed success and fell by the treachery of his kinsmen. He was without a doubt the liberator of Germania and one who fought not against the emergence of the Roman people, as had other kings and generals, but against the empire at its greatest. In battle his fortunes may have varied, but in war he was never conquered. He lived 37 years, for 12 he held power,

and he is still commemorated in song among the barbarian tribes. He is wholly unknown to Greek historians, who admire only their own, and not duly celebrated by Romans since we extol the past and are uninterested in recent times.[35]

Minos grants that Arminius be forever honoured. 'Although the *Arminius* was written in Latin and was therefore accessible only to a relatively narrow circle of the educated,' says Rhiannon Ash, 'it put Arminius on the map as an ardent patriot endorsed by the credentials of antiquity and realised his potential as a character relevant to the contemporary political scene.'[36]

Ulrich von Hutten was the first to refer to Arminius as a forefather of the Germans, and the *Arminius* was the first of what was to become an entire Arminius/Hermann literary tradition. Daniel Casper von Lohenstein wrote a novel of over 3,000 pages, *Großmüthiger Feldherr Arminius oder Hermann* (*The Greathearted General Arminius or Hermann*), which was unfinished when he died, completed by another author and published posthumously in 1689.[37] Friedrich Gottlieb Klopstock wrote the lyric poems 'Hermann und Thusnelda' (1752) and 'Hermann' (1767), and the dramas *Die Hermannsschlacht* (*The Arminius Battle,* 1769), *Hermann und die Fürsten* (*Arminius and the Princes,* 1784) and *Hermanns Tod* (*Arminius' Death*, 1787). In fact, the Battle of the Teutoburg Forest is the subject of no fewer than 82 German dramas.[38] One of the most well known was written in 1809 by Heinrich von Kleist as a call for resistance to the French and a prime example of anti-Napoleonic propaganda and German Romanticism. Dedicated in 1875, the Hermannsdenkmal ('Arminius Monument') crowns the Grotenberg Mountain near the city of Detmold, where it commemorates the crushing defeat of the Romans. It inspired the Hermann Heights Monument, dedicated in New Ulm, Minnesota in 1897 and rededicated in 2011.[39] There were 75 operas performed on the theme of Arminius between 1676 and 1910 in opera houses from London to Dresden to Rome; Handel's *Arminio* was revived in 1972.[40] According to Wolfgang Schlüter, archaeological research at Kalkriese near Osnabrück conclusively proves the site of the battle, and in 2003 the Kalkriese Museum opened to the public. However, undoubtedly the most quirky incarnation of the Roman battle is the 1996 satirical camp film *Die Hermannsschlacht*, in Latin with German subtitles.[41]

Under the Ancien Régime, Michel de Montaigne (1533–92) was perhaps the most sympathetic to Tacitus. In his essay 'Of the art of discussion', he offers reflections upon reading the *Annals* and *Histories* that are still valid today: 'It is not a book to read, it is a book to study and learn'; 'You would often say that it is us he is describing and decrying.' As for Tacitus not being Christian, 'that was his misfortune, not his fault.'[42] Not all French readers of the era were so agreeable. René Rapin (1621–87) was a Jesuit theologian and literary critic. In his 'Reflections upon history', Tacitus compares poorly to Livy and Thucydides, although we might agree with Rapin that Tacitus 'thinks finely, but seldom expresses himself clearly.'[43] Likewise in a literary dialogue by Dominique Bouhours, a Jesuit grammarian and contemporary of Rapin, Tacitus is criticized for his lack of clarity: 'He has neither the simplicity nor the clarity that history demands.' There is more at stake in these criticisms than aesthetics. Tacitus' perceived lack of clarity results in his not being properly understood and therefore potentially misused by princes and statesmen. Furthermore, the issue matters as much now as it ever did in seventeenth-century France. Bouhours issues the warrant for the *Understanding Classics* series when he states that classical authors 'have not written for the whole world [...] so it is not their fault but that of their readers if they cannot understand'.[44] So the authors in this series have a duty to make their classical authors more accessible.

In sixteenth- and seventeenth-century England, the divide between Tudors and Stuarts, Protestants and Catholics was yet another dichotomy onto which Tacitus was mapped. Under the Tudors (Henry VII to Elizabeth I, 1485–1603), England enjoyed prosperity that allowed humanism to flourish. Sir Henry Savile, a member of Elizabeth's court, published the first translation of Tacitus' *Histories* into English, for which he was knighted in 1604. He also composed *The End of Nero and Beginning of Galba*, an account of the events that transpired between the end of the *Annals* and beginning of the *Histories*. In his preface to the reader, Savile acknowledges the same concerns that were voiced by Rapin and Bouhours, but reaches a different conclusion of Tacitus: 'He is hard. *Difficilia quae pulchra*' ('beautiful things are difficult').[45] On the occasion of Savile's knighthood, his friend Ben Jonson composed an epigram that celebrates Savile's talent and likens him to Tacitus:

> If, my religion safe, I durst embrace
> That stranger doctrine of Pythagoras
> I should believe the soul of Tacitus
> In thee, most weighty Savile, lived to us:
> So hast thou rendered him in all his bounds
> And all his numbers, both of sense and sounds.[46]

When James VI of Scotland succeeded Elizabeth in 1603, he inaugurated the Jacobean era as James I, eponymous king of Jamestown, the capital of the English colony of Virginia. Under his rule, the liberal arts continued to flourish, and Tacitus was read and appreciated by Francis Bacon, John Hobbes and John Locke.[47] At Oxford, Degory Wheare – the first Camden Professor of Ancient History – delivered lectures on Tacitus; at Cambridge, Isaac Dorislaus did the same.[48]

The succession of James by Charles I in 1625 ushered in a period of civil unrest and religious persecution, and once again Tacitus provided useful paradigms. Sir John Eliot was a member of Parliament who sought the enforcement of the laws against Roman Catholics, demanded an investigation into a recent defeat in Spain and pursued the impeachment of the Marquis of Buckingham. On 10 May 1626 he delivered a speech to the House of Commons comparing the Marquis to Sejanus: 'Of all the precedents I can find, none so near resembles him as doth Sejanus, and him Tacitus describes thus.'[49] The king was quick to perceive in this speech his own analogy with the tyrannical and debauched Tiberius, and the next day Eliot was imprisoned and eventually died in the Tower.

After Charles I was executed, John Milton published his *First Defence of the People of England*, a direct response to the royalist *Defensio Regia pro Carolo I* written by the French author Claudius Salmasius. Milton draws on Tacitus to demonstrate the dangers of monarchy and the need for political liberty; as a result, the work was burned in Paris but popular among American revolutionaries.[50] Algernon Sidney, tried and executed for conspiring to assassinate Charles II, refers to the *Germania* in his *Discourses Concerning Government*, a treatise that argues for revolution against monarchy that was published posthumously in 1698.

It is no surprise that Napoléon Bonaparte hated Tacitus, both for political and stylistic reasons. His nephew and heir Napoléon III was roundly condemned by Victor Hugo, who concludes his pamphlet 'Napoleon the Small' with this vivid image of Tacitus as a zookeeper:

> History has its tigers. The historians, immortal keepers of wild beasts, exhibit this imperial menagerie to the nations. Tacitus alone, that great showman, captured and confined eight or ten of these tigers in the iron cage of his style. Look at them: they are terrifying and superb; their spots are an element in their beauty [...] this, Nero, the burner of Rome, who smeared Christians with wax and pitch, and then set them alight as torches; this, Tiberius, the man of Capraea; this, Domitian...

Compared with these villains, Napoléon III is a jackal, and history 'keeps apart the disgusting beasts.'[51]

Eventually, Tacitus was dragged into politics less frequently; in the eighteenth and nineteenth centuries he was claimed by translators, historians and philosophers. In addition to the translations by our duelling Gordon and Hunter, John Dryden also rendered Tacitus into elegant English prose, and between 1776 and 1789 (the signing of the Declaration of Independence and the First Continental Congress) Edward Gibbon composed and published his magisterial *History of the Decline and Fall of the Roman Empire*. According to Paul Cartledge, Gibbon admired and empathized with Tacitus 'even to the point of self-identification', evident in his objectives, theme, subject matter, style and interpretations.[52] In *The New Science*, Giambattista Vico quotes or refers to Tacitus nearly 60 times, and in his *Autobiography* he gives us the insight that 'Tacitus contemplates man as he is, Plato as he should be.'[53] Hegel, Nietzsche and Weber refer to Tacitus; Marx and Engels knew and cited him.[54]

This cursory survey of European intellectual history from the Italian Renaissance to the end of the Victorian era reveals one important fact:

Tacitus was read almost exclusively by educated men of the upper and ruling classes; we have next to no evidence that the works of Tacitus were read by women or by children in schools or in homes. After the Industrial Revolution resulted in the rise of the middle class Tacitus found his way into novels and eventually onto Hollywood screens, even if his influence is not obvious or openly acknowledged. As we pay for the consequences of the twentieth century and face the grim challenges of the twenty-first, Tacitus continues to describe us, decry us and inspire us.

Today

Seven years before Himmler's detail looted the Villa Fontedamo, the Oxford scholar Ronald Syme began writing *The Roman Revolution*. It was 1937, and in Italy Mussolini was clearing the Mausoleum of Augustus and reconstructing the Ara Pacis in anticipation of the bimillenary of the birth of Augustus. Syme was wary: 'A memorable and alarming anniversary looms heavily upon us. [...] These anniversaries, being mere accidents of our numerical system, may often prove to be tedious or noxious.'[55] *The Roman Revolution* was then published in September 1939, just a few days after the outbreak of World War II. In the book, Syme chronicles the period after the assassination of Julius Caesar and the violent transition from Republic to the rule of Augustus and his regime. Syme takes a grim view of the Augustan achievement, born of civil war and maintained by means of tightly controlled propaganda. Augustus was 'a chill and mature terrorist', his constitution 'a screen and a sham'.[56] *The Roman Revolution* bears the imprint of its times. During the war, Syme served in British embassies in Belgrade and Ankara, where he was a professor of classical philology for three years and published only book reviews. He returned to Oxford and was appointed Camden Professor of Ancient History in 1949. In 1958, he published his monumental two-volume *Tacitus*, still unsurpassed for its thoroughness, detail and critical stance. A year after its publication, Syme was knighted. Sombre, pessimistic, reclusive, penetrating: the impression we have of Tacitus today derives in large part from the portrait framed by Syme's *Tacitus*. Yet Mark

Toher documents examples when Syme detects in Tacitus a personality remarkably like his own: 'The Tacitus that emerges from *Tacitus* has features that were characteristic of Syme himself.'[57] A cursory glance through the endnotes of this very volume will reveal that the impact of *Tacitus* is, even today, inescapable. Thus from the pre-war years to the outset of the Cold War, Syme was engaged in scholarship that would permanently change the study of Roman history.

During these same momentous years, several novelists were bringing Tacitus to the page for more general consumption. In 1964, John B. Hainsworth remarked that Tacitus' preferences to begin his histories *in medias res* was a move 'more suitable for the novelist than historian'.[58] Indeed, much of Tacitus' material and arrangement lends itself to a genre characterized above all by an inward turn to psychological motivations. Martha Malamud has examined three novelists writing between the two world wars who find in the histories of Tacitus material for expressing their growing concerns with the disintegration of European politics, society and culture.[59] The first is Robert Graves, whose *I, Claudius* and *Claudius the God* were originally published in May and November of 1934. According to Sandra Joshel, the novels

> inscribe a particular version of Roman history at a moment of crisis for the British empire that included the loss of Ireland in 1922–3, the growth of the Indian Congress Party in the 1920s and 1930s and the total failure of the expected recovery of the imperial economy during the Depression.[60]

Graves openly acknowledges the influence of Tacitus in the epigraph of the first novel by quoting from the *Annals*. The novels recount the reigns of Augustus, Tiberius, Caligula and Claudius, himself the narrator and historian. In 1977–8, the BBC series was aired in the United States as part of *Masterpiece Theatre*, and while it adheres closely to Graves' novels, it too betrays its unmistakable cultural and temporal milieu. In contrast to the big-screen productions of the 1950s that featured scenes of epic proportions, the television series concentrated on scenes of domesticity, as the television itself was an apparatus deeply embedded in home life. *I, Claudius* was above all a family drama whose form resembled the serial soap operas that were growing in popularity in the 1970s.[61]

Second is Naomi Mitchison, whose *The Blood of the Martyrs* was published in 1939. Like Syme's *Roman Revolution*, this novel also takes a grim view of the present through the lens of the past. Unlike Sienkiewicz's *Quo Vadis*, with its heroic protagonist Marcus Vinicius and its romantic depiction of early Christianity, Mitchison's novel is a political and social allegory. As Nero persecuted Christians, so Hitler and Mussolini were tyrannizing Europe. Furthermore, while most historical novels – in keeping with the surviving sources – centre on elite figures, Mitchison, sympathetic to the socialist cause, deliberately brings slaves, women and foreigners to the forefront.[62]

Third is the prolific German-Jewish author Lion Feuchtwanger, an early and outspoken critic of the Nazi party. As a result, he was put on Hitler's list of Germans to be deprived of citizenship. Feuchtwanger moved to France, where he was imprisoned; in the 1933 Nazi book-burning, his works were destroyed. The three novels of his Josephus Trilogy, *Josephus* (1932), *The Jew of Rome* (1935) and *Josephus and the Emperor* (1942), follow the life of the Jewish historian Josephus, a priest of royal descent who was a leader in the revolt against Rome in 66–73 CE. Josephus commanded forces in Galilee against Vespasian and survived the 47-day siege of Jotapata in north-western Galilee and was taken prisoner. Because his prophecy that Vespasian would become emperor was fulfilled, Josephus was released and granted freedom. He followed Vespasian to Rome, where he was given a villa and a generous pension. Under these circumstances he produced an immense body of history. Unlike Graves and Mitchison, for whom Tacitus is a source and a model, Feuchtwanger puts Tacitus in the third novel as a character, in which he appears to embark on his literary career, composing the *Agricola* as a response to the political despotism that surrounded him. Thus while Feuchtwanger, assimilated German Jew, may be compared to Josephus, assimilated Roman Jew, he, like Tacitus, also turns to literature as a refuge from his political trials.[63]

Of a different ilk is Marguerite Yourcenar's *Memoirs of Hadrian*, conceived in Europe sometime between 1924 and 1929 but not finished until

1950 on Mount Desert Island, off the coast of Maine. The novel begins as a letter from the aged Hadrian to the young Marcus Aurelius, his successor, but quickly turns into 'a project for telling you about my life'.[64] Yourcenar seeks to recreate Hadrian's inner reality. She reimagines for us his childhood, adolescence and the successes and twists of fate of his adulthood, all with meticulous attention to historical fact, as attested in the 'Bibliographical Note' appended to the novel and which catalogues her ancient sources and their value.[65] Therefore, although Tacitus is mentioned by Hadrian only in passing ('I have never greatly relished the pompous affability of Pliny; and the sublime rigidity of Tacitus seemed to me to enclose a Republican reactionary's view of the world, unchanged since the death of Caesar'[66]), the novel accurately recreates the world he inhabited.

While Tacitus would thus recognize many of the people, places and events in the *Memoirs of Hadrian* in which he was barely an aside, according to Malamud he would hardly recognize the world recreated 'in the popular fantasy novels by Manda Scott in her Boudica series'.[67] Between 2003 and 2006, Scott published, at the rate of one per year, *Dreaming the Eagle*, *Dreaming the Bull*, *Dreaming the Hound* and *Dreaming the Serpent Spear*. These four novels recreate the world of Boudicca, the leader of the Iceni who led the rebellion against the Romans under Suetonius Paulinus in 61 CE. Long before Manda Scott, Boudicca had enjoyed a vibrant legacy in literature and art as well as movies and documentaries, ever since her revival by Tennyson in his poem 'Boadicea'; she became Queen Victoria's namesake, since both mean 'victory'.[68] Any woman who concludes a battle exhortation by acknowledging the willingness of her fellow women to risk their lives ('as for the men, let them live and become slaves'[69]) is welcome in popular feminist camps. In her 1979 installation piece *The Dinner Party*, Judy Chicago creates a triangular dinner table with 39 place settings for 39 mythical and historical women.[70] Thanks to her luminous depiction in Tacitus, Boudicca has a place between Aspasia and Hypatia.

Of the great seventeenth-century French dramatists, Jean Racine wrote the *Britannicus*, in the preface of which he says, 'I have copied my characters from the greatest painter of antiquity – I mean Tacitus.'[71] Pierre

Corneille's *Othon*, on the other hand, departs significantly from Tacitus despite claims of faithfulness to the characters; most notably, Otho is not driven to usurp the throne but is merely installed by the army. In England, William Shakespeare was instrumental in bringing stories from classical literature to popular audiences. While he drew on Plutarch for the plot of *Julius Caesar* and Ovid for the star-crossed lovers of *Romeo and Juliet*, Tacitus is less influential (although no less artfully deployed). In *Henry V*, the king, in a borrowed cloak, canvasses his men's sentiments the night before battle. Similarly, the night before the battle of Idistaviso, Germanicus put on a cloak of rough pelt worn by commoners and walked through the camp to ascertain his men's opinions of him. The assumption is that Shakespeare had read Tacitus, and given that Richard Grenawey's 1598 translation of the *Annals* had recently been published, this is likely.[72] While Shakespeare drew on the extant *Annals*, his drinking buddy Ben Jonson sought material in the tatters of *Annals* Books 5 and 6. His play *Sejanus His Fall*, performed at the Globe in 1603 (Shakespeare played Tiberius), was a flop in its day. But in the autumn of 2005, the Royal Shakespeare Company production of *Sejanus His Fall* found favourable reviews among post-9/11 audiences who perceived something all too familiar in the depiction of ruthless, bloodthirsty evil and the pursuit of absolute power.[73]

Although Arminius, Boudicca and Nero the persecutor of Christians may be the most memorable of Tacitus' characters in Early Modern and Modern European literature, the story of Germanicus also provides rich material for creative impulses. In 1956, the Afrikaans verse play *Germanicus* by Nicolaas Petrus van Wyk Louw was staged for the first time in the Western Cape, and in 2013 Jo-Marie Claassen published the first English translation of the play in eight scenes. The first four scenes take place in the territory of Germania, where Germanicus is campaigning successfully. The scenes adhere to the content of the *Annals* and re-enact the Pannonian revolt, Agrippina the Elder's activity among the soldiers, the Roman victories over the Chatti and Cherusci, and an embassy from the Cheruscan noble Segestes and his daughter Thusnelda, wife of Arminius. Two central scenes take place in Rome, where Livia and Tiberius react to Germanicus' homecoming. In these scenes, Louw uses the tone of the *Annals* to inspire his inventive recreation of the things Tacitus did not narrate. For example, Scene vi expands upon the brief paragraph in the *Annals* recounting the appearance and demise of Clemens, the false Agrippa Postumus. Tacitus simply states that Clemens was arrested and then interviewed by Tiberius. In contrast, Louw inserts a conversation between Tiberius and Germanicus, followed by an exchange between Tiberius and the torturer. Louw also invents a 28-line speech for Clemens, where Tacitus provides only the sneer, 'The same way you became Caesar', when Tiberius asks how he became Agrippa Postumus.[74] The final two scenes take place in the Roman Near East, where Piso breaks with Germanicus, whose health declines rapidly until he dies. Whereas in Tacitus Piso and Germanicus are enemies, Louw presents a long-term friendship in greater depth and probes the reasons for its ultimate dissolution.

Germanicus is an exploration of power, in all of its manifestations. At first reluctant, Tiberius eventually wielded his power ruthlessly. Germanicus never wanted power and repeatedly attempted to throw it off. Piso is the most complex character; he clearly wants power for himself, but only after Germanicus refuses it. Then there are the women: Livia, who sacrificed her humanity for power; Agrippina the Elder, who gloried in her husband's possibilities; and Plancina, wife of Piso, reduced to a mere puppet figure. Yet more striking than the exposition of individual attitudes towards power is the portrayal of the brutality of empire and its consequences. For example, the reaction of the captive queen Thusnelda is a plausible invention by Louw:

> I am no longer human. I am all hate.
> One solid piece of rancid, stone blind hatred.
> This you do to us, you shrink all life to this,
> you make it narrow, one dark dungeon: hate,
> and struggle, breaking-out,
> We do not want to hate forever: we are human:
> we want to love, have children, care for them...[75]

Such a speech belongs to anyone whose rights, liberty and personal dignity have been systematically stripped away. Yet even the emperor himself loathes the consequences of empire. Tiberius is no less damning:

> We are tied down
> by Fate in the stinking sewer of this Empire
> and the filth of our era washes over all of us.[76]

It is tempting to hear in the words of the vulnerable captive and the oppressive despot a scathing condemnation of apartheid, but nowhere does Louw make contemporary politics explicit, and in point of fact the play was composed in 1944 but the National Party that instituted the system of apartheid was not elected until 1948. Yet, as Jo-Marie Claassen concedes,

> if one accepts that an author of genius often reaches out in a wider sweep than he himself may be aware of, Louw's vatic portrayal of the dangers inherent in absolute power can be taken to have reflected both the South Africa of his time and the world for all time.[77]

More direct in his use of the Roman imperial imagination to take a political stand is Anselm Kiefer, whose 1976 painting *Varus* is both a tribute to the Battle of the Teutoburg Forest and a gesture towards the Holocaust.[78] The snowy path splattered with blood diminishes in perspective through blood-red trees that carry the viewer back in time. While the vanishing point adds depth to the painting, it also suggests the futility of war and violence that lead nowhere. Yet without any guidance from the artist, the viewer is left to imagine what lies at the end of the path. The shadows behind the trees play upon the imagination such that the forest conjures haunts familiar from *Grimm's Fairy Tales* that could just as easily have been the hideaways of victims of Nazi persecution. The blood is fresh but the corpses are absent, so that only the inhumanity of slaughter is visible: this is not a wasteland of peace.

The painting is inscribed, so that at first glance the names 'Hermann', 'Thusnelda' and 'Varus' (the only Roman and the only name inscribed in black) invite the viewer to imagine the Roman defeat which Tacitus described in retrospect, for the battle is recalled by the survivors who returned six years later:

Therefore a desire to perform the obsequies for the soldiers and their leader seized Germanicus Caesar; the entire army which was present was moved to pity because of their relatives, friends, and in the end because of the misfortunes of war and the lot of mankind. While Caecina was sent in advance in order to examine the hidden areas of the forest and to construct bridges and causeways over the damp marshes and deceptive plains, they penetrated into the mournful places unsightly in appearance and memory. Varus' first camp with broad circumference and measured headquarters was evidence of the work of three legions; thereupon from the half-levelled rampart and the shallow trench it was understood that the already diminished remnants of the legions had pitched there. In the middle of the plain the whitening bones were scattered or heaped as the men had fled or stood their ground. Lying nearby were the broken pieces of weapons and the limbs of horses; likewise, human heads were nailed to the trunks of trees. In the neighbouring groves were the barbarian altars near which they had immolated the tribunes and centurions of the first ranks. And the survivors of this disaster, having escaped battle or capture, were recounting that here the legates fell, there the eagles were taken; where the first wound inflicted Varus, where he met death with an unlucky right hand from his own blow; on which platform Arminius harangued his men, how many yokes for the captives, the mass graves, and that in his arrogance he mocked the standards and eagles.[79]

One can see the appeal of such a paradigmatic narrative to a German of Kiefer's generation, born in 1945. The army of Varus is likened to the victims of the concentration camps. As Tacitus substantiates the massacre with testimony from the soldiers who returned to the site, so the history of the Holocaust depends on the testimony of survivors.

Whereas Louw expands upon the material provided by Tacitus to create entire scenes in his play *Germanicus*, Kiefer reduces this paragraph of Tacitus to its bare essentials and adds instead in white paint in the heights of the trees the names of philosophers Martin Luther, Johann Gottlieb Fichte and

Friedrich Schleiermacher; poets Friedrich Hölderlin, Friedrich Klopstock, Heinrich von Kleist, Christian Dietrich Grabbe and Rainer Maria Rilke; and imperial field marshal Alfred von Schlieffen. We are already familiar with some of these thinkers and writers who helped create the Arminius legend from the pages of Tacitus.

Thus the painting documents the battle and its reception across two millennia; it also calls for reflection on empire. The modern German nation was born of the slaughter of three legions of Romans – who themselves obliterated native tribes in pursuit of an empire that lasted for centuries. The Germans lost World War II, but by murdering six million Jews in the concentration camps of the Holocaust they permanently changed the population of Europe and set the course for the Palestinian–Israeli conflict at the heart of today's Middle East. *Varus* offers a representation of the scars of empire.

For the American poet Frank Bidart, Tacitus' return to the Teutoburg Forest provokes a different response. As part of the 1997 collection *Desire*, 'The Return' is a five-page quasi-translation of *Annals* 1.60–3; some of the lines of the poem are purely Tacitean, although at times Bidart omits some sentences while repeating others that convey his unique meaning of the poem, distinct from the Tacitean original. Another poem in *Desire*, 'Borges and I', opens and closes with a statement that could be taken to describe the method of composing 'The Return': 'We fill pre-existing forms and when we fill them we change them and are changed.' So Bidart fills Tacitus' pre-existing narrative with his own poem, by which Tacitus is changed: but then so are we.

Bidart transforms Tacitus from history into lyric. He seizes upon the first words of paragraph 61 quoted above, *igitur cupido*, 'therefore a desire', as yet another avenue to explore the theme of the collection. The desire to return is not mere nostalgia; instead the poem asks the reader to ponder the impossibility of ever returning to a place in time against the persistent longing to do so.

Bidart follows Tacitus closely. As the soldiers advance, every step forward leads them further back in time, until they arrive at the battle-field itself:

on the open ground between them

were whitening bones, free
from putrefaction,–

scattered where men had been struck down
fleeing, heaped up

where they had stood their ground before the slaughter.[80]

At the end of the poem, Bidart twice reprises these lines but with slight changes in form and content. Still, the repetition drives home the notion of the open ground that testifies to the violence. Thus three times Bidart calls on the image of the whitening bones scattered or heaped, evidence of men who fled or persisted. In the penultimate couplet, Bidart adds words not found in Tacitus:

I have returned here a thousand times,
though history cannot tell us its location.[81]

Voices are of course the essence of lyric. With the first person, Bidart has inserted himself into the poem, but the result is not an intrusion but rather a fusion of his voice with Tacitus and ultimately with his reader. Haven't we all returned in the mind's eye (since precise locations are impossible) to some traumatic event to analyse it, or purge it – or, as Germanicus, to purify it? To undertake the writing of history is to commit to returning to places and events that are irretrievable but irresistible. Tacitus is a poet too. So the final couplet belongs to him:

Arminius, relentlessly pursued by
Germanicus, retreated into pathless country.[82]

In this translation of *Annals* 1.63.1, the original active voice is transposed to passive, with the result that Arminius is rendered more sympathetic and enigmatic. Yet the change of voice also reminds the Latinist that this is Bidart's poem, and Tacitus is merely the pre-existing form.

Bidart was not the first poet to put Tacitus into verse, nor the last. In 1628, Alessandro Adimari produced a book of 50 sonnets based on *sententiae* from Tacitus. On 5 January 2016 at Trinity Wall Street, New York, Scott Ordway debuted 'North Woods', a ten-minute a cappella piece that adapts sentences selected from the *Agricola* and *Germania*. 'North Woods' was commissioned by Lorelei Ensemble, whose mission is to expand the repertoire for women's voices (here at last is Tacitus for women). The piece is part of their larger project, *Reconstructed: The New Americana*. New works by four emerging composers engage with well-known sacred and folk melodies from the American music tradition. The first is centred on the 'Battle Hymn of the Republic', the second captures stories of Native American women, the third is an arrangement of an English ballad that was preserved by Appalachian oral traditions, and 'North Woods' is the final piece. So how does Tacitus fit into *Reconstructed: The New Americana*?

Scott Ordway began working on the piece in 2013 when he was living in Maine. He explains his motivation:

> In *Germania* and *Agricola* [...] the author describes territories to the north of the Roman Empire. He was ignorant in two important ways, though: he had never personally traveled to either Britain or the German lands, and he didn't understand how the planet was shaped or how it related to the sun. Because of this, his writings about the North are infused with an almost mystical reverence that still feels intuitively correct. Vast woods and waters shrouded in endless twilight acquire a moral significance that grows from the landscape itself: because they are frozen and dark, they are unwelcoming to humanity, and this makes them pure. This, to me, is the idea of the North, and it resounds everywhere in the way that people discuss the northern peripheries of the places they live and know.[83]

As a result, 'North Woods' draws on parts of the *Agricola* and *Germania* that are usually overlooked by scholars more interested in the history of imperial expansion or colonization. Instead, in Part I Ordway extracts sentences that describe the climate of the northern reaches, sentences that most Latin students would rather ignore because of the dense language that expresses astronomical phenomena in unfamiliar, if not illogical, ways. The eight voices begin in a discordant chant that almost sounds like beating wings. The voices are both icy and ethereal as they sing: 'The nights are not dark; the earth casts only a low shadow. The level edge does not project the darkness high aloft (and so) the shades of night do not reach the sky and stars above.' By recasting these words from *Agricola* 12 across the rugged landscape of Maine, Ordway has solved Tacitus' problem: the earth is round, not flat. Britannia is not the terminus of one empire but the beginning of another.

In Part II, Ordway combines sentences from the *Agricola* and *Germania* that express the isolation of the north. Although the voices seem to migrate from wild to civilized, the rivers run to an infinite nowhere: 'To the north of it no land exists whatever, and upon that face beat the waves of a vast and shoreless sea. And the rivers bend gently away to lose themselves in the northern Ocean.'

Then in Part III, an extract from the *Germania* suffuses all that preceded with a sense of divinity:

> They do not imprison their gods within walls, or represent them with
> human features; instead they consecrate woods and groves and they
> call by the names of gods the hidden presence that they see only by
> the eye of reverence.

Throughout 'North Woods', the minimalist style with its slowly changing progressions in long arching phrases on an environmental theme calls to mind the experimental film *Koyaanisqatsi,* a harsh indictment of the industrial degradation of the environment. Perhaps I am overreaching, but in the context of Ordway's composition, Tacitus' words seem to caution those who ignore the innate sanctity of the natural world.

It is not enough any more to admit to having created a wasteland and calling it peace, whether in Vietnam or Afghanistan. While Tacitus forces us to take responsibility for war and imperialism, his pervasive discourses on the limitations of freedom of action and the difference between social and antisocial conduct speak to our ethical duty towards each other and even towards the environment. To understand Tacitus, 'after you are acquainted with his manner and subject', is to risk perceiving some uneasy, inconvenient truths, and so those who understand Tacitus will probably at some point, in the words of Reverend Thomas Hunter, 'throw him by'. But not for long.

NOTES

I. PREFACING A LIFE

1   Thomas Gordon, *The Works of Tacitus. With Political Discourses Upon That Author* (1728), as cited in *Heritage*, p. 176.

2   Thomas Hunter, *Observations on Tacitus. In Which his Character as a Writer and an Historian, is Impartially Considered, and Compared with that of Livy* (1752), as cited in *Heritage*, p. 186.

3   See Howard D. Weinbrot, 'Politics, taste, and national identity: some uses of Tacitism in eighteenth-century Britain', in *Tacitus and the Tacitean Tradition*, pp. 168–84; *Heritage*, pp. xliii–xliv.

4   Peter Burke, 'Tacitism', in Thomas A. Dorey (ed.), *Tacitus* (New York, 1969), p. 150.

5   Christopher B. Krebs, *A Most Dangerous Book: Tacitus's Germania from the Roman Empire to the Third Reich* (New York and London, 2011).

6   *Ag.* 30.5; Stanley Karnow, *Vietnam: A History* (New York, 1983).

7   *Ag.* 1.1.

8   *G.* 1.1.

9   *Dial.* 1.1.

10   *Hist.* 1.1.1.

11   *Ann.* 1.1.1.

12   Emily Dickinson, *Collected Poems* (Philadelphia, PA, 1991), p. 223.

13   Michel de Montaigne, *Essays* (1588), as cited in *Heritage*, p. 134.

14   Pedro de Ribadeneyra, *Religion and the Virtues of the Christian Prince against Machiavelli* (1595), as cited in *Heritage*, p. 67.

15   Vespasian's rule, *Dial.* 17.3; Tacitus as a young man, *Dial.* 1.2.

16   *Ag.* 9.6.

17   *Hist.* 1.1.3.

18   *Ann.* 11.11.1.

19   *Ag.* 45.5.

20   Pliny, *Epistles* 2.1.6.

21   Ibid. 2.11.

22 Anthony R. Birley, 'The life and death of Cornelius Tacitus', *Historia* 49.2 (2000), pp. 231–4.

23 Nerva, *Ag.* 3.1; Trajan, *Ag.* 44.5.

24 *G.* 37.2.

25 C. O. Brink, 'Can Tacitus' *Dialogus* be dated? evidence and historical conclusions', *Harvard Studies in Classical Philology* 96 (1994), p. 275.

26 Pliny, *Epistles* 6.16, 20; *Ann.* 2.61.2.

27 David S. Potter, 'The inscriptions on the bronze Herakles from Mesene: Vologeses IV's war with Rome and the date of Tacitus' *Annales*', *Zeitschrift für Papyrologie und Epigraphik* 88 (1991), pp. 277–90; Steven H. Rutledge, 'Trajan and Tacitus' audience: reader reception of *Annals* 1–2', *Ramus* 27 (1998), pp. 141–3.

28 Moses Hadas, *Gibbon's the Decline and Fall of the Roman Empire* (New York, 1962), p. 38.

29 Dylan Sailor, *Writing and Empire in Tacitus* (Cambridge, 2008), p. 34.

30 Krebs, *A Most Dangerous Book*, pp. 41–2.

31 Suetonius, *Domitian* 11.1.

32 Pliny, *Epistles* 8.14.8. See Brian W. Jones, *The Emperor Domitian* (London and New York, 1992), pp. 180–92 on Domitian's relationship with the Senate.

33 On Domitian's paranoia, see Victoria E. Pagán, *Conspiracy Theory in Latin Literature* (Austin, TX, 2012), pp. 114–16.

34 Carole E. Newlands, *Statius: Poet Between Rome and Naples* (London, 2012), pp. 20–36 illuminates the difficulties in assessing the relationship between Domitian and the poet Statius, especially against a bias that has been in place for centuries.

35 Ronald Syme, *Tacitus*, 2 vols (Oxford, 1958), p. 11.

36 See Pagán, *Conspiracy Theory*, pp. 119–21.

37 On the achievements of Trajan, see Julian Bennett, *Trajan* Optimus Princeps: *a Life and Times* (Bloomington, IN, 1997).

38 On the achievements of Hadrian, see Anthony Everitt, *Hadrian and the Triumph of Rome* (New York, 2009).

39 See Tore Janson, *Latin Prose Prefaces: Studies in Literary Conventions* (Stockholm, 1964).

40 See James B. Rives, *Tacitus: Germania* (Oxford, 1999), pp. 48–9 on the absence of prefatory statements.

41 Four lines are preserved in a scholium to Juvenal 4.94; see Susanna Morton Braund, *Juvenal: Satires Book I* (Cambridge, 1996), p. 251.

42 *Ag.* 39.1.

43 Rhiannon Ash, 'Act like a German! Tacitus' *Germania* and national characterisation in the historical works', in Devillers, p. 187. See also Rives, *Tacitus: Germania*, pp. 51–3.

44 *Dial.* 1.3.

45 *Ag.* 2.1–2.

46 Anthony J. Woodman with Christina S. Kraus, *Tacitus: Agricola* (Cambridge, 2014), pp. 76–7.

47 *Ag.* 2.3.

48 Ibid.

49 On amnesty in fourth-century Athens, see Andrew Wolpert, *Remembering Defeat: Civil War and Civic Memory in Ancient Athens* (Baltimore, 2002), pp. 76–84.

50 On *damnatio memoriae* in Roman culture, see Harriet Flower, *The Art of Forgetting: Disgrace and Oblivion in Roman Political Culture* (Chapel Hill, NC, 2011).

51 *Ag.* 3.1.

52 Ibid.

53 Woodman with Kraus, *Tacitus: Agricola*, pp. 88–9.
54 *Ag.* 3.2.
55 See Holly Haynes, 'Survival and memory in the *Agricola*', *Arethusa* 39.2 (2006), pp. 152–3 on the enigmatic phrase 'survivors of ourselves'.
56 *Ag.* 45.1.
57 Ibid.
58 Suetonius, *Domitian* 10.4.
59 *Ag.* 43.2–3.
60 Sailor, *Writing and Empire*, pp. 103–18, especially p. 115 on Agricola's death.
61 Syme, *Tacitus*, pp. 686–7.
62 *Hist.* 1.1.3.
63 Cynthia Damon, *Tacitus: Histories I* (Cambridge, 2003), p. 81.
64 *Hist.* 1.1.4.
65 *Ag.* 3.3.
66 *Ann.* 11.11.1.
67 Ibid. 3.24.3.
68 Anthony J. Woodman, *Rhetoric in Classical Historiography: Four Studies* (London and Sydney, 1988), p. 167.
69 Jones, *The Emperor Domitian*, p. 124.
70 Christopher Pelling, 'Tacitus' personal voice', in *Cambridge Companion*, p. 150. Frederick M. Ahl, 'The art of safe criticism in Greece and Rome', *American Journal of Philology* 105 (1984), p. 207 warns against Tacitean optimism: 'The verdict of extant literature is very different. Latin poetry flourished under Domitian. The closest thing to epic Trajan's reign has left is his column.'
71 *Ann.* 1.1.1.
72 Ibid. 1.1.2.
73 Ibid. 4.34.3.
74 Pliny, *Epistles* 9.19.5; on the historical events to which the remark eludes, see D. C. A. Shotter, 'Tacitus and Verginius Rufus', *Classical Quarterly* 17.2 (1967).
75 John B. Hainsworth, 'The starting-point of Tacitus' *Historiae*: fear or favor by omission?', *Greece & Rome* 11.2 (1964) argues that because Tacitus wanted to avoid treating this embarrassing allegiance to Nero, he chose to begin the *Histories* in the middle of Galba's reign.
76 Syme, *Tacitus*, p. 178.
77 *Ann.* 1.1.2.
78 Cynthia Damon (trans.), *Tacitus, Annals* (London and New York, 2012), p. liii.
79 Origin of law, *Ann.* 3.25.2–3.28.2; luxury, ibid. 3.52–5.
80 Syme, *Tacitus*, p. 481.
81 Donald R. Kelley, '*Tacitus noster*: the *Germania* in the Renaissance and Reformation', in *Tacitus and the Tacitean Tradition*, p. 153.

II. NOBLES AND NOBODIES

1 Thomas Hunter, *Observations on Tacitus. In Which his Character as a Writer and an Historian, is Impartially Considered, and Compared with that of Livy* (1752), as cited in *Heritage*, p. 180.

2   Ronald Syme, *Tacitus*, 2 vols (Oxford, 1958), p. 379.

3   *Ann.* 3.24.2.

4   Timothy P. Wiseman, 'Calpurnius Siculus and the Claudian civil war', *Journal of Roman Studies* 72 (1982), pp. 58, 67.

5   *Ann.* 4.44.2.

6   Ibid. 4.75.

7   Ibid. 3.19.3.

8   Ibid. 1.3.3.

9   Ibid. 1.6.1.

10   Ibid. 6.25.1. Tacitus goes on to record that Tiberius falsely accused her of adultery so that he could allege that the death of her paramour was the cause of her grief and subsequent death.

11   *Ann.* 3.56. On Tacitus' treatment of Drusus, see Jane Bellemore, 'The identity of Drusus: the making of a *princeps*', in Alisdair G. G. Gibson (ed.), *The Julio-Claudian Succession: Reality and Perception of the 'Augustan Model'* (Leiden, 2013), pp. 79–94.

12   Ellen O'Gorman, 'Alternate empires: Tacitus' virtual history of the Pisonian principate', *Arethusa* 39.2 (2006), pp. 281–301; I am indebted to her study in what follows, although my conclusions arrive at a different end.

13   Elimar Klebs et al., *Prosopographia imperii romani* (Berlin, 1897–8; 2nd ed. 1933–), numbers C 224–50.

14   Patrick Kragelund, Mette Moltesen and Jan Stubbe Østergaard, *The Licinian Tomb: Fact or Fiction?* (Copenhagen, 2003).

15   *Ann.* 2.43.2–3.

16   Ibid. 2.43.4.

17   See Werner Eck, A. Caballos and F. Fernandez, *Das senatus consultum de Cn. Pisone patre* (Munich, 1996); for a translation, see David S. Potter and Cynthia Damon, 'The senatus consultum de Cn. Pisone patre', *American Journal of Philology* 120.1 (1999) 13–41.

18   *Ann.* 15.48.2–3.

19   Ibid. 15.48–59.

20   Cynthia Damon, *Tacitus: Histories I* (Cambridge, 2003), p. 126.

21   *Hist.* 1.14.2.

22   Ibid. 1.47.2.

23   Kragelund, Moltensen and Østergaard, *The Licinian Tomb*, p. 30. Piso's eldest brother perished under Claudius; see Barbara Levick, *Claudius* (New Haven, CT, and London, 1990), p. 58. The second, M. Licinius Crassus Frugi, was the enemy of Aquilius Regulus, who secured his death; see Steven H. Rutledge, *Imperial Inquisitions: Prosecutors and Informants from Tiberius to Domitian* (London and New York, 2001), p. 193. Of his third brother, Crassus Scribonianus, only his name is known from Tacitus, *Hist.* 1.47.2. For the burial, see *Hist.* 1.46, 47. For the tomb, see Kragelund, Moltesen and Østergaard, *The Licinian Tomb*.

24   *Hist.* 4.11.2.

25   O'Gorman, 'Alternate empires', p. 285.

26   *Hist.* 4.50.1–2.

27   Juvenal 1.33–5, translation by Susanna Morton Braund, *Juvenal and Persius* (Cambridge, MA, 2004), pp. 133–4.

28   *Ag.* 45.1 as per Rutledge, *Imperial Inquisitions*, p. 203.

29   Pliny, *Epistles* 7.33; on Pliny's appointment to the case see Leanne Bablitz, 'The selection

of advocates for *repetundae* trials: the cases of Pliny the Younger', *Athenaeum* 97 (2009), pp. 200–1.

30   Elisabeth Henry (Bessie) Walker, *The Annals of Tacitus: A Study in the Writing of History* (Manchester, 1952), pp. 204–34.

31   Ibid., p. 213.

32   Rutledge, *Imperial Inquisitions*, pp. 52–3.

33   Ibid., p. 234.

34   *Ann.* 2.28.3.

35   Ibid. 2.31.3.

36   Ibid. 3.19.1.

37   Ibid. 5.11.

38   Joseph Roisman, *The Rhetoric of Conspiracy in Ancient Athens* (Berkeley, CA, 2006), p. 5.

39   *Ann.* 6.4.

40   For a more nuanced view of prosecutors in imperial society, see Sander M. Goldberg, 'The faces of eloquence: the *Dialogus de oratoribus*', in *Cambridge Companion*, pp. 77–8.

41   *Ann.* 13.15.2.

42   Ibid. 13.16.4.

43   Romans traditionally had three names: *praenomen*, or personal name; the *nomen*, or name of the *gens*; and the *cognomen*, or family name. In Marcus Tullius Cicero, Marcus is the given name, Tullius denotes the *gens*, and Cicero is the family name, which is often in origin a nickname.

44   Rubellius Plautus, *Ann.* 14.59; Rubellius Blandus, ibid. 6.27.

45   *Ann.* 1.16.3.

46   Ibid. 1.22.1.

47   Ibid. 1.23.3.

48   Ibid. 1.35. In his 'Notes on the *Annals* by Tacitus', the Russian poet Pushkin regarded the soldier's suggestion as 'a cold-blooded challenge, not an inappropriate joke'; cited in *Heritage*, p. 207.

49   Francis R. D. Goodyear, *The Annals of Tacitus Books 1–6*, vol. I: *Annals 1.1–54* (Cambridge, 1972), p. 195.

50   *Ag.* 14.1.

51   *Ann.* 15.49.3. Lateranus owned property on the Caelian Hill.

52   Statius, *Silvae* 2.7.60–1; Frederick M. Ahl, *Lucan: An Introduction* (Ithaca, NY, and London, 1976), pp. 333–53.

53   *Ann.* 15.49.4.

54   Ibid. 15.66.2.

55   Ibid. 15.67.4.

56   Ibid. 15.69.

57   On the dramatic structure of the Pisonian conspiracy, see Anthony J. Woodman, 'Amateur dramatics at the court of Nero: *Annals* 15.48–74', *Tacitus and the Tacitean Tradition*, pp. 104–28.

58   *Ann.* 15.71.4, *in agmen et numerum*.

59   *Hist.* 1.25.1.

60   Ibid. 1.25.2.

61   Rhiannon Ash, *Tacitus: Histories Book II* (Cambridge, 2007), p. 111.

62   *Hist.* 2.12.

63   Ibid. 2.13.2.

64 Ash, *Tacitus: Histories Book II*, p. 112.

65 Victoria E. Pagán, 'Teaching torture in Seneca *Controversiae* 2.5', *Classical Journal* 103.2 (2007), pp. 165–82.

66 See Ellen O'Gorman, *Irony and Misreading in the* Annals *of Tacitus* (Cambridge, 2000), p. 141 for a discussion of the scene at *Ann.* 14.8.5.

67 See also Rhiannon Ash, 'Fission and fusion: shifting Roman identities in the *Histories*', in *Cambridge Companion*, pp. 93–5 for a discussion of the ways morality is polarized along lines of gender and identity in this episode.

68 *Ann.* 15.57.2.

69 *Ag.* 4.2, 4.3.

70 Anthony J. Woodman with Christina S. Kraus, *Tacitus: Agricola* (Cambridge, 2014), p. 101.

71 *Ag.* 7.1.

72 Ash, *Tacitus: Histories Book II*, p. 113.

73 Gwyn Morgan, *69 A.D.: The Year of Four Emperors* (Oxford, 2006), p. 104.

74 René Rapin, *Reflections Upon History* (*c.*1674), as cited in *Heritage*, p. 136.

III. WORDS AND DEEDS

1 For a thoroughgoing study of the Greek origins of Latin literature, see Denis Feeney, *Beyond Greek: The Beginnings of Latin Literature* (Cambridge, MA, 2016).

2 Cicero, *De Oratore* 2.52.

3 *Ann.* 3.30.2.

4 Thomas Gordon, *The Works of Tacitus. With Political Discourses Upon That Author* (1728), as cited in *Heritage*, p. 173.

5 *Ag.* 10.3; *Ann.* 4.34.3.

6 Judith Ginsburg, *Tradition and Theme in the* Annals *of Tacitus* (New York, 1981). On the influence of Sallust and Livy on Tacitus see Alain M. Gowing, 'From the annalists to the *Annales*: Latin historiography before Tacitus', in *Cambridge Companion*, pp. 22–3. Ronald Martin, *Tacitus* (Bristol, 1981), p. 23 is doubtful: 'What influence any of the above historians may have exercised on Tacitus defies rational explanation.'

7 Timothy P. Wiseman, 'Lying historians: seven types of mendacity', in Christopher Gill and Timothy P. Wiseman (eds), *Lies and Fiction in the Ancient World* (Austin, TX, 1993), p. 146. See also the seminal work of Anthony J. Woodman, *Rhetoric in Classical Historiography: Four Studies* (London and Sydney, 1988).

8 Aristotle, *Poetics* 1451b1.

9 *Hist.* 1.12.1–3.

10 Thucydides, *The Peloponnesian War* 1.22, translation revised and edited by Terry E. Wick as *Thucydides: The Peloponnesian War* (New York, 1982), p. 13.

11 Cicero, *De Inventione* 9, as quoted in Woodman, *Rhetoric in Classical Historiography*, p. 87.

12 *Hist.* 1.1.1; cf. *Ann.* 1.1.2.

13 Holly Haynes, 'Tacitus' history and mine', in *Blackwell Companion*, p. 288 is especially perceptive: 'Tacitus' histories are less a narrative of events that took place during the first century of the Roman principate than a documentary of the narratives that went on in people's heads during that time.'

14 Olivier Devillers, 'The concentration of power and writing history: forms of historical persuasion in the *Histories* (1.1–49)', in *Blackwell Companion*, p. 183.

15 For a quantitative study of trials in the *Annals*, see Leanne Bablitz, 'Tacitus on trial(s)', in Lee Brice and Daniëlle Slootjes (eds), *Aspects of Ancient Institutions and Geography: Studies in Honour of Richard J. A. Talbert* (Leiden, 2015), pp. 65–83.

16 *Ag.* 15.1.

17 Ibid. 15.1–5.

18 *Ann.* 14.29.

19 Ibid. 14.31.2–4.

20 *Hist.* 2.37.1.

21 Ibid. 2.60.

22 *Ag.* 29.4.

23 Ibid. 30.3; on the difficulties of translating this sentence, see Anthony J. Woodman with Christina S. Kraus, *Tacitus: Agricola* (Cambridge, 2014), pp. 240–1.

24 *Ag.* 30.4–5.

25 Ibid. 32.4.

26 Stephen J. V. Malloch, *The* Annals *of Tacitus Book 11* (Cambridge, 2013), pp. 338–41.

27 *Ann.* 11.23.2.

28 Ibid.

29 Ibid. 11.24.1.

30 For an examination of Tacitus' response to the problem of access to information, see Devillers, 'The concentration of power'.

31 Kenneth Wellesley, 'Can you trust Tacitus?', *Greece & Rome* 1 (1954), p. 25 regards this not as a technique of managing limited access to information but as an 'arbitrary or wilful literary device'.

32 *Ann.* 11. 24.4.

33 Ibid. 11.24.5–6.

34 Ibid. 11.24.7.

35 Norma P. Miller, 'The Claudian tablet and Tacitus: a reconsideration', *Rheinisches Museum* 99 (1956), p. 307.

36 Miller, 'The Claudian tablet', p. 312.

37 *Ann.* 11.24.4.

38 Stephen J. V. Malloch, '*Hamlet* without the prince? the Claudian *Annals*', in *Cambridge Companion*, p. 116 n. 4; Malloch, *The* Annals *of Tacitus Book 11*, pp. 3–9. Barbara Levick, *Claudius* (New Haven, CT, and London, 1990), p. 83 argues that Claudius was not dominated by his freedmen; rather, he recognized their abilities and used them to his best advantage. Miriam T. Griffin, 'The Lyons Tablet and Tacitean hindsight', *Classical Quarterly* 32.2 (1982), p. 410 suggests that the sentence 'could be a generalization' of a point made in the Tablet; Ronald Syme, *Tacitus*, 2 vols (Oxford, 1958), p. 707 suggests that it may derive from Suetonius. Either way, freedmen are prominent in Tacitus' narrative of Claudius.

39 *Ann.* 11.25.1; the assumption is that the Aedui were admitted first and other *primores Galliae* followed. See Malloch, *The* Annals *of Tacitus Book 11*, p. 379.

40 *Ann.* 1.12.2.

41 Ibid. 1.74.5.

42 See David C. A. Shotter, 'Tiberius and Asinius Gallus', *Historia* 20.4 (1971).

43 *Ann.* 2.40.3.

44 Ibid. 6.46.4.

45 Ibid. 14.9.3.

46 *oderint dum metuant*: Cicero, *Philippics* 1.34; Suetonius, *Caligula* 30; Seneca, *de Ira* 1.20; *de Clementia* 1.12.4, 2.2.2.

47 *Ann.* 14.8.5; see also Chapter II.

48 *Ann.* 15.62.2.

49 Ibid. 15.63.2.

50 Ibid. 15.64; for observations on Paulina's death see Mario Erasmo, *Reading Death in Ancient Rome* (Columbus, OH, 2008), pp. 27–30.

51 *Ann.* 15.63.3.

52 Andrew Laird, *Powers of Expression, Expressions of Power: Speech Presentation and Latin Literature* (Oxford, 1999), p. 129.

53 *Ann.* 14.59.3.

54 Dio 62.14.1.

55 *Ann.* 15.67.4; see Chapter II.

56 *Ann.* 15.67.2.

57 Ibid. 15.67.3.

58 Ibid. 16.35.1.

59 Ibid. 15.64.4; Miriam T. Griffin, *Seneca: A Philosopher in Politics* (Oxford, 1976), pp. 369–72.

60 For example, the contents of *Ann.* 1.12.2 and 1.74.5 are also found in Dio; see Francis R. D. Goodyear, *The Annals of Tacitus Books 1–6*, vol. I: *Annals* 1.1–54 (Cambridge, 1972), pp. 179–80.

61 Laird, *Powers of Expression*, pp. 116–52 dismantles such assumptions, and I follow his conclusions.

62 Thomas Hunter, *Observations on Tacitus. In Which his Character as a Writer and an Historian, is Impartially Considered, and Compared with that of Livy* (1752), as cited in *Heritage*, p. 183.

63 Ginsburg, *Tradition and Theme*, p. 98.

64 Syme, *Tacitus*, p. 304.

65 *Ann.* 1.61; *Hist.* 3.71–2.

66 On Tacitus' use of *enargeia* to develop certain themes in the *Agricola* and *Annals*, see Elizabeth Keitel, 'No vivid writing, please: *euidentia* in the *Agricola* and the *Annals*', in Devillers, pp. 59–70.

67 *Ann.* 14.2; *Hist.* 4.81. On the value of anecdotes as historical evidence, see Richard Saller, 'Anecdotes as historical evidence for the principate', *Greece & Rome* 27 (1980), pp. 69–83.

68 *Ann.* 13.31.1.

69 Henry Furneaux, *The Annals of Tacitus*, vol. II: Books XI–XVI (Oxford, 1907), p. 193; Erich Koestermann, *Cornelius Tacitus: Annalen*, vol. III: Books 11–13 (Heidelberg, 1967), p. 294.

70 For the significance of empty years in chronicles, see Hayden White, *The Content of the Form: Narrative Discourse and Historical Representation* (Baltimore, MA, 1987), p. 11.

71 *Ann.* 4.32. The Latin particle *quippe* (the root of our English word 'quip') inflects the adjective 'unbroken' with a deep sense of sarcasm, which I have indicated with the parenthetical interjection; we might say, 'unbroken – yeah right'.

72 Ronald H. Martin and Anthony J. Woodman, *Tacitus: Annals Book IV* (Cambridge, 1989), p. 169.

73   *Ann.* 4.69.1.
74   Ibid. 5.9.1.
75   Ibid. 5.9.2.
76   Ibid. 6.23.2.
77   Henry Furneaux, *The* Annals *of Tacitus*, vol. I: Books I–VI, 2nd ed. (Oxford, 1896), p. 624; Erich Koestermann, *Cornelius Tacitus: Annalen. Band II: Buch 4–6* (Heidelberg, 1965), p. 296.
78   *Ann.* 13.25.
79   Ibid. 15.37.
80   Ibid. 13.35.3. For Montaigne, this is an example of Tacitus at his best; *Heritage*, p. 134: 'We may find him bold in his testimony, as when he maintains of a soldier who was carrying a load of wood that his hands became stiff with cold and stuck to his burden, so that they remained there attached and dead, having separated from his arms.'
81   *Ann.* 15.57.2.
82   Ibid. 1.65.7.
83   Goodyear, *The* Annals *of Tacitus Books 1–6*, vol. 1, p., 342–5 acknowledges that Tacitus will use periphrasis, but he wisely cautions against overanalysis.
84   Syme, *Tacitus*, p. 500; for an analysis of the shared literary culture of Tacitus and Juvenal, see Catherine Keane, 'Historian and satirist: Tacitus and Juvenal', in *Blackwell Companion*, pp. 403–27.
85   *Hist.* 3.25.3; cf. Juvenal 1.74: 'honesty is praised, and shivers'.
86   Patrick Sinclair, *Tacitus the Sententious Historian: A Sociology of Rhetoric in* Annales *1–6* (University Park, PA, 1995), p. 89 and *passim* for Tacitus' use of *sententiae* in the Tiberian hexad.
87   Cynthia Damon, *Tacitus: Histories Book I* (Cambridge, 2003), pp. 302–4.
88   *Ag.* 42.3.
89   *Hist* 1.49.4.
90   Ibid. 1.4.2.
91   *Ann.* 3.65.1; according to Anthony J. Woodman, '*praecipuum munus annalium*: the construction, convention and context of Tacitus, *Annals* 3.56.1', *Museum Helveticum* 52 (1995), pp. 111–26 Tacitus is not defining but defending the function of history.
92   Anthony J. Woodman and Ronald H. Martin, *The Annals of Tacitus Book 3* (Cambridge, 1996), p. 455.

IV. ROMANS AND OTHERS

1   Caesar, *Gallic Wars* 6.11–28; Sallust, *War Against Jugurtha* 17–19; Sallust, *Histories* fragments 2.1–11, 2.82–6, 3.10–15, 3.61–80; Tacitus, *Ag.* 10–17.
2   Velleius Paterculus 2.96.3 promised to write of Pannonians and Dalmatians, and Seneca the Younger wrote of India and Egypt, although these writings are now lost; see James B. Rives, *Tacitus: Germania* (Oxford, 1999), pp. 13–14.
3   Rives, *Tacitus: Germania*, p. 50.
4   James B. Rives, 'Germania', in *Blackwell Companion*, pp. 45–61.
5   For Rives, *Tacitus: Germania*, p. 55 the *Germania* moves from general to specific, from genus to species; for Ellen O'Gorman, 'No place like Rome: identity and difference in the *Germania* of Tacitus', *Ramus* 22 (1993), p. 136 the two halves undermine each other,

since the first half unites Germania and the second divides it. On the periegetic tradition, see James S. Romm, *The Edges of the Earth in Ancient Thought: Geography, Exploration, and Fiction* (Princeton, NJ, 1992), pp. 26–31.

6 Rives, *Tacitus: Germania*, p. 125.
7 *G.* 27.2.
8 Richard F. Thomas, 'The *Germania* as literary text', in *Cambridge Companion*, pp. 62–3.
9 Thomas, 'The *Germania* as literary text', p. 63.
10 *G.* 45.5.
11 Ibid. 46.4.
12 See Andrew G. Nichols, *Ctesias: on India* (London, 2011).
13 *Ann.* 2.41.1.
14 Pliny, *Epistles* 3.5.4.
15 Rives, *Tacitus: Germania*, p. 39.
16 *G.* 28.1.
17 Ibid. 2.1, 4.1.
18 Ibid. 18.1, 19.2, 20.1.
19 Ibid. 46.1.
20 Christopher B. Krebs, *A Most Dangerous Book: Tacitus's* Germania *from the Roman Empire to the Third Reich* (New York and London, 2011), pp. 182–3; see also Chapter VI.
21 Nancy Shumate, 'Postcolonial approaches to Tacitus', in *Blackwell Companion*, p. 479.
22 Rives, *Tacitus: Germania*, pp. 51, 63.
23 Rugii and Lemovii: *G.* 44.1; Sitones: *G.* 45.6.
24 *Ann.* 3.65.3.
25 Rhiannon Ash, 'Act like a German! Tacitus' *Germania* and national characterisation in the historical works', in Devillers, p. 187–8.
26 Caesar, *Gallic Wars* 1.1.3.
27 Ibid. 1.1.4.
28 *G.* 37.2.
29 Ibid. 2.1.
30 Ibid. 2.1.
31 Christopher Pelling, 'Tacitus' personal voice', in *Cambridge Companion*, p. 153.
32 Virgil, *Georgics* 2.149–50; for 'incessant', see Richard F. Thomas, *Virgil: Georgics*, vol. 1 (Cambridge, 1988), p. 184.
33 *G.* 26.4.
34 Virgil, *Georgics* 2.155: *egregias urbes*; G. 16.1: *nullas* [...] *urbes*.
35 See Timothy Joseph, 'Tacitus and epic', in *Blackwell Companion*, pp. 369–85.
36 Rives, *Tacitus: Germania*, p. 14.
37 Thomas, 'The *Germania* as literary text', p. 66.
38 Ibid., p. 62.
39 Virgil, *Georgics* 2.142.
40 *G.* 4.1.
41 Virgil, *Georgics* 2.136–8.
42 Ibid. 2.165–6.
43 *G.* 5.2.
44 Pelling, 'Tacitus' personal voice', p. 153.
45 *G.* 46.4.
46 Virgil, *Georgics* 2.174–6.

47 *G.* 6.2.
48 Ibid. 11.1.
49 Ibid. 16.1.
50 Ibid. 25.1.
51 Ibid. 19.1.
52 Several examples are collected by Rives, *Tacitus: Germania*, pp. 202–3; on the discourses of immorality in ancient Rome, see Catharine Edwards, *The Politics of Immorality in Ancient Rome* (Cambridge, 1993). On Ovid, see Carole E. Newlands, *Ovid* (London and New York, 2015), pp. 26–35.
53 *G.* 20.3.
54 Rives, *Tacitus: Germania*, p. 209; on legacy hunters in ancient Rome, see Keith Hopkins, *Death and Renewal: Sociological Studies in Roman History*, vol. 2 (Cambridge, 1983), pp. 238–47.
55 *G.* 22.3.
56 *Ag.* 43.3.
57 *Ann.* 1.11.2.
58 *G.* 27.1.
59 Rives, *Tacitus: Germania*, p. 224.
60 *Ann.* 2.83; 3.6.
61 *Ag.* 46.1.
62 *Ann.* 3.76.2.
63 Ronald Mellor, *Tacitus* (London and New York, 1993), p. 133.
64 *G.* 29.1.
65 Holly Haynes, *The History of Make-Believe: Tacitus on Imperial Rome* (Berkeley, 2003), p. 148. 'Julius' denotes he was among the many to receive Roman citizenship under Caesar, Augustus or Tiberius; by coincidence 'Civilis' befits his role in the civil wars.
66 *Hist.* 4.12.2–3.
67 *Ag.* 36.1.
68 *Corpus Inscriptionum Latinarum*, vol. III, no. 3676; Michael P. Speidel, *Riding for Caesar: The Roman Emperors' Horse Guards* (Cambridge, MA, 1994), p. 32.
69 Speidel, *Riding for Caesar*, pp. 1–24.
70 *Ann.* 2.6.3–4.
71 Ash, 'Act like a German!', p. 198.
72 Ronald Syme, *Tacitus*, 2 vols (Oxford, 1958), pp. 128–9.
73 Syme, *Tacitus*, p. 222.
74 Pliny, *Panegyricus* 14.5; Brian W. Jones, *The Emperor Domitian* (London and New York, 1992), p. 148.
75 *Ag.* 39.1.
76 *G.* 37.5.
77 Ash, 'Act like a German!', p. 187; see also Krebs, *A Most Dangerous Book*, p. 38 on Tacitus' impulse to write the *Germania* 'to disclose that all of *Germanien* was not yet conquered'.
78 Syme, *Tacitus*, p. 222.
79 Pliny, *Epistles* 8.4.1–2.
80 *G.* 37.2.
81 Ibid. 37.3.
82 Tim Cornell, 'The end of Roman imperial expansion', in John Rich and Graham Shipley (eds), *War and Society in the Roman World* (London, 1993), p. 141; for a review of the

theory of defensive imperialism see Eric Adler, *Valorizing the Barbarians: Enemy Speeches in Roman Historiography* (Austin, TX, 2011), pp. 1–4.

83 *G.* 37.4.

84 See Rives, *Tacitus: Germania*, p. 277 on Tacitus' misidentification of Cassius.

85 *Ann.* 1.11.4.

86 *G.* 37.4.

87 Ibid. 37.4–5.

88 *Ag.* 30.1; *Ann.* 12.34, 14.35.1.

89 *Ann.* 1.59.6.

90 Victoria E. Pagán, 'Distant voices of freedom in the *Annales* of Tacitus', *Studies in Latin Literature and Roman History* X (2000), pp. 358–69.

91 *Ann.* 12.37.2.

92 *Ag.* 21.

93 Alexandra Gajda, 'Tacitus and political thought in early modern Europe, c. 1530–c. 1640', in *Cambridge Companion*, p. 263.

94 E.g., Dylan Sailor, 'The *Agricola*', in *Blackwell Companion*, p. 31.

95 *Ag.* 41.2.

V. THEN AND NOW

1 Stephen Greenblatt, *The Swerve: How the World Became Modern* (New York and London, 2011) provides an engaging account of the discovery.

2 On the textual tradition of the minor works, see Charles E. Murgia, 'The textual transmission', in *Blackwell Companion*, pp. 16–21; Michael Winterbottom, 'The transmission of Tacitus' *Dialogus*', *Philologus* 116 (1972), pp. 114–28; on the survival and rediscovery of the *Germania* in particular, see Christopher B. Krebs, *A Most Dangerous Book: Tacitus's Germania from the Roman Empire to the Third Reich* (New York and London, 2011), pp. 56–80.

3 Alfred Gudeman, *P. Cornelii Taciti Dialogus de Oratoribus* (Boston, 1894), pp. xiii–xxii surveys early scholarship; Ronald H. Martin, *Tacitus* (Bristol, 1981), pp. 58–9 summarizes recent.

4 Pliny, *Epistles* 9.10.2. For the date, see Adrian N. Sherwin-White, *The Letters of Pliny: A Historical and Social Commentary* (Oxford, 1966), p. 487.

5 *Dial.* 9.6, 12.1.

6 Rebecca Edwards, 'Hunting for boars with Pliny and Tacitus', *Classical Antiquity* 27.1 (2008), pp. 35–58 examines intertextual references between the *Dialogue* and letters of Pliny to suggest that Tacitus may have revised the *Dialogue* over the years, thus making it even more difficult to ascertain the date of publication. For further correspondences between Tacitus and the letters of Pliny, see Christopher Whitton, '"Let us tread our path together": Tacitus and the Younger Pliny', in *Blackwell Companion*, pp. 345–68.

7 Charles E. Murgia, 'The length of the lacuna in Tacitus' *Dialogus*', *California Studies in Classical Antiquity* 12 (1979), p. 232.

8 Roland Mayer, *Tacitus: Dialogus de Oratoribus* (Cambridge, 2001), pp. 49–50.

9 *Ag.* 2.3, 3.1.

10 Ronald Syme, *Tacitus*, 2 vols (Oxford, 1958), pp. 670–3; Martin, *Tacitus*, pp. 59–60;

Steven H. Rutledge, 'Tacitus' *Dialogus de oratoribus*: a socio-cultural history', in *Blackwell Companion*, pp. 63–4.

11   *Ann.* 2.88.3.

12   Ibid. 3.55.5.

13   On the displaced aristocrat, see Nancy Shumate, *Nation, Empire, Decline: Studies in Rhetorical Continuity from the Romans to the Modern Era* (London, 2006), pp. 122–6.

14   *Ann.* 3.55.5; Judith Ginsburg, '*in maiores certamina*: past and present in the *Annals*', in *Tacitus and the Tacitean Tradition*, pp. 86–8.

15   Syme, *Tacitus*, p. 565.

16   *Ann.* 3.55.1–5.

17   Livy 39.6.7–9; Polybius 9.10; Sallust, *War Against Catiline* 11.6.

18   Anthony J. Woodman and Ronald H. Martin, *The Annals of Tacitus Book 3* (Cambridge, 1996), pp. 404–5; Anthony J. Woodman (trans.), *Tacitus: The Annals* (Indianapolis, IN, 2004), p. 110, note 117.

19   *Ann.* 13.1.1, 1.6.1.

20   *Dial.* 1.1.

21   Ibid. 1.2. Cf. Sander M. Goldberg, 'The faces of eloquence: the *Dialogus de Oratoribus*' in *Cambridge Companion*, p. 74: 'The question never receives an unequivocal answer in an authorial voice.'

22   *Dial.* 1.3.

23   See Erik Gunderson, *Declamation, Paternity, and Roman Identity: Authority and the Rhetorical Self* (Cambridge, 2003), pp. 29–31 for his observations on the role of memory in Seneca the Elder.

24   Plutarch, *Otho* 9; Quintilian, *Institutes of Oratory* 12.10.11.

25   Christopher van den Berg, *The World of Tacitus' Dialogus de Oratoribus: Aesthetics and Empire in Ancient Rome* (Cambridge, 2014), p. 58.

26   Cf. Goldberg, 'The faces of eloquence', p. 82.

27   *Dial.* 11.2.

28   *Hist.* 1.37.5.

29   *Ann.* 15.34.2.

30   See Timothy D. Barnes, 'Curiatius Maternus', *Hermes* 109.3 (1981), pp. 382–4 and 'The significance of Tacitus' *Dialogus de Oratoribus*', *Harvard Studies in Classical Philology* 90 (1986), pp. 225–44.

31   Teacher: *D.* 2.1; 'new man' and provincial: ibid. 7.1; in Britain: ibid. 17.4; Syme, *Tacitus*, p. 799; see also Barnes, 'The significance of Tacitus' *Dialogus*', p. 236–7.

32   For rehabilitations of Aper see Craig Champion, '*Dialogus* 5.3–10.8: a reconsideration of the character of Marcus Aper', *Phoenix* 48 (1994), pp. 152–63; Sander M. Goldberg, 'Appreciating Aper: the defence of modernity in Tacitus' *Dialogus de Oratoribus*', *Classical Quarterly* 49.1 (1999), pp. 224–37.

33   'Objectionable': Barnes, 'The significance of Tacitus' *Dialogus*', p. 236; *arriviste*: Goldberg, 'The faces of eloquence', p. 77; 'brashness [...] vulgar sense of values': Gordon Williams, *Change and Decline: Roman Literature in the Early Empire* (Berkeley, CA, 1978), p. 28.

34   Goldberg, 'Appreciating Aper', p. 237.

35   C. O. Brink, 'History in the *Dialogus de Oratoribus* and Tacitus the historian: a new approach to an old source', *Hermes* 121.3 (1993), p. 339; 'champion of the modern day', Mayer, *Tacitus: Dialogus de Oratoribus*, p. 45.

36   Mayer, *Tacitus: Dialogus de Oratoribus*, p. 47.

37 Ronald Syme, *The Augustan Aristocracy* (Oxford, 1986), pp. 241–2.
38 *Hist.* 3.9.3.
39 *Hist.* 3.9.3, 3.18.2; Gwyn Morgan, *69 A.D.: The Year of Four Emperors* (Oxford, 2006), pp. 282–3.
40 *Hist.* 3.25.2, 3.28.
41 Ibid. 4.42.2.
42 Ibid. 4.44.
43 Syme, *Tacitus*, p. 102; Goldberg, 'Appreciating Aper', p. 228.
44 On the reception of Cato in the Neronian period, see John P. Sullivan, *Literature and Politics in the Age of Nero* (Ithaca, NY, and London, 1985), pp. 117–19.
45 *Dial.* 3.2, 3.3.
46 Mayer, *Tacitus: Dialogus de Oratoribus*, p. 96.
47 Suetonius, *Domitian* 10.4.
48 *Dial.* 4.1.
49 Eleventh wealthiest Roman on record according to Steven H. Rutledge, *Imperial Inquisitions: Prosecutors and Informants from Tiberius to Domitian* (London and New York, 2001), pp. 225–8.
50 Martial, *Epigrams* 4.54.7; Suetonius, *Domitian* 3.1.
51 Rhiannon Ash, *Tacitus: Histories Book II* (Cambridge, 2007), pp. 102–3.
52 *Hist.* 2.10.
53 Juvenal, 4.81–93, translation by Susanna Morton Braund, *Juvenal and Persius* (Cambridge, MA, 2004), pp. 203–5.
54 *Dial.* 11.1.
55 Virgil, *Aeneid* 1.254.
56 *Dial.* 12.6.
57 Ibid. 13.5; Virgil, *Georgics* 2.475.
58 *Dial.* 13.6.
59 Arrival of Alcibiades: Plato, *Symposium* 212c3–215a3. June Allison, 'Tacitus' *Dialogus* and Plato's *Symposium*', *Hermes* 127.4 (1999), pp. 479–92 argues for Tacitus' direct engagement with Plato, deliberately bypassing Cicero so as to underscore the uselessness of political oratory.
60 *Dial* 14.2.
61 Ibid. 16.7.
62 Edwards, 'Hunting for boars', p. 51.
63 *Dial.* 26.8.
64 *Ann.* 4.33.4.
65 Juvenal, 1.170–1; on the implications of the promise see Catherine Keane, 'Historian and satirist: Tacitus and Juvenal', in *Blackwell Companion*, p. 408.
66 *Ann.* 4.34.
67 *Dial.* 27.1.
68 Ibid. 27.3.
69 On the significance of the interstitial passages of the *Dialogue*, see van den Berg, *The World of Tacitus'* Dialogus, pp. 98–123.
70 On the *Dialogue* as a rich source of social history see Rutledge, 'Tacitus' *Dialogus de oratoribus*: a socio-cultural history', pp. 64–6, and on Messalla pp. 75–6.
71 *G.* 20.1; *Dial.* 28.5.
72 *Dial.* 29.1.

73 *Ag.* 4.2.
74 *Dial.* 29–30.
75 Ibid. 32.4.
76 Ibid. 34.1.
77 Ibid. 35.1.
78 In fact a corpus of Roman declamations survives for us to evaluate for ourselves against Messalla's wholly negative attitude towards the practice; see Gunderson, *Declamation, Paternity, and Roman Identity.*
79 *Dial.* 40.2.
80 Thomas John Keeline, 'A rhetorical figure: Cicero in the early Empire', Ph.D. diss. (Harvard University, 2014), p. 24. Shadi Bartsch, *Actors in the Audience: Theatricality and Doublespeak from Nero to Hadrian* (Cambridge, MA, 1994), pp. 110–14 proposes that Maternus is employing 'doublespeak', that is, he offers two meanings to two different audiences.
81 *Dial.* 42.
82 See Elizabeth Keitel, '"Is dying so very terrible?" The Neronian *Annals*', in *Cambridge Companion*, p. 143 on another example of Tacitus' reconsidering a judgement 'nearly two decades later'.
83 *Dial.* 21.2: *auribus iudicum accommodata*; *Ann.* 13.3.1: *temporis eius auribus accommodatum.*
84 Suetonius, *Nero* 8; Dio 61.3.1.
85 Such agreement in detail suggests a common source, hostile to Seneca, according to Ettore Paratore, *Tacito* (Rome, 1962), p. 468.
86 Ronald Mellor, *Tacitus* (London and New York, 1993), p. 131; Miriam T. Griffin, *Seneca: A Philosopher in Politics* (Oxford, 1976), p. 416; Christopher Star, *The Empire of the Self: Self-Command and Political Speech in Seneca and Petronius* (Baltimore, MA, 2012), p. 149; Paul Plass, *Wit and the Writing of History: The Rhetoric of Historiography in Imperial Rome* (Madison, WI, 1988), p. 8.
87 Humour is not unusual at the end of a dialogue: Mayer, *Tacitus: Dialogus de Oratoribus*, p. 216. Holly Haynes, 'The in- and outside of history: Tacitus with Groucho Marx', in Devillers, p. 31, highlights the themes of inclusion and exclusion inherent in the change of subjects (*they* [...] *we*).
88 *Dial.* 1.4.
89 Ibid. 15.1, 21.1, 23.1, 39.1.
90 Cf. van den Berg, *The World of Tacitus'* Dialogus, p. 34: 'The kernel of criticism seems to take aim at Nero's reliance on someone who cannot adequately differentiate between form and content.'
91 Gérard Genette, *Palimpsests: Literature in the Second Degree*, trans C. Newman and C. Doubinsky (Lincoln, NE, 1997), pp. 229–35.
92 *Dial.* 3.1.
93 Ibid.; Olivier Devillers, 'Les *opera minora* "laboratoire" des opera maiora', in Devillers, p. 21; Syme, *Tacitus*, p. 591; Thomas E. Strunk, 'Offending the powerful: Tacitus' *Dialogus de Oratoribus* and safe criticism', *Mnemosyne* 63 (2010), p. 249.
94 *Ann.* 13.4.2.
95 See Leanne Bablitz, 'Bringing the law home: the Roman house as courtroom', in K. Tuori (ed.), *Public and Private in the Roman House* (*Journal of Roman Archaeology* Supplement, 2015), p. 66 on the use of the *cubiculum* as a space for Roman juridical proceedings.

96 *Ag.* 3.3: 'I shall not regret, even if in language unskilled and plain, recounting the history of our earlier servitude and the testimony of our present happiness'; for Anthony J. Woodman with Christina S. Kraus, *Tacitus: Agricola* (Cambridge, 2014), p. 92 'our earlier servitude' is a reference to the age of Domitian, which was covered in the lost books of the *Histories*. Tacitus is more specific at *Hist.* 1.1.4: 'But if my life should last long enough, I have set aside for my old age the principate of Divine Nerva and the imperial command of Trajan, material richer and safer.' *Ann.* 3.24.3: 'As for the deaths of the others, I shall recount the rest of that era, should I live long enough for more work, once the present undertakings are completed'; this promise to narrate the age of Augustus was never fulfilled. Anthony J. Woodman, 'Questions of date, genre, and style in Velleius: some literary answers', *Classical Quarterly* 25 (1975), p. 288: 'no one really believes that any of these authors themselves intended actually to write such future works.'

97 *Dial.* 3.4; Mayer, *Tacitus: Dialogus de Oratoribus*, p. 97; Syme, *Tacitus*, p. 110.

98 Dial. 42.1; Mayer, *Tacitus: Dialogus de Oratoribus*, p. 216.

99 *Dial.* 2.1.

100 Ibid. 26.2: 'Indeed, neither for an orator or even a man is that style becoming which is adopted by many of the speakers of our age, and which, with its redundancy of words, its meaningless periods and licence for expression, imitates the art of an actor.' Ibid. 29.3: 'a liking for actors and a passion for gladiators and horses' are inborn, according to Messalla; we might compare this *equorum studia* for Nero's *regimen equorum* at 13.3.3. Acting as a cause of Nero's downfall: *Ann.* 15.67.2.

101 *Dial.* 9.1, 9.4.

102 Cf. van den Berg, *The World of Tacitus'* Dialogus, p. 34: 'Tacitus [...] demonstrates the association of eloquence with government in the Roman mind, as well as the desire to see coherent patterns of development that can be thought of in moral terms.' Otho is the only other *princeps* whom Tacitus records as needing a ghostwriter, and the portrait is not flattering at all, *Hist.* 1.90.2.

103 Devillers, 'Les *opera minora* "laboratoire" des opera maiora', p. 27. We might take *Dial.* 17.3 and *Ann.* 13.3.2 as evidence of Syme's perennial contention that Tacitus made a mistake by beginning the *Annals* with the death of Tiberius instead of an earlier date: Syme, *Tacitus*, pp. 368–74, 427–31; idem, *Ten Studies in Tacitus* (Oxford, 1970), p. 6; idem, 'History or biography: the case of Tiberius Caesar', *Historia* 23 (1974), pp. 483–4; idem, *History in Ovid* (Oxford, 1978), pp. 197–8; idem, 'How Tacitus wrote *Annals* 1–3', in Anthony Birley (ed.), *Roman Papers*, vol. 3 (Oxford, 1984), pp. 1027–8, 1041–2; idem, *The Augustan Aristocracy* (Oxford, 1986), pp. 115, 161, 212, 234, 433. Whether Tacitus reckons from Octavian (*Dial.* 17.3), Julius Caesar (*Ann.* 13.3.2), or the death of Augustus (*Ann.* 1.11), his periodization always corresponds to a principate.

104 Devillers, 'Les *opera minora* "laboratoire" des opera maiora', p. 30.

VI. YESTERDAY AND TODAY

1 Francesco Guicciardini, *Ricordi* (1512–30), as cited in Daniel Kapust, 'Tacitus and political thought', in *Blackwell Companion*, p. 504.

2 The labels were first applied in 1921 by Giuseppe Toffanin; see also Ronald Mellor, *Tacitus* (London and New York, 1993), p. 145; and Kapust, 'Tacitus and political thought', p. 504.

3   Pedro de Ribadeneyra, *Religion and the Virtues of the Christian Prince against Machiavelli* (1595), as cited in *Heritage*, p. 67.

4   *Heritage*, p. 31.

5   Suetonius, *Gaius (Caligula)* 24.

6   Tertullian, *Apologeticum* 16.

7   *Ann.* 15.44.2–5.

8   Gillian Clark, *Christianity and Roman Society* (Cambridge, 2004), pp. 47–53.

9   *Ann.* 15.39.3.

10   Monica Silveira Cyrino, *Big Screen Rome* (Malden, MA, 2005), pp. 21, 30. See also the interpretation of 'toga movies' by William Fitzgerald, 'Oppositions, anxieties and ambiguities in the toga movie', in *Imperial Projections*, pp. 23–49, and problems faced by the makers of the movie *Spartacus*, as discussed by Alison Futrell, 'Seeing Red: Spartacus as domestic economist', in *Imperial Projections*, pp. 77–118.

11   Catherine Keane, 'Historian and satirist: Tacitus and Juvenal', in *Blackwell Companion*, pp. 411–12; Voltaire appreciated Tacitus for his satirical twist: 'I regard Tacitus as a satirist sparkling with wit, knowledgeable of men and courts, and skewering an emperor for all eternity in a few words', as cited in *Heritage*, p. 152.

12   Clarence W. Mendell, *Tacitus: The Man and his Works* (New Haven, CT, and London, 1957), pp. 225–6. It is also possible that Dio and Tacitus were drawing on the same, now lost, source: see David S. Potter, 'Tacitus' sources', in *Blackwell Companion*, pp. 130–5.

13   *Scriptores Historiae Augustae, Tacitus* 10.3. By *historiae Augustae* we assume Vopiscus means a history of emperors after Augustus, and not a history of the age of Augustus, which Tacitus promised but never delivered.

14   Friedrich Leo, 'Tacitus' (1896), as cited in *Heritage*, p. 229.

15   Jerome, *Commentary on Zacchariah*, as cited in Mendell, *Tacitus*, p. 228.

16   Mendell, *Tacitus*, pp. 229–30.

17   Cassiodorus, *Variarum Libri* 5.2, citing *G.* 45.4–5; Mendell, *Tacitus*, p. 232; Ronald H. Martin, *Tacitus* (Bristol, 1981), p. 236.

18   Christopher B. Krebs, *A Most Dangerous Book: Tacitus's Germania from the Roman Empire to the Third Reich* (New York and London, 2011), 63–4; Mendell, *Tacitus*, p. 235.

19   Ronald H. Martin, 'From manuscript to print', in *Cambridge Companion*, pp. 244, 248.

20   Martin, *Tacitus*, p. 238; idem, 'From manuscript to print', p. 244.

21   For a complete history of the printed text, see Mendell, *Tacitus*, pp. 349–78.

22   *G.* 4.1.

23   On the Nazi hunt for the manuscript, see Simon Schama, *Landscape and Memory* (New York, 1996), pp. 75–81; quote from p. 81.

24   Charles E. Murgia, 'The textual transmission', *Blackwell Companion*, p. 17. On the Liceo, see http://tinyurl.com/zrgmnpx (last accessed 3 October 2016). Please note that the text on the web page is in Italian.

25   Leo, 'Tacitus', as cited in *Heritage*, p. 226.

26   Cary Nederman, 'Niccolò Machiavelli', in Edward N. Zalta (ed.), *The Stanford Encyclopedia of Philosophy*, winter 2014 edition. Available at http://plato.stanford.edu/archives/win2014/entries/machiavelli/ (last accessed 3 October 2016).

27   *Ann.* 13.19.1.

28   *Hist.* 4.3.2.

29   Arnaldo Momigliano, *The Classical Foundations of Modern Historiography* (Berkeley, CA, 1990), p. 122.

30 Giovanni Botero, *Reason of State* (1589), as cited in *Heritage*, p. 51.

31 Traiano Boccalini, *News from Parnassus* (1612), as cited in *Heritage*, p. 55.

32 *Heritage*, p. 52.

33 Krebs, *A Most Dangerous Book*, pp. 83–91.

34 Herbert Benario, 'Conrad Celtis and the city of Nürnberg', *Classical Outlook* 82.3 (2005), p. 103.

35 *Ann.* 2.88.2–3.

36 Rhiannon Ash, *Tacitus (Ancients in Action)* (Bristol, 2006), p. 134.

37 Ash, *Tacitus*, p. 135.

38 James Booker, 'The major Hermansschlacht dramas', Ph.D. diss. (University of Nebraska, 1975).

39 Martin Winkler, *Arminius the Liberator: Myth and Ideology* (Oxford, 2016), pp. 65–79; H. Kesting, *Die Befreier Arminius im Lichte der geschichtlichen Quellen und der wissenschaftlichen Forschung* (Detmold, 1962), pp. 112–27.

40 P. Barbon and B. Plachta, '"Chi la dura la vince" – "Wer ausharrt, siegt." Arminius auf der Opernbühne des 18. Jahrhunderts', in R. Wiegels and W. Woesler (eds), *Arminius und die Varusschlacht: Geschichte – Mythos – Literatur* (Paderborn, 1995); Herbert Benario, 'Arminius into Hermann: history into legend', *Greece & Rome* 51.1 (2004), p. 89.

41 Walter Schlüter, 'The Battle of the Teutoburg Forest: Archaeological Research at Kalkriese near Osnabrück', in John D. Creighton and R. J. A. Wilson (eds), *Roman Germany: Studies in Cultural Interaction (Journal of Roman Archaeology* Supplement, 1996), pp. 123–59. On the film, see Cornelius Völker, 'Monumental, magisch, masslos: Deutschland im Jahr 9! Die Hermansschlacht Der Spielfilm', *Grabbe-Jahrbüch* 15 (1996), pp. 38–47 and Winkler, *Arminius the Liberator*, pp. 218–26.

42 Michel de Montaigne, 'Of the art of discussion' (1580), as cited in *Heritage*, pp. 132, 132, 133.

43 René Rapin, 'Reflections upon history', as cited in *Heritage*, p. 137.

44 Dominique Bohours, 'La manière de la bien pensée dans les ouvrages d'esprit', as cited in *Heritage*, p. 138.

45 Sir Henry Savile, *The End of Nero and Beginning of Galba* (1598), as cited in *Heritage*, p. 83.

46 Ben Jonson, 'Epigram 95 "To Sir Henry Savile"' (1604), lines 1–6, as cited in *Heritage*, p. 102.

47 Kapust, 'Tacitus and political thought', pp. 512–14.

48 *Heritage*, pp. 116–21.

49 Sir John Eliot, 'Speech to the House of Commons' (1626), as cited in *Heritage*, p. 122.

50 *Heritage*, p. 125.

51 Victor Hugo, *Napoleon the Little (The Works of Victor Hugo)* (Boston, 1909), p. 293.

52 Paul Cartledge, 'Gibbon and Tacitus', in *Cambridge Companion*, p. 270.

53 In Max Harold Fisch and Thomas Goddard Bergin (trans.), *The Autobiography of Giambattista Vico* (Ithaca, NY, 1963), pp. 138–9.

54 Kapust, 'Tacitus and political thought', p. 517.

55 Ronald Syme, 'Augustus and Agrippa', *Classical Review* 51.5 (1937), p. 194.

56 Idem, *The Roman Revolution* (Oxford, 1939), pp. 191, 15.

57 Mark Toher, 'Tacitus' Syme', in *Cambridge Companion*, p. 325.

58 John B. Hainsworth, 'The starting-point of Tacitus' *Histories*: fear or favor by omission?', *Greece & Rome* 11.2 (1964), p. 128.

59 Martha Malamud, 'Tacitus and the twentieth-century novel', in *Cambridge Companion*, pp. 300–16.

60   Sandra R. Joshel, '*I, Claudius*: projection and imperial soap opera', in *Imperial Projections*, p. 124; Malamud, 'Tacitus and the twentieth-century novel', pp. 300–1. Both provide vivid background on Graves' personal experience in World War I that surely shaped his literary output. On Graves' profound influence on the reception of classics in the twentieth century, see the contributions in Alisdair G. G. Gibson (ed.), *Robert Graves and the Classical Tradition* (Oxford, 2015).

61   See Joshel, '*I, Claudius*'.

62   Malamud, 'Tacitus and the twentieth-century novel', pp. 308–9.

63   Ibid., p. 315; see also Mellor, *Tacitus*, pp. 229–35.

64   Marguerite Yourcenar, *The Memoirs of Hadrian and Reflections on the Composition of the Memoirs of Hadrian*, translated from the French by Grace Frick in collaboration with the author (New York, 1974), p. 20.

65   Ibid., pp. 297–315.

66   Ibid., p. 60.

67   Malamud, 'Tacitus and the twentieth-century novel', p. 316.

68   Herbert Benario, 'Boudicca Warrior Queen', *Classical Outlook* 84.2 (2007), p. 72.

69   *Ann.* 14.35.2.

70   See Judy Chicago, photography by Donald Woodman, *The Dinner Party: From Creation to Preservation* (London, 2007).

71   Jean Racine, '"Second Preface" to *Britannicus*' (1676) as cited in *Heritage*, p. 140.

72   *Ann.* 2.12–13. Herbert Benario, 'Tacitus, Germanicus, and *Henry V*, *Notes and Queries* 255 (2010) pp. 372–3; idem, 'Shakespearean debt to Tacitus' *Histories*', *Notes and Queries* 253 (2008), pp. 202–5 on Shakespeare's debt to Tacitus' *Histories* in *Richard II*.

73   Gary Taylor, 'The butcher of Rome', *The Guardian*, 18 July 2005, maps George Bush onto Sejanus with alarming accuracy: https://www.theguardian.com/stage/2005/jul/18/theatre.stage (last accessed 3 October 2016).

74   *Ann.* 2.40; Jo-Marie Claassen, *N. P. van Wyk Louw: Germanicus* (Dragonfly eBook, 2013), Scene vi. The original play does not have scene or line numbers, so in the preface Claassen recommends that quotations be found in the eBook using the search function.

75   Claassen, *Germanicus*, Scene v.

76   Ibid., Scene vi.

77   Ibid., introduction.

78   On Kiefer's explorations of postwar German national identity, see Andreas Huyssen, 'Anselm Kiefer: the terror of history, the temptation of myth', *October* 48 (1989); Schama, *Landscape and Memory*, pp. 120–34; Winkler, *Arminius the Liberator*, pp. 210–13.

79   *Ann.* 1.61.

80   Frank Bidart, 'The Return', in *Desire* (New York, 1997), pp. 18–19.

81   Ibid., p. 22.

82   Ibid.

83   Scott Ordway, 'Composer's Note', 'North Woods: eight women's voices' (Philadelphia, PA, 2014).

BIBLIOGRAPHY

Adler, Eric, *Valorizing the Barbarians: Enemy Speeches in Roman Historiography* (Austin, TX, 2011).

Ahl, Frederick M., *Lucan: An Introduction* (Ithaca, NY, and London, 1976).

—— 'The art of safe criticism in Greece and Rome', *American Journal of Philology* 105 (1984), pp. 174–208.

Allison, June, 'Tacitus' *Dialogus* and Plato's *Symposium*', *Hermes* 127.4 (1999), pp. 479–92.

Ash, Rhiannon, *Tacitus (Ancients in Action)* (Bristol, 2006).

—— *Tacitus: Histories Book II* (Cambridge, 2007).

—— 'Fission and fusion: shifting Roman identities in the *Histories*', in *Cambridge Companion*, pp. 85–99.

—— 'Act like a German! Tacitus' *Germania* and national characterisation in the historical works', in Devillers, pp. 185–200.

Bablitz, Leanne, 'The selection of advocates for repetundae trials: the cases of Pliny the Younger', *Athenaeum* 97 (2009), pp. 197–208.

—— 'Tacitus on trial(s)', in Lee Brice and Daniëlle Slootjes (eds), *Aspects of Ancient Institutions and Geography: Studies in Honor of Richard J. A. Talbert* (Leiden, 2015), pp. 65–83.

—— 'Bringing the law home: the Roman house as courtroom', in Kaius Tuori (ed.), *Public and Private in the Roman House* (*Journal of Roman Archaeology* Supplement, 2015), pp. 63–76.

Barbon, Paolo and Bodo Plachta, '"Chi la dura la vince" – "Wer ausharrt, siegt". Arminius auf der Opernbühne des 18. Jahrhunderts', in Rainer Wiegels and Winfried Woesler (eds), *Arminius und die Varusschlacht: Geschichte – Mythos – Literatur* (Paderborn, 1995), pp. 265–90.

Barnes, Timothy D., 'Curiatius Maternus', *Hermes* 109.3 (1981), pp. 382–4.

———'The significance of Tacitus' *Dialogus de Oratoribus*', *Harvard Studies in Classical Philology* 90 (1986), pp. 225–44.

Bartsch, Shadi, *Actors in the Audience: Theatricality and Doublespeak from Nero to Hadrian* (Cambridge, MA, 1994).

Bellemore, Jane, 'The identity of Drusus: the making of a princeps', in Alisdair G. G. Gibson (ed.), *The Julio-Claudian Succession: Reality and Perception of the 'Augustan Model'* (Leiden, 2013), pp. 79–94.

Benario, Herbert, 'Arminius into Hermann: history into legend', *Greece & Rome* 51.1 (2004), pp. 83–94.

———'Conrad Celtis and the city of Nürnberg', *Classical Outlook* 82.3 (2005), pp. 101–4.

———'Boudica warrior queen', *Classical Outlook* 84.2 (2007), pp. 70–3.

———'Shakespearean debt to Tacitus' *Histories*', *Notes and Queries* 253 (2008), pp. 202–5.

———'Tacitus, Germanicus, and *Henry V*', *Notes and Queries* 255 (2010), pp. 372–3.

Bennett, Julian, *Trajan Optimus Princeps: A Life and Times* (Bloomington, IN, 1997).

Bidart, Frank, *Desire* (New York, 1997).

Birley, Anthony R. 'The life and death of Cornelius Tacitus', *Historia* 49.2 (2000), pp. 230–47.

Booker, James, 'The major Hermannsschlacht dramas', Ph.D. diss. (University of Nebraska, 1975).

Braund, Susanna Morton, *Juvenal: Satires Book 1* (Cambridge, 1996).

———*Juvenal and Persius* (Cambridge, MA, 2004).

Brink, Charles O., 'History in the *Dialogus de Oratoribus* and Tacitus the historian: a new approach to an old source', *Hermes* 121.3 (1993), pp. 335–49.

———'Can Tacitus' *Dialogus* be dated? Evidence and historical conclusions', *Harvard Studies in Classical Philology* 96 (1994), pp. 251–80.

Burke, Peter, 'Tacitism', in Thomas A. Dorey (ed.), *Tacitus* (New York, 1969), pp. 149–71.

Cartledge, Paul, 'Gibbon and Tacitus', in *Cambridge Companion*, pp. 269–79.

Champion, Craig, '*Dialogus* 5.3–10.8: a reconsideration of the character of Marcus Aper', *Phoenix* 48 (1994), pp. 152–63.

Chicago, Judy, *The Dinner Party: From Creation to Preservation*, photography by Donald Woodman (London, 2007).

Claassen, Jo-Marie, *N. P. van Wyk Louw: Germanicus* (Dragonfly eBook, 2013).

Clark, Gillian, *Christianity and Roman Society* (Cambridge, 2004).

Cornell, Tim, 'The end of Roman imperial expansion', in John Rich and Graham Shipley (eds), *War and Society in the Roman World* (London, 1993), pp. 139–71.

Cyrino, Monica Silveira, *Big Screen Rome* (Malden, MA, 2005).

Damon, Cynthia, *Tacitus: Histories Book 1* (Cambridge, 2003).

———(trans.), *Tacitus, Annals* (London and New York, 2012).

Devillers, Olivier, 'The concentration of power and writing history: forms of historical persuasion in the *Histories* (1.1–49)', in *Blackwell Companion*, pp. 162–86.

———'Les *opera minora* "laboratoire" des opera maiora', in Devillers, pp. 13–30.

Dickinson, Emily, *Collected Poems* (Philadelphia, PA, 1991).

Eck, Werner, Antonio Caballos and Fernando Fernández (eds), *Das senatus consultum de Cn. Pisone Patre* (Munich, 1996).

Edwards, Catharine, *The Politics of Immorality in Ancient Rome* (Cambridge, 1993).

Edwards, Rebecca, 'Hunting for boars with Pliny and Tacitus', *Classical Antiquity* 27.1 (2008), pp. 35–58.

Erasmo, Mario, *Reading Death in Ancient Rome* (Columbus, OH, 2008).

Everitt, Anthony, *Hadrian and the Triumph of Rome* (New York, 2009).

Feeney, Denis, *Beyond Greek: The Beginnings of Latin Literature* (Cambridge, MA, 2016).

Fisch, Max Harold and Thomas Goddard Bergin (trans.), *The Autobiography of Giambattista Vico* (Ithaca, NY, 1963).

Fitzgerald, William, 'Oppositions, anxieties, and ambiguities in the toga movie', in *Imperial Projections*, pp. 23–49.

Flower, Harriet, *The Art of Forgetting: Disgrace and Oblivion in Roman Political Culture* (Chapel Hill, NC, 2011).

Furneaux, Henry, *The* Annals *of Tacitus*, vol. I: Books I–VI, 2nd ed. (Oxford, 1896).

—— *The* Annals *of Tacitus*, vol. II: Books XI–XVI (Oxford, 1907).

Futrell, Alison, 'Seeing red: Spartacus as domestic economist', in *Imperial Projections*, pp. 77–118.

Gajda, Alexandra, 'Tacitus and political thought in early modern Europe, c. 1530–c. 1640', in *Cambridge Companion*, pp. 253–68.

Genette, Gérard, *Palimpsests: Literature in the Second Degree*, translated by Channa Newman and Claude Doubinsky (Lincoln, NE, 1997).

Gibson, Alisdair G. G. (ed.), *Robert Graves and the Classical Tradition* (Oxford, 2015).

Ginsburg, Judith, *Tradition and Theme in the* Annals *of Tacitus* (New York, 1981).

—— '*In maiores certamina*: past and present in the *Annals*', in *Tacitus and the Tacitean Tradition*, pp. 86–103.

Goldberg, Sander M., 'Appreciating Aper: the defense of modernity in Tacitus' *Dialogus de Oratoribus*', *Classical Quarterly* 49.1 (1999), pp. 224–37.

—— 'The faces of eloquence: the *Dialogus de Oratoribus*', in *Cambridge Companion*, pp. 73–84.

Goodyear, Francis R. D., *The Annals of Tacitus, Books 1–6*, vol. 1: *Annals* 1.1–54 (Cambridge, 1972).

Gowing, Alain M., 'From the annalists to the *Annales*: Latin historiography before Tacitus', in *Cambridge Companion*, pp. 17–30.

Greenblatt, Stephen, *The Swerve: How the World Became Modern* (New York and London, 2011).

Griffin, Miriam T., *Seneca: A Philosopher in Politics* (Oxford, 1976).

—— 'The Lyons Tablet and Tacitean hindsight', *Classical Quarterly* 32.2 (1982), pp. 404–18.

Gudeman, Alfred, *P. Cornelii Taciti: Dialogus de Oratoribus* (Boston, MA, 1894).

Gunderson, Erik, *Declamation, Paternity, and Roman Identity: Authority and the Rhetorical Self* (Cambridge, 2003).

Hadas, Moses, *Gibbon's The Decline and Fall of the Roman Empire* (New York, 1962).

Hainsworth, John B., 'The starting-point of Tacitus' *Historiae*: fear or favor by omission?', *Greece & Rome* 11.2 (1964), pp. 128–36.

Haynes, Holly, *The History of Make-Believe: Tacitus on Imperial Rome* (Berkeley, CA, 2003).

—— 'Survival and memory in the *Agricola*', *Arethusa* 39.2 (2006), pp. 149–70.

—— 'Tacitus' history and mine', in *Blackwell Companion*, pp. 282–304.

—— 'The in- and outside of history: Tacitus with Groucho Marx', in Devillers, pp. 31–44.

Hopkins, Keith, *Death and Renewal: Sociological Studies in Roman History*, vol. 2 (Cambridge, 1983).

Hugo, Victor, *The Works of Victor Hugo* (Boston, MA, 1909).

Huyssen, Andreas, 'Anselm Kiefer: the terror of history, the temptation of myth', *October* 48 (1989), pp. 25–46.

Janson, Tore, *Latin Prose Prefaces: Studies in Literary Conventions* (Stockholm, 1964).

Jones, Brian W., *The Emperor Domitian* (London and New York, 1992).

Joseph, Timothy, 'Tacitus and epic', in *Blackwell Companion*, pp. 369–85.

Joshel, Sandra R. '*I, Claudius*: projection and imperial soap opera', in *Imperial Projections*, pp. 119–61.

Kapust, Daniel, 'Tacitus and political thought', in *Blackwell Companion*, pp. 504–28.

Karnow, Stanley, *Vietnam: A History* (New York, 1983).

Keane, Catherine, 'Historian and satirist: Tacitus and Juvenal', in *Blackwell Companion*, pp. 403–27.

Keeline, Thomas John, 'A rhetorical figure: Cicero in the early Empire', Ph.D. diss. (Harvard University, 2014).

Keitel, Elizabeth, '"Is dying so very terrible?" The Neronian *Annals*', in *Cambridge Companion*, pp. 127–43.

—— '"No vivid writing please!": *Evidentia* in the *Agricola* and the *Annals*', in Devillers, pp. 59–70.

Kelley, Donald R., '*Tacitus Noster*: The *Germania* in the Renaissance and Reformation', in *Tacitus and the Tacitean Tradition*, pp. 152–67.

Kesting, H., *Die Befreier Arminius im Lichte der geschichtlichen Quellen und der wissenschaftlichen Forschung* (Detmold, 1962).

Koestermann, Erich, *Cornelius Tacitus: Annalen*, vol. II: Books 4–6 (Heidelberg, 1965).

—— *Cornelius Tacitus: Annalen*, vol. III: Books 11–13 (Heidelberg, 1967).

Kragelund, Patrick, Mette Moltesen and Jan Stubbe Østergaard, *The Licinian Tomb: Fact or Fiction?* (Copenhagen, 2003).

Krebs, Christopher B., *A Most Dangerous Book: Tacitus's Germania from the Roman Empire to the Third Reich* (New York and London, 2011).

Laird, Andrew, *Powers of Expression, Expressions of Power: Speech Presentation and Latin Literature* (Oxford, 1999).

Levick, Barbara, *Claudius* (New Haven, CT, and London, 1990).

Malamud, Martha, 'Tacitus and the twentieth-century novel', in *Cambridge Companion*, pp. 300–16.

Malloch, Simon J. V., '*Hamlet* without the prince? The Claudian *Annals*', in *Cambridge Companion*, pp. 116–26.

—— *The Annals of Tacitus: Book 11* (Cambridge, 2013).

Martin, Ronald H., *Tacitus* (Bristol, 1981).

—— 'From manuscript to print', in *Cambridge Companion*, pp. 241–52.

Martin, Ronald H. and Anthony J. Woodman, *Tacitus: Annals Book IV* (Cambridge, 1989).

Mayer, Roland, *Tacitus: Dialogus de Oratoribus* (Cambridge, 2001).

Mellor, Ronald, *Tacitus* (London and New York, 1993).

Mendell, Clarence W., *Tacitus: The Man and his Work* (New Haven, CT, and London, 1957).

Miller, Norma P., 'The Claudian tablet and Tacitus: a reconsideration', *Rheinisches Museum* 99 (1956), pp. 304–15.

Momigliano, Arnaldo, *The Classical Foundations of Modern Historiography* (Berkeley, CA, 1990).

Morgan, Gwyn, *69 A.D.: The Year of Four Emperors* (Oxford, 2006).

Murgia, Charles E., 'The length of the lacuna in Tacitus' *Dialogus*', *California Studies in Classical Antiquity* 12 (1979), pp. 221–40.

—— 'The textual transmission', in *Blackwell Companion*, pp. 15–22.

Nederman, Cary, 'Niccolò Machiavelli', in Edward N. Zalta (ed.), *The Stanford Encyclopedia of Philosophy*, winter 2014 edition. Available at http://plato.stanford.edu/archives/win2014/entries/machiavelli/ (last accessed 27 September 2016).

Newlands, Carole, *Statius: Poet Between Rome and Naples* (London, 2012).

—— *Ovid* (London and New York, 2015).

Nichols, Andrew, *Ctesias: On India* (London, 2011).

O'Gorman, Ellen, 'No place like Rome: identity and difference in the *Germania* of Tacitus', *Ramus* 22 (1993), pp. 135–54.

—— *Irony and Misreading in the* Annals *of Tacitus* (Cambridge, 2000).

—— 'Alternate empires: Tacitus's virtual history of the Pisonian principate', *Arethusa* 39.2 (2006), pp. 281–301.

Ordway, Scott, 'North Woods: eight women's voices' (Philadelphia, PA, 2014).

Pagán, Victoria Emma, 'Distant voices of freedom in the *Annales* of Tacitus', *Studies in Latin Literature and Roman History* X (2000), pp. 358–69.

—— 'Teaching torture in Seneca *Controversiae* 2.5', *Classical Journal* 103.2 (2007), pp. 165–82.

—— *Conspiracy Theory in Latin Literature* (Austin, TX, 2012).

Paratore, Ettore, *Tacito* (Rome, 1962).

Pelling, Christopher, 'Tacitus' personal voice', in *Cambridge Companion*, pp. 147–67.

Plass, Paul, *Wit and the Writing of History: The Rhetoric of Historiography in Imperial Rome* (Madison, WI, 1988).

Potter, David S., 'The inscriptions on the bronze Herakles from Mesene: Vologeses IV's war with Rome and the date of Tacitus' *Annales*', *Zeitschrift für Papyrologie und Epigraphik* 88 (1991), pp. 277–90.

—— 'Tacitus' sources', in *Blackwell Companion*, pp. 125–40.

Potter, David S. and Cynthia Damon, 'The *Senatus Consultum de Cn. Pisone Patre*', *American Journal of Philology* 120.1 (1999), pp. 13–41.

Rives, James B., *Tacitus: Germania* (Oxford, 1999).

—— 'Germania', in *Blackwell Companion*, pp. 45–61.

Roisman, Joseph, *The Rhetoric of Conspiracy in Ancient Athens* (Berkeley, CA, 2006).

Romm, James S., *The Edges of the Earth in Ancient Thought: Geography, Exploration, and Fiction* (Princeton, NJ, 1992).

Rutledge, Steven H., 'Trajan and Tacitus' audience: reader reception of *Annals* 1–2', *Ramus* 27 (1998), pp. 141–59.

—— *Imperial Inquisitions: Prosecutors and Informants from Tiberius to Domitian* (London and New York, 2001).

—— 'Tacitus' *Dialogus de Oratoribus*: a socio-cultural history', in *Blackwell Companion*, pp. 62–83.

Sailor, Dylan, *Writing and Empire in Tacitus* (Cambridge, 2008).

—— 'The *Agricola*', in *Blackwell Companion*, pp. 23–44.

Saller, Richard, 'Anecdotes as historical evidence for the principate', *Greece & Rome* 27 (1980), pp. 69–83.

Schama, Simon, *Landscape and Memory* (New York, 1996).

Schlüter, Walter, 'The Battle of the Teutoberg Forest: archaeological research at Kalkriese near Osnabrück', in John D. Creighton and Roger J. A. Wilson (eds), *Roman Germany: Studies in Cultural Interaction* (*Journal of Roman Archaeology* Supplement, 1999), pp. 123–59.

Sherwin-White, Adrian N., *The Letters of Pliny: A Historical and Social Commentary* (Oxford, 1966).

Shotter, David C. A., 'Tacitus and Verginius Rufus', *Classical Quarterly* 17.2 (1967), pp. 370–81.

—— 'Tiberius and Asinius Gallus', *Historia* 20 (1971), pp. 443–57.

Shumate, Nancy, *Nation, Empire, Decline: Studies in Rhetorical Continuity from the Romans to the Modern Era* (London, 2006).

—— 'Postcolonial approaches to Tacitus', in *Blackwell Companion*, pp. 476–503.

Sinclair, Patrick, *Tacitus the Sententious Historian: A Sociology of Rhetoric in* Annales *1–6* (University Park, PA, 1995).

Speidel, Michael P., *Riding for Caesar: The Roman Emperor's Horse Guards* (Cambridge, MA, 1994).

Star, Christopher, *The Empire of the Self: Self-Command and Political Speech in Seneca and Petronius* (Baltimore, MD, 2012).

Strunk, Thomas E., 'Offending the powerful: Tacitus' *Dialogus de Oratoribus* and safe criticism', *Mnemosyne* 63 (2010), pp. 241–67.

Sullivan, John P., *Literature and Politics in the Age of Nero* (Ithaca, NY, and London, 1985).

Syme, Ronald, 'Augustus and Agrippa', *Classical Review* 51.5 (1937), pp. 194–5.

—— *The Roman Revolution* (Oxford, 1939).

—— *Tacitus*, 2 vols (Oxford, 1958).

—— *Ten Studies in Tacitus* (Oxford, 1970).

—— 'History or biography: the case of Tiberius Caesar', *Historia* 23 (1974), pp. 481–96.

—— *History in Ovid* (Oxford, 1978).

—— 'How Tacitus wrote *Annals* 1–3', in Anthony Birley (ed.), *Roman Papers*, vol. 3 (Oxford, 1984), pp. 1014–42.

—— *The Augustan Aristocracy* (Oxford, 1986).

Taylor, Gary, 'The butcher of Rome', *The Guardian*, 18 July 2005, https://www.theguardian.com/stage/2005/jul/18/theatre.stage (last accessed 3 October 2016).

Thomas, Richard F., *Virgil: Georgics*, vol. 1 (Cambridge, 1988).

—— 'The *Germania* as literary text', in *Cambridge Companion*, pp. 59–72.

Toher, Mark, 'Tacitus' Syme', in *Cambridge Companion*, pp. 317–29.

van den Berg, Christopher, *The World of Tacitus' Dialogus de Oratoribus: Aesthetics and Empire in Ancient Rome* (Cambridge, 2014).

Völker, Cornelius, 'Monumental, magisch, masslos: Deutschland im Jahr 9! Die *Hermansschlacht* Der Spielfilm', *Grabbe-Jahrbüch* 15 (1996), pp. 38–47.

Walker, Elisabeth Henry (Bessie), *The Annals of Tacitus: A Study in the Writing of History* (Manchester, 1952).

Weinbrot, Howard D., 'Politics, taste, and national identity: some uses of Tacitism in eighteenth-century Britain', in *Tacitus and the Tacitean Tradition*, pp. 168–84.

Wellesley, Kenneth, 'Can you trust Tacitus?', *Greece & Rome* 1 (1954), pp. 13–33.

White, Hayden, *The Content of the Form: Narrative Discourse and Historical Representation* (Baltimore, MD, 1987).

Whitton, Christopher, '"Let us tread our path together": Tacitus and the Younger Pliny', in *Blackwell Companion*, pp. 345–68.

Wick, Terry E. (trans.), *Thucydides: The Peloponnesian War* (New York, 1982).

Williams, Gordon, *Change and Decline: Roman Literature in the Early Empire* (Berkeley, CA, 1978).

Winkler, Martin, *Arminius the Liberator: Myth and Ideology* (Oxford, 2016).

Winterbottom, Michael, 'The transmission of Tacitus' *Dialogus*', *Philologus* 116 (1972), pp. 114–28.

Wiseman, Timothy Peter, 'Calpurnius Siculus and the Claudian Civil War', *Journal of Roman Studies* 72 (1982), pp. 57–67.

—— 'Lying historians: seven types of mendacity', in Christopher Gill and Timothy P. Wiseman (eds), *Lies and Fiction in the Ancient World* (Austin, TX, 1993), pp. 122–46.

Wolpert, Andrew, *Remembering Defeat: Civil War and Civic Memory in Ancient Athens* (Baltimore, MD, 2002).

Woodman, Anthony J., 'Questions of date, genre, and style in Velleius: some literary answers', *Classical Quarterly* 25 (1975), pp. 272–306.

—— *Rhetoric in Classical Historiography: Four Studies* (London and Sydney, 1988).

—— 'Amateur dramatics at the court of Nero: Annals 15.48–74', in *Tacitus and the Tacitean Tradition*, pp. 104–28.

—— '*Praecipuum munus annalium*: the construction, convention and context of Tacitus, *Annals* 3.56.1', *Museum Helveticum* 52 (1995), pp. 111–26.

—— (trans.), *Tacitus: The Annals* (Indianapolis, IN, 2004).

Woodman, Anthony J. and Ronald H. Martin, *The Annals of Tacitus: Book 3* (Cambridge, 1996).

Woodman, Anthony J. with Christina S. Kraus, *Tacitus: Agricola* (Cambridge, 2014).

Yourcenar, Marguerite, *The Memoirs of Hadrian*, translated from the French by Grace Frick in collaboration with the author (New York, 1974).

INDEX